London School of Economics
Monographs on Social Anthropology

Managing Editor: David McKnight

The Monographs on Social Anthropology were established in 1940 and aim to publish results of modern anthropological research of primary interest to specialists.

The continuation of the series was made possible by a grant in aid from the Wenner-Gren Foundation for Anthropological Research, and more recently by a further grant from the Governors of the London School of Economics and Political Science. Income from sales is returned to a revolving fund to assist further publications.

The Monographs are under the direction of an Editorial Board associated with the Department of Anthropology of the London School of Economics and Political Science.

London School of Economics
Monographs on Social Anthropology
No 65

Hierarchy and Egalitarianism

*Caste, Class and Power in
Sinhalese Peasant Society*

Tamara Gunasekera

THE ATHLONE PRESS
London and Atlantic Highlands, NJ

First published 1994 by
THE ATHLONE PRESS
1 Park Drive, London NW11 7SG
and 165 First Avenue,
Atlantic Highlands, NJ 07716

British Library Cataloguing in Publication Data
*A catalogue record for this book is available
from the British Library*

ISBN 0 485 19565 8

Library of Congress Cataloging in Publication Data
Cataloging in Publication Data applied for

Typeset by
Bibloset, Chester

Printed and bound in Great Britain by
Bookcraft Ltd, Bath, England

TO JEREMY

Contents

List of Tables

List of Figures

List of Maps

Note on the Transliteration of Sinhalese Words

For many of the Sinhalese words used in this book there are one or more generally accepted English renditions. In such cases I have used one such rendition. For example, although the transliterated rendition for the high-ranking cultivator caste would be 'goyigama', in this book it appears in one of its common English renditions – Goigama.

All other Sinhalese words, including caste names, which do not have common English renditions, are represented according to the standard Roman transliteration found in Gair and Karunatilaka's *Literary Sinhala Inflected Forms: A Synopsis*.

For typographical simplicity, colloquial phrases, although not found in written Sinhalese, are also presented according to the above romanization.

Except for caste names, names of bureaucratic offices and words which have an accepted English rendition, all Sinhalese words are italicized. The only exception is the English rendition for 'manor house' – walawwe – which is italicized in order to avoid confusion with a similar caste name. All Sinhalese words are explained in the text when they first appear. Words that appear more than once in the text are listed in the Glossary, which also contains the transliteration of Sinhalese words the English renditions of which appear in the text.

Personal names and surnames have not been transliterated but presented in the way they would commonly be written in English.

Glossary

amuna, *pl.* amunu	Sinhalese land measure, here equivalent to 2½ acres of paddy land.
anda	Crop-sharing tenancy in paddy cultivation where crop is divided equally between landlord and tenant.
Aracci (*Sin.* āracci)	Goigama caste minor headman with jurisdiction over a *vasama*.
ästom	From English phrase 'at home'; a celebration on a special occasion.
aswedum (*Sin.* äsväddum)	The process of bringing land into cultivation as a paddy field.
attam	Cooperative labour arrangement used in paddy cultivation.
badda	State department in the Kandyan kingdom.
banda (*Sin.* banḍa)	Suffix meaning 'prince' attached to personal name of high-caste males.
bās	Masons, carpenters, etc.; used as a suffix to the personal name when addressing or referring to such artisans, e.g. Piyadasa bäs.
Batgam	Literally rice villages. Name of low-ranking caste commonly known as Padu.
binna	Uxorilocal marriage; carries with it connotations of shame and poverty for the groom.
caritaya	Character
dhanaya	Wealth
Dissava (*Sin.* disāve)	Governor of a province in the Kandyan kingdom.
Gallat	Caste name of group who were tradi-

	tionally blacksmiths.
gamsabhāva	Village committee/village tribunal/ village council.
gatiguna	Character
gedera	House
goḍa iḍam	High land
Goigama (*Sin.* goyigama)	Caste name of high-ranking 'cultivator' caste.
Grama Sevaka (*Sin.* grāma sēvaka)	Literally village servant – bureaucrat in charge of the smallest unit of local administration, the *vasama*.
hatara	Four
hēn	High land on which swidden agriculture is practised.
Hēna	Caste name of group who were traditionally washermen.
kachchery (*Sin.* Kaccēriya)	District administrative headquarters.
kankāni	Overseer on plantations.
kannamāru	Tenurial arrangement on paddy land where co-owners of a field rotate the parcels each year.
karu anda	Crop-sharing tenancy in paddy cultivation where the tenant carries out half the tasks and receives ¼ the crop.
konḍe	Hair gathered into a knot at the back of the head.
Korala (*Sin.* kōrāla)	Bureaucrat in charge of pattuwa.
korale (*Sin.* kōrāle)	Administrative division in the Kandyan kingdom.
kulaya	Caste
kurakkan	A type of millet.
kuruni	Sinhalese land measure, here equivalent to ¹⁄₁₆ acre of paddy land.
lās	Sinhalese land measure. 1 lās = 1 kuruni (see above).
maḍa iḍam	Literally mud land; paddy land.
madaran	Tenancy fee
maha	Principal paddy cultivation season.
mahatmaya	A respectful title (and vocative) for a

(*Sin.* mahatmayā)	person with some education.
māma/māmandi	Mother's brother
manike (*Sin.* mänike)	Suffix meaning 'jewel' attached to personal name of high-caste females; vocative used by lower castes when addressing the former.
mudalali (*Sin.* mudalāli)	A polite term (and vocative) for those engaged in trade.
nända/nändamma	Father's sister
nikāya	Sect of the Buddhist monkhood in Sri Lanka.
niyara	Low ridges separating parcels of land within a paddy field.
Padu	See Batgam.
päla, *pl.* päl	Sinhalese land measure, here equivalent to ⅝ acre of paddy land.
patabändi	A form of *vāsagama* name referring to a title bestowed upon an ancestor by a Sinhalese king.
Patti	Caste name of group whose traditional occupation was cattle herding.
pattuwa (*Sin.* pattuva)	Administrative division in charge of a Korala.
pinkama, *pl.* pinkam	Buddhist merit-making occasion.
pirit	Sacred texts chanted in order to make merit at domestic and *vihāra* religious rituals.
Radala	Caste name of regionally famous aristocrats.
rajakāriya	Customary service or duty to the king.
Ratemahatmaya (*Sin.* ratemahatmayā)	Chief native headman under the British.
sangha (*Sin.* saṃgha)	Buddhist monkhood
sannasa	Copper plate or stone slab on which royal grants of land were recorded.
tattumāru	Tenurial arrangement on paddy land where co-owners of a field take it in turns to cultivate the whole field.
Vahal	Slave; caste name of lowest caste in the

	Rangama/Devideniya community.
Vahumpura	Caste name of group whose traditional occupation was juggery making.
vāsagama	Literally village of residence; surname.
vasama	Smallest unit of local administration comprising 2,000 – 4,000 people in one or more villages; in charge of an Aracci until 1963 and since then of a Grama Sevaka.
vatu	Garden land
Vel Vidane (*Sin.* vel vidāne)	Irrigation headman
Vidāna Dēvaya	Vahumpura caste minor headman
Vidāna Duraya	Batgam caste minor headman
vihāraya, *pl.* vihāra	Buddhist temple; refers to a complex which includes the bo tree (*Ficus religiosia*), the monk's residence, and the chief Buddhist shrine which houses sacred relics.
walawwe (*Sin.* valavva)	Manor house of aristocrats; caste name used in the Rangama/Devideniya community for village aristocrats.
yala	Secondary paddy cultivation season.

1 Introduction

This book is a study of stratification and social change in a Sinhalese peasant society. Treating caste, class and power not only as important ways of structuring relations between people but also as prominent ideologies, the book examines the complex interplay of these hierarchies both within and between the social and cultural realms over a period of almost one hundred years. In order to do so, comparison is made between the social structure and ideology of inequality prevailing at two distinct points in time: the contemporary period and the period spanning the turn of the century.

The contemporary period refers to the late 1970s and early 1980s, a time before the eruption of violent conflict in Sri Lanka. Nevertheless this study's analysis of the politicization of everyday life in rural Sri Lanka does contribute to an understanding of the sense of frustration felt by those excluded in the process.

The way in which local political processes and the agrarian hierarchy are here analysed will, I hope, demonstrate the importance of avoiding a caste bias in the understanding of power and class. Not least among the advantages of avoiding caste bias is that South Asian studies need not then retain the status of a geographical special case. For instance, changes in the community-region relationship in Sri Lanka, which are taking place through the growth of patronage politics and the party politicization of local power structures, bear certain interesting similarities to the situation in parts of rural Europe.[1] But although the impact of democracy and party politics on local power structures in South Asia has been the subject of extensive writings, the caste bias in the analysis of power has been difficult to eliminate. Changes in the composition of local-level power elites is often interpreted as a shift of power from rich, numerically small, high-caste groups, to larger castes (composed of relatively wealthy peasants) which occupy an intermediate position in the caste hierarchy. In other words one 'dominant caste'[2] is seen to replace another. As the analysis of power in this study will show, discussion of power in terms of the imprecise and misleading 'dominant caste' concept[3] obscures the fundamental changes that are taking place in developing democracies like Sri Lanka.

Over the past century divisiveness has come to permeate group relationships in the peasant community I studied. Despite, or even because of redistributive policies and the emphasis on egalitarianism of national governments, disunity and antagonism created by class and caste have become marked features of contemporary life. In post-independence years there has been an attenuation in the salience of local inequalities – the economic dependence of the poor on the rich has decreased as have the privileges and obligations based on caste status. Paradoxically, however, these changes have not fostered a sense of unity but have on the contrary exacerbated class and caste tensions.

The analysis of stratification in this book challenges the familiar argument that class is replacing caste in South Asia. The structure of inequality has indeed undergone change, but in Sri Lanka it is not taking the form of an emerging class hierarchy replacing a decaying caste hierarchy. One of the central arguments of this book is that the decline in caste discrimination and the presence of class antagonism in a given society do not necessarily imply the decay of caste, the rise of class consciousness or a rejection of hierarchy.

More significant than those in caste and class have been the changes that have taken place in the sphere of power. It is here that one of the most fundamental changes in post-independence Sri Lanka has taken place. Democracy and party competition have led to the demise of village leadership. This fact has significant implications for the future of rural development based on popular participation, a significance which is often overlooked because observers fail to distinguish between the concepts of power and leadership. The new rural power elite, the basis of whose power lies not in caste or wealth but rather in political connection, cannot assume the role of leaders. The inability to foster collective action in communities divided by caste, class and party allegiance is in large part responsible for the moribund nature of many rural development organizations in Sri Lanka.

A resurgence of village leadership in the future seems unlikely.

For not only are contemporary power holders not leaders, but in recent decades the cultural conceptions of inequality, influenced by external factors, have made people increasingly unwilling to act out the role of follower. Principal among these external influences has been the democratic and socialist ideology espoused by national governments since independence. Exposure to this egalitarian ideology has entailed a rejection of hierarchy in the dimension of power at the local level. However, this has not been matched by an equivalent rejection of the hierarchies of caste and class. As this study shows, despite declining caste discrimination and rising class antagonism, notions of hierarchy may coexist with those of equality in ways which render liberal hopes of a caste-free society or Marxist hopes of peasant revolution little short of wishful thinking.

THEORETICAL FRAMEWORK

This study of stratification eschews the use of models which assign primacy to one or other type of inequality in a given society. It uses instead a more complex model which incorporates without preferential emphasis the three basic dimensions of stratification. The three-dimensional model of stratification used in this study, which borrows from Weber's work[4] and more directly from Runciman's development of it,[5] is based on the theoretical premise that inequalities of class, status and power are conceptually distinct. As such there is no justification for the a priori assignment of causal priority to any one type of inequality. The model thus makes an analytical distinction between the hierarchies of class, status and power which leads to the separate analysis of each hierarchy. The analytical separation of the hierarchies of inequality does not reject the possibility of interplay between class, status and power, but on the contrary facilitates examination of the relationship between them. The three-dimensional model takes the relationship between the hierarchies to be not logical or necessary but rather contingent. It ensures that the interaction between class, status and power is empirically verified rather than theoretically assumed.

   Caste, class and power are significant for rural Sinhalese not just in the realm of action and behaviour but also in that of ideas and cultural conceptions. But to treat either behaviour or ideas as a causally prior form of social reality is unwarranted. This study attaches importance to making an analytical distinction between ideas and behaviour and thus may be said broadly to follow Schneider's[6] approach to the relationship between the social and cultural realms of reality. Distinguishing social from cultural analysis enables us to examine the degree to which ideas and behaviour are dependent, interdependent or independent of each other. Hence the social structure of stratification (hierarchical groups and the interaction between strata) is differentiated from, and analysed separately from, the cultural realm of stratification (systems of ideas and meanings). Moreover the three-dimensional model is applied not just to the social realm but also to the cultural (i.e. the ideologies[7] of caste, class and power are analysed separately) making possible the examination of the interplay between caste, class and power both within and between the different realms of social reality.

DEFINITION OF CONCEPTS

The term stratification as used in this study is not synonymous with inequality. Certain types of inequality stratify society while others merely differentiate it. Stratification involves the notion of hierarchy and the ability to locate individuals in different groups or strata ranked one above the other. By contrast there exist in any given society a number of human attributes which, though possessed by people in unequal degrees, serve only to differentiate rather than stratify the society in the above sense. For instance, 'education does not by definition stratify society, it only differentiates it. Polymaths do not constitute a high ranking stratum in the way that the rich, or the social aristocracy, or the holders of governmental office do.'[8] The same is true of attributes such as piety, helpfulness, generosity, etc, which in most societies bestow upon their possessors a degree of admiration, but do not stratify society into high and low strata, and hence logically find no place in an analysis of stratification. Class, status and power, however, are types of inequality which create cleavages in society, divide people into ranked strata, and structure the relations between people belonging to the various strata. Along with Weber and Runciman, I shall therefore take class, status and power to constitute the three basic dimensions of stratification.

Class

Class in this study is defined in relation to control over valuable assets.

In this definition the 'value' of an asset is not used synonymously with its cash or market value. Rather an asset is deemed to be valuable only to the extent that it contributes to the material well-being of the person who has control over it. Thus, for instance, in a situation where poorly-developed trade and markets result in the uncertainty of the supply of a good considered necessary for material well-being, control over that good (or the means to obtain it) would be more significant for the demarcation of class categories than another good which had a higher market value but was not considered necessary for material well-being. In other words, receipt of a large cash income may not be a good index of class position if it cannot readily secure goods which locally are considered 'essential'. The term 'control' in this definition need not be synonymous with ownership. Legal title of ownership does not necessarily confer rights to the full income-yielding potential of the asset in question. In the case of some types of land mortgage, for example, apart from the initial loan, the owner receives no regular stream of income from his asset.

Classes can be identified along a continuum of differential control over valuable assets by the extent to which members of a group thus depicted interact in a consistent way with members of other groups. Determination of the 'cutting points' of class thus becomes a matter for empirical investigation.

Groups will be termed classes whether or not this interaction is a result of consciousness of class position and of a desire to act upon common class interest. Hence this is an objective definition of class which does not entail the notion of 'class consciousness'. Nor is it strictly a Marxist one. It is a more generalized definition which allows that the Marxist formulation of relationship to the means of production may, in a given place and time, be the most useful way of demarcating groups possessing differential degrees of wealth. But it is a definition in which denies that this is necessarily at all times and in all places the appropriate formula for identifying such groups.

Status

The term status is ill-defined and ambiguous as a result of the wide range of its application both in popular usage and in the literature of stratification. In this study I restrict its scope to a particular meaning. Status is used here as synonymous with social honour and prestige and conceptually distinct from power and class. As Runciman points out, there is a self-evident conceptual distinction between status, power and class. For example, when people desire status they clearly wish for something distinct from control over men (power) or resources (class), though control over these things may be, in a given society, a precondition for the achievement of higher status. Thus, although in a particular society a relation may exist between these it is a contingent and not a necessary one.[9]

Castes as Status Groups

No clear definition of caste has emerged from the literature despite the proliferation of theoretical writings on the subject. The religious justification of the caste system in India has led some anthropologists to perceive it primarily as an ideology.[10] Others, though not denying the religious aspect, see it as a system of social stratification. The absence of a uniform definition of caste is also evidenced in the long-standing debate about the appropriateness of using the term caste outside India. In this study the term caste is not used as if it were only applicable to India, as Dumont would have it; nor is it confined exclusively to the South Asian region as Leach, Ryan and Yalman insist it should be.[11] A structural rather than cultural definition of caste is proposed here but it differs significantly from those propounded by Barth and Berreman.[12] In their loose, catch-all notion of caste, a person's caste rank reflects his status, power and economic position, such that within a single caste there is a 'status summation'. But this definition of caste is inadequate. If 'status summation' is taken to be the characteristic structural feature of the caste system, one would be hard put to locate caste systems even in the classic caste context of India. For not only is perfect congruency between the hierarchies of caste, class and power extremely rare in contemporary India, but, as historical studies are increasingly making evident, it was also rare in Indian society at the turn of the century.[13]

The definition of caste employed in this study is more focused and specific than customary definitions. Castes are defined as groups possessing differential degrees of social honour and prestige. These groups place restrictions on marriage with individuals in other such groups, and membership in them is hereditary, depending on one or both parents being members of a given caste. In societies where caste is present, therefore, social honour and prestige or status accrue to an individual by virtue of his birth in a particular caste. Thus, in such societies, the status hierarchy consists of the caste hierarchy.

Power

The notion of power has been a proverbially problematic one for the social sciences in general. In this study, power will be defined as the ability to influence the actions of others and/or the ability to bring about an intended state of affairs. According to this definition, power holders are not limited to those who, by virtue of their position in the institutional political structure, have formal authority to influence the lives of others. They are also those whose bases of power lie outside the formal structure. Neither does this definition limit power relationships to those where influence and authority over others is exercised overtly. If an individual has the ability to bring about an intended state of affairs he is a power holder regardless of whether he achieves his aims overtly or covertly.

In this study the concept of power is distinguished from that of leadership. Although there is a close relationship between power and leadership these concepts are not synonymous and it is important to distinguish clearly between them. A local-level leader is here defined as a member of the local power elite who is able to command a following and direct collective activity because he is respected and admired, and because his power is deemed to be relatively permanent. Thus although leadership at the local level implies membership of the power elite, power holders need not always be leaders.

Chapter 1 has set out the objectives of the study, the theoretical framework used and the definitions of the principal concepts used throughout the book. Chapter 2 describes the research setting and discusses the reasons for selecting the two adjacent villages of Rangama and Devideniya in the Kandyan highlands.

The arrangement of the rest of the book in two main parts reflects its diachronic perspective. Each part examines the social structure and ideology of stratification in the Rangama/Devideniya community at a specific point in time. The internal organization of both parts is similar and is patterned on the study's theoretical framework, which makes analytical distinctions between society and culture, and within each realm between the three dimensions of caste, class and power.

Part I (Chapters 3 to 7) examines stratification at the turn of the century, during what I have called the 'baseline period'. The analysis of this period is based on the information of older informants and archival sources and is necessarily less exhaustive and contains less detail than that of the contemporary period.

Part II (Chapters 8 to 12) examines the nature of stratification as it applies to the Rangama/Devideniya community during the period of fieldwork in the late 1970s and early 1980s. My use of the ethnographic present tense in these chapters refers to that period. The analysis here is carried out in a historical context, with reference being made to the patterns of stratification in the baseline period and the changes that have occurred in the intervening years.

In the conclusion I examine the complex ways in which the social structure and ideology of stratification have interacted over the past century and draw together the findings of the previous chapters to construct an overall picture of social change.

2 Research Setting

The peasant community with which this book is concerned is situated in the central highlands of Sri Lanka, a region principally populated by a group of people known as the Kandyan Sinhalese. This chapter discusses the ways in which the theoretical objectives of the study influenced the selection of the general locale and the specific community within which field research was carried out.

THE KANDYAN SINHALESE AND THE KANDYAN KINGDOM

Sri Lanka is a multiethnic and multireligious society.[1] The most prominent group in the island is made up of Sinhalese Buddhists constituting approximately 70 per cent of the population. The Sinhalese people are divided by historical experience into two main groups – the Kandyan Sinhalese and the Low Country Sinhalese. The distinctiveness of these two groups is mainly the result of European colonial rule in Sri Lanka. The Low Country Sinhalese live in the maritime regions of the island which were continuously under European rule from the sixteenth century until Sri Lanka's independence in 1948.[2] The Kandyan Sinhalese are those who reside within the boundaries of the former Kandyan kingdom in the interior of the island, which remained independent until the British conquest in 1815. It is their lesser exposure to Western European influence that constitutes the basis of Kandyan feelings of superiority *vis-à-vis* Low Country Sinhalese. Although the latter live in a more commercialized society and are in general wealthier and more sophisticated, the Kandyans claim superiority as the proud upholders of Sinhalese customs, traditions and religion within the Kandyan kingdom.

A knowledge of the Kandyan kingdom is a necessary beginning to this study of stratification. It not only provides historical background for the study, but also helps to make clear why the Kandyan highlands were selected as the most suitable research locale.

The Kandyan kingdom lasted from 1469 to 1815.[3] Although it was continually at war with the European powers which controlled the coastal regions, it included within its boundaries the greater part of the island (see Map 1, p.11). When the kingdom finally fell in 1815 it was not due to military weakness, but to the perfidy of the Kandyan nobles who, disenchanted by the way the king was usurping their power, conspired with the British to overthrow him.

The Kandyan kingdom was an absolute monarchy. As 'lord of the soil', the king had complete control over the disposal of land. He appointed members of the bureaucracy and was the highest judicial authority in the land.

In a largely non-monetary economy the king obtained the services of his subjects by distributing land in exchange for services. The services of the highest officers of state as well as those of the most menial labourers were rewarded by land grants. This system of service tenure was known as *rajakāriya* (duty to the king) and was based on the caste system – each caste being obliged to perform a specific service as a condition of tenure. Security of tenure, and the extent and value of landholdings, were inversely related to the onerousness of services rendered, and were directly related to one's general position (superior or inferior) in the caste hierarchy. For instance, in exchange for participating in ceremonial processions and paying homage to the king, some aristocrats of the Radala caste were granted rights over vast extents of land.

The caste system was also the foundation of the centrally-organized state departments and the provincial bureaucracy – an important source of power in the kingdom. Each state department (*badda*) was responsible for organizing the traditional caste services owed to the state by a particular caste group. The head of each *badda* was invariably of Radala caste. The Radala people also occupied the apex of the provincial bureaucracy, which was composed of a hierarchy of officials who wielded executive as well as judicial power over successively smaller areas of jurisdiction. Those of the Goigama caste (second only to the Radala aristocrats) could aspire to middling positions in the bureaucracy, but all those of lower birth could hope for nothing higher than headmanship of an exclusively low-caste village.

The salience of caste in the Kandyan kingdom was not mitigated

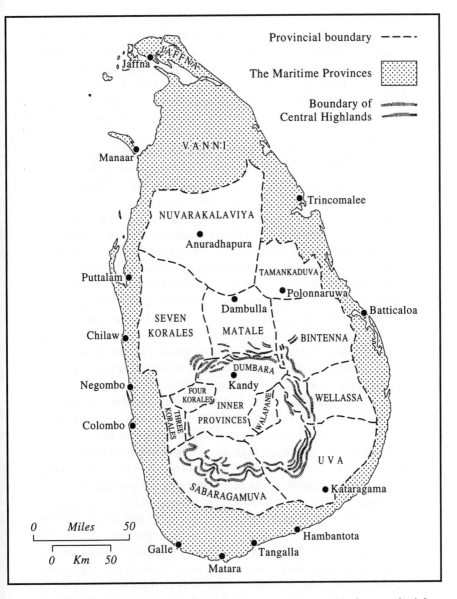

Map 1: The Kandyan kingdom in the early eighteenth century, showing provincial boundaries. After G. Powell, **The Kandyan Wars, The British Army in Ceylon 1803-1818**, London, Lee Cooper, 1973, 8.

by the supposedly egalitarian nature of the Buddhist religion. Buddhism in Sri Lanka has always operated through the framework of caste. During the Kandyan period, entrance to the Buddhist monkhood (sangha) was confined to the Radala and Goigama castes, the higher ranks of the ecclesiastical hierarchy being drawn exclusively from the aristocracy. Moreover, Buddhist monasteries and temples were recipients of vast estates from the king, the organization of which was based on the caste system. These grants consisted of whole villages, and the land was cultivated by tenants of the monastery or temple who, according to their caste, provided materials and services required for the maintenance of the religious institutions and the performance of rituals.

Not only was Buddhism permeated by caste, it was also intimately linked with the Kandyan state which officially sanctioned caste as the correct order of society. Buddhism was the state religion, and a relationship of interdependence obtained between Buddhism and the polity – the king protected and defended the faith and the sangha legitimized the king. Chief monks often participated in the political councils of Kandy (the capital city) and the king consulted them prior to making important decisions of state. Thus Buddhism's close association with the state served to legitimize the monarchy and its role as perpetuator of the caste system.

The prominence of caste in the Kandyan kingdom should not lead one to assume that the hierarchies of power and class were insignificant. Caste groups by no means constituted the only unequal strata in society. The relation between the owner of the land and the cultivator of the land was, for instance, an equally fundamental relationship of inequality. But this landlord–tenant relationship was not an exclusively economic one. Grantees of royal villages (i.e. Buddhist monasteries and temples, high officials and nobles) obtained the right not only to the land but also to the services and dues of the tenants living in those villages. As in feudal Europe the lord of the manor possessed extensive influence over the lives of his tenants.

If by caste hierarchy one meant only the general dichotomous division of people into those of superior birth (Radala and Goigama) and those of inferior birth (all other castes), then it could be maintained that class and power were functions of caste in the Kandyan kingdom. When, however, the caste hierarchy is seen in terms of the individual castes ranked one above the other, it is apparent that there was no perfect congruence between the three dimensions of stratification. For below the Radala and Goigama a variety of lower castes of clearly differential status possessed inferior (relative to Radala and Goigama) but roughly equivalent rights to land and bureaucratic positions. There was, however, a high degree of congruence between the highest strata of the hierarchies of class, caste and power. Membership of the Radala caste was a prerequisite for entrance into the highest stratum of the power and class hierarchies. Thus the Radala aristocrats, and to a lesser extent the Goigama people, occupied an enviable position in Kandyan society, enjoying not only caste superiority but also superiority of wealth and power.

SELECTION OF THE RESEARCH LOCALE

Suitability of the Kandyan Highlands

In order to pursue the theoretical objectives of the study the research locale had to be one which satisfied three criteria. It was in the region known as 'the Kandyan Highlands' that these three criteria could be met most satisfactorily.

Firstly, I required a community where caste-based cleavages were significant. This criterion introduced a potential source of bias, in so far as the salience of caste in a community might be inversely related to the emergence of other identities (e.g. class); but its employment was essential from a theoretical standpoint. This was because a major objective of the research – to show the importance of avoiding a caste bias in the understanding of power and class in South Asian society – could best be achieved in a research locale where caste itself was salient. To choose a research locale where caste was no longer important as a basis stratifying society would have frustrated this ambition.

Recent ethnographic research indicates that of the Sinhalese regions of Sri Lanka, caste, as a basis for structuring relations between people, is more important in the Kandyan regions than it is in the Low Country.[4] The greater salience of caste among the Kandyans may be attributable to the survival until 1815 of the Kandyan kingdom, the social, political and economic organization of which was founded on, and functioned through, the caste system. This in all probability resulted in the perpetuation of Sinhalese values and ideas in the Kandyan regions long after they were challenged by foreign ideologies in the maritime regions. Equally significant is the fact that caste-based feudal service tenure still exists in the Kandyan regions on the large landholdings of Buddhist monasteries and temples.[5] In the Low Country by contrast, the proselytizing actions of the Portuguese and the Dutch and in particular the former Christian power's aggressive attitude towards Buddhism, resulted in a decline in Buddhism. Buddhist monasteries were converted into churches or confiscated, and the spread of Christianity was accompanied by the demise of the feudal Sinhalese institution of 'monastic landlordism'.[6] The British were the only Europeans to colonize the Kandyan regions and their attitude to Buddhism was characterized throughout by non-interference, and, in the early years, even by protection and support. Thus, despite legislation that has effected far-reaching changes in the tenure of secular landholdings,[7] vast tracts of land in the Kandyan regions are even today controlled by Radala aristocrats[8] and cultivated by low-caste tenants.

The second criterion I used in selecting a community was related to the size of the community. I needed a research locale where the relevant groups in the class, caste and power hierarchies were in interaction within an area and a population sufficiently small to be susceptible to intensive analysis.

Although localized power and class hierarchies may be found in many parts of the island, localized caste hierarchies are less common. This is because in most Sinhalese areas (including the north-central and south-eastern regions of the former Kandyan kingdom) single caste villages are the norm. In such areas a number of adjacent villages would have to be incorporated into the scope of the study in order to analyse the local caste hierarchy – a task too onerous for a single researcher. The phenomenon of diverse castes interacting within a small local area is, however, commonly found in the Kandyan highlands,[9] where many villages are characterized by a high degree of caste differentiation.

Finally, I required a research locale where the three dimensions of stratification were dispersed rather than cumulative, and where the discrepancy (or increase in discrepancy) was of recent enough origin to be within the living memory of older informants. Such a research locale would not only facilitate study of changes that might have taken place in the system of stratification, but would also afford an opportunity to examine how conflicts of wealth, power and status were resolved.

Owing to the rapid socio-economic changes that have taken place throughout rural Sri Lanka in the last century, this was not an exacting criterion. Among other changes, the breakdown of the feudal political structure, the emergence of a land market and the establishment of a plantation sector in the economy, have resulted in a situation where power and wealth are no longer associated with caste status as they were during the Kandyan kingdom. Thus the phenomenon of dispersed hierarchies is not uncommon in many parts of contemporary Sri Lanka, the Kandyan highland region being no exception.

The Rangama/Devideniya Community

The 'community' I selected was composed primarily of two adjacent villages in the Kegalle district, the larger one being a multi-caste village named Rangama. It would have been inappropriate, given the objectives of my research, to restrict the focus of study to the boundaries of this village, for the relevant groups in interaction in the hierarchies of stratification could only be encompassed by including within the 'community' the neighbouring, virtually caste-exclusive village of Devideniya, as well as four households from two other neighbouring villages.

The close geographical and interactional links between Rangama and Devideniya are largely a result of a change in the pattern of land-ownership that took place between 1910 and 1950. This change took the form of increasing ownership of land in Rangama by the Batgam (very low-caste) people of Devideniya and the concomitant impoverishment of the Rangama Goigama. The changing fortunes of different castes gave rise to further changes which not only rendered the administrative boundary between the two villages artificial, but also led to changes in the officially recognized boundaries of these villages. For one thing many Batgam migrated to Rangama, and some who reside within the Rangama village limits still consider themselves Devideniya people. Moreover, parts of what was known as Devideniya at the turn of the century were, by the 1930s, being included within Rangama in official land registers. Thus, whilst those who claim Walawwe[10] (aristocratic) status today insist that their village is Rangama, at the turn of the century the Walawwe people in this community, as well as their lands, were exclusively associated with Devideniya.

The Rangama/Devideniya community[11] satisfied all three criteria which were considered necessary to pursue the theoretical objectives of the study. Firstly, the concepts and structures of caste play a significant role in the life of the inhabitants of this community. Secondly, in the Rangama/Devideniya community the relevant groups in interaction within the local caste, class and power hierarchies were contained in 236 households. The community was therefore of suitable size to be analysed intensively by a single researcher. Finally, national-level politics and the intervention of government in rural affairs, together with changing economic conditions at the local level, have resulted in a situation in this community where the hierarchies of caste, class and power are dispersed rather than cumulative.

Geographically the Rangama/Devideniya community is situated in the western part of the central highlands (see Map 2, p.17), an area characterized by the juxtaposition of plantations on the higher reaches of the hillsides, and Sinhalese villages in the valleys. Despite the fact that plantations, since their inception in the nineteenth century, have had an impact on certain aspects of village life (for example Sinhalese have worked on them as casual labourers), these valley settlements cannot, in any sense, be considered simply as adjuncts of the plantations. They are ancient Kandyan villages which were in existence long before the plantations were opened up in the forests surrounding the villages. The Rangama/Devideniya community is in close proximity to the Berawila and Natha Kande plantations, but its inhabitants are today, and have always been, essentially peasant cultivators with their own social life and institutions.

The central highland region is in the wet zone of Sri Lanka and receives rainfall (100–200 inches annually) from both the

Map 2: Sri Lanka, showing central highlands, district boundaries and the location of the Rangama/Devideniya community.

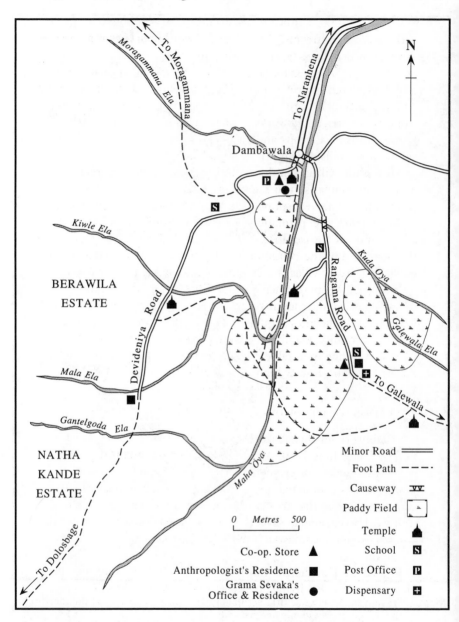

Map 3: Rangama and Devideniya

north-east and the south-west monsoons. The area is criss-crossed with rivers and streams. The village of Rangama lies in a valley through which flows a large river, the Maha Oya. Devideniya lies due west of Rangama on a hillside (see Map 3, p.18). Rice, the staple food, is grown in paddy fields situated in the valley. These paddy fields are not only rain-fed but also receive water from minor irrigation works – dams across rivers and streams. Other subsistence crops and cash crops are grown on the lower slopes of the hillsides known as 'high land'.

Most of the villages in the central highland region are relatively isolated in comparison to their Low Country counterparts. This community is no exception. On the hillside above the village of Devideniya are plantations extending from the west to the south, and on the south-eastern side an enormous rock forms the boundary of the community. To the east beyond an outcrop of rocks lie a few villages accessible only by narrow footpath. It is only through the north therefore that the community is connected to the bazaars and population centres. The closest of these is Dambawala, which lies about one-and-a-half miles from the centre of the community. Dambawala itself is linked to larger centres by a narrow, winding motorable road, which runs due north to a town on the Colombo-Kandy highway.

CONDITIONS OF FIELDWORK

The fieldwork for this book was conducted during the period February 1979 to June 1980. Although I carried out archival research at the Sri Lanka Government Archives in Colombo, most of the fieldwork was conducted on location in the Rangama/Devideniya community. For the greater part of my residence in the community I lived alone, save for the presence of a middle-aged woman whom I employed in the capacity of cook and general chaperon.

I lived in Devideniya for five months and in Rangama for eleven months. By living in the virtually caste-exclusive village of Devideniya I was able to establish very close relationships with a number of people from the low-ranked Batgam caste. Rangama had no unoccupied houses, so on moving there I had to settle for living in a section of a house owned by rich people of intermediate caste status. As I expected, this constrained my interaction with the high-caste group. Even though I was a tenant rather than a lodger (I cooked and ate separately) and deliberately maintained a friendly but distant relationship with the landlord's family, I experienced a certain amount of difficulty overcoming the reluctance of some high-caste people to visit me in these 'low-caste premises'.

Being an anthropologist in one's own country brings with it disadvantages as well as advantages. Although Sinhalese myself, I was a Low Country urbanite from Colombo working in a rural, Kandyan community, and the people of Rangama and Deivdeniya found it difficult at first to classify me. (Their confusion as to my identity was exacerbated by the fact that my husband was English.) Gaining acceptance as a Sinhalese was only one of the problems. Another was the matter of establishing a rapport with different caste groups. This is a difficult task at the best of times. It requires exceptional delicacy when one happens to belong to a particular caste group oneself.

Despite these drawbacks, however, in my case at least the advantages of being Sinhalese far outweighed the disadvantages. For one thing, being a speaker of Sinhalese, I did not need an interpreter. Equally important was the fact that I was sensitive to the nuances and inferences of speech and was able to judge fairly accurately the veracity of information given me by informants.

Perhaps due in part to the sensitivity of the subjects I was pursuing (caste relationships, land ownership, conceptions of inequality, etc.) I experienced some difficulty in eliciting certain kinds of information. I found villagers to be hospitable and friendly but in general suspicious of outsiders and, initially at least, reluctant to talk about inequality in the community. People in this community are jealous and distrustful of each other and do not display the 'vertical solidarity' one associates with the 'village community'. Many people were reluctant to talk freely for fear that what they said would be misconstrued and criticized by fellow villagers. I stopped using my tape recorder when I sensed that its presence unnerved people and inhibited conversation. In such a research climate it was only after expending considerable effort in breaking down reserve and establishing rapport, that I was able to obtain the information I needed.

Participant observation is difficult in these non-nucleated villages where houses are scattered on hillsides so thick with vegetation that often one cannot see one's neighbour's house. Tea shops are possibly the only places were unsolicited information may be gathered but my position as a female anthropologist precluded sitting around in tea shops – a preserve of the Sinhalese male. I collected most of my information through informal interviews. I eschewed random interviewing in favour of interviewing selected informants. The monk of the Rangama *vihāraya* – a powerful and influential man in the community – was indispensable, both as an informant and as a means of contact with other people in the community. By the middle of the fieldwork period I had established good relations with the majority of people and excellent rapport with about fifteen families which between them represented all the castes and class groups in the community. I was therefore able to obtain from the latter all the more sensitive quantitative data required (e.g. land ownership) without resorting to a house-to-house socio-economic survey, the results of which in this situation would have been highly dubious.

I lived for sixteen months in the Rangama/Devideniya community, a sufficiently long period of time in which to observe the production of paddy in both the principal (*maha*) season and the secondary (*yala*) season, as well as the cultivation and marketing of high-land crops. The timing of the fieldwork turned out to be fortunate. This was a period (1979–80) of considerable political significance, since it occurred shortly after the return to power of the United National Party following a seven-year term of office by the rival Sri Lanka Freedom Party. I was therefore able to observe the effect of the many changes in local-level institutions which came about as a result of this change in national government. The timing of the fieldwork was also fortunate in that it saw the introduction of a major development project into the Rangama/Devideniya community – the supply of electricity.

Apart from the monsoon seasons, which bring torrential showers and an abundance of leeches, the Rangama/Devideniya community was a pleasant research locale, being surrounded by breathtakingly beautiful scenery and favoured by a pleasant climate.

Part I

Stratification During the Baseline Period

3 The Baseline Period

In order to give a diachronic perspective to this study, the social structure and ideology of stratification in the Rangama/Devideniya community was examined at two specific points in time. The contemporary period constitutes one of these points, analysis of which is contained in part II. The earlier period, which was selected as a baseline for comparison, was the turn of the century. In this chapter I explain why I chose the years 1885 to 1910 to constitute the baseline period, and construct a general picture of this community at the turn of the century.

DEFINING THE BASELINE

Over the past 100 years the Rangama/Devideniya community has undergone changes which have significantly increased the divergence between the hierarchies of caste, class and power. In order to examine the process of socio-cultural change and the effect it had on this community, I chose to define the baseline as a period prior to that in which these changes had taken place.

Although radical change has occurred in local-level power structures in post-independence years, the divergence between the caste and power hierarchies in this community had begun as early as 1912, when the high-caste monopoly of power was eroded by the appointment of a low-caste headman in Devideniya. The decades after 1910 also witnessed a significant divergence between the hierarchies of caste and class as a result of increasing Batgam landownership. I decided to situate the baseline period prior to these early twentieth-century changes. By so doing I was able to increase the scope of the diachronic perspective, as well as include analysis of the rise of low-caste prosperity. This would not have been possible had the baseline been situated in the period immediately prior to independence.

Situating the baseline period prior to the changes in the early twentieth century meant that the upper limit of the baseline had to be 1910. The lower limit, 1885, was determined in relation to the availability of a vital archival source – the Grain Tax Assessment Registers. The Grain Tax was abolished in 1892 and since these registers were essential for constructing a picture of landownership at the time, I found it necessary to push back the lower limit to 1885, thereby allowing inclusion of the last available Grain Tax Assessment Register compiled in 1888.

Older informants in the contemporary Rangama/Devideniya community remember the economic decline of the high castes and the Batgam rise to prosperity well. A few also recall the appointment of the low-caste headman in Devideniya. They were, however, of a very young age during the baseline period, so in using this source of information I relied not only upon their own experiences but also on their recollections of what their elders had told them. In constructing a picture of stratification in the baseline period, I supplemented this kind of information with archival information gathered from the Ceylon National Archives and, to a lesser extent, the Colombo Museum Library. These archival sources consisted principally of British Colonial government documents and included Census Reports, Administrative Reports, Land Registers, Grain Tax Assessment Registers and Registers of Temple Lands. Although time-consuming, the diaries of the Assistant Government Agents of the Kegalle district turned out to be one of the most interesting and fruitful archival sources. The detailed accounts of the day-to-day activities and official duties of these indefatigable British administrators convey a remarkably vivid picture of life in the Kegalle district at the turn of the century.

THE RANGAMA/DEVIDENIYA COMMUNITY AT THE TURN OF THE CENTURY

During the baseline period Sri Lanka was under British colonial rule. For purposes of administration the British regrouped the Kandyan territorial divisions into administrative districts. The Rangama/Devideniya community belonged to the Kandyan province (*disāvani*) of Hatara Korale, which in British times was included in the administrative district of Kegalle.

The contemporary population of this community is 1,230, but

Table 1   *Demography of the community 1881–1911*

Year	Houses	Population
1881	54	302
1891	66	404
1901	59	376
1911	85	455

Source: Census Reports, 1881, 1891, 1901, 1911.

at the turn of the century less than five hundred people lived in Rangama and Devideniya (see Table 1). With the exception of a single Low Country Sinhalese family and two Muslim families, the population of the community was exclusively Kandyan Sinhalese.

Living conditions in the Rangama/Devideniya community today are by Western standards low. There is no running water, only one house has electricity, and transport is rudimentary – even the ubiquitous bicycles and bullock carts of Low Country villages are a rarity here. Nevertheless, conditions have improved dramatically since the baseline period. At that time the Dambawala 'bazaar' consisted of two small shops owned by Muslims[1] which sold a few basic household items but were not well enough stocked to satisfy the demands (minimal though they were) of the inhabitants of this community. Thus people were obliged to depend on itinerant Muslim door-to-door traders to purchase essential items such as salt, dry fish and cloth.

Today a plethora of government institutions and services have penetrated the community, but during the baseline period geographical isolation was accompanied by government neglect.[2] There were no schools and literacy was rare.[3] Despite the fact that the many waterways in the region made it susceptible to regular flooding, there were no bridges of any sort. To reach most parts of the community it was necessary to wade across rivers and streams, often in water chest high, during the monsoons. Although British rule had been in force in the Kandyan Provinces since 1815, the few public services that this community received were not due to the beneficence of government but the community's good fortune in being located close to the Berawila and Natha

Kande tea plantation.[4] By the end of the nineteenth century the inhabitants of this community and other Sinhalese villagers in the area had the use of a post office and a dispensary. These were established in Naranhena (a village two-and-a-half miles away from the community) to serve the needs of the sixteen British plantations in the region.

Despite the presence of the plantations, the focus of rural life remained the Buddhist temple (*vihāraya*). The Rangama *vihāraya* served the inhabitants of four villages – Rangama, Devideniya, Galewala and Naranhena. It is claimed that King Valagamba dedicated land and founded this *vihāraya* in the first century B.C., and that the village of Rangama was originally a royal endowment to the Rangama *vihāraya*. The royal grant (*sannasa*)[5] – an inscribed granite slab dedicating land to the *vihāraya* – is still in existence, but during the baseline period, as now, there were few other reminders of the grandeur achieved by the Rangama *vihāraya* in its earliest days. Its fortunes had declined over the centuries until at the end of the nineteenth century the *vihāraya* owned virtually no paddy land and only one-and-a-half acres of high land.[6] The incumbent of the Rangama *vihāraya* during the baseline period could therefore hardly be described as a monastic landlord. Indeed the activities of the present incumbent (see Chapter 11) appear all the more remarkable when one takes into account the fact that his operational base, like that of his recent predecessors, is no more than an impoverished *vihāraya*.

Although the focus of community life was located in Rangama, which in terms of population and land area[7] was twice as large as Devideniya (see Table 2), it was Devideniya which could, at the turn of the century, lay claim to fame not merely locally but also regionally. In marked contrast to the present situation, where the name Devideniya is tainted with the stigma of low-caste status, during the baseline period it was famous for its aristocratic associations. For Devideniya was the location of one of the eighteen principal manor houses (*walawwes*)[8] of Hatara Korale. These *walawwes* could be distinguished from the *walawwes* of village aristocrats (many of which are little more than modest two-room houses) by their grandeur, size, wealth and regional reputation. The inhabitants of these famous *walawwes* were known as Radala people.

Table 2   *Land in Rangama and Devideniya during the baseline period*

	Rangama			Devideniya		
	A	R	P(a)	A	R	P
Paddy	68	2	35	34	2	20
High	131	2	10	57	0	00

Sources: Grain Tax Assessment Register, Kegalle District 1888. High Land Register, Rangama Vasama, Kegalle District, 1897.
(a) I use measures officially recognized in contemporary Sri Lanka.
A = Acres (1 acre = 0.4 hectare)
R = Roods (4 roods = 1 acre)
P = Perches (40 perches = 1 rood)

The presence of the Devideniya *walawwe* and its dissolution just prior to the baseline period have been significant factors in the history of this community, and have played a part in shaping its contemporary social structure. It is therefore not out of place to present here a brief account of this *walawwe*.

The Devideniya Walawwe

The multi-caste character of the present Rangama/Devideniya community is in large part due to the historical impact of the Devideniya *walawwe*. Older informants claim that the aristocrats of the *walawwe* brought in families of blacksmiths and washermen and gave them land to cultivate in exchange for their services. Certain paddy fields in the Rangama/Devideniya community retain to this day caste-associated names (e.g. *radā wela* – washerman's field). Even more significant was the fact that two Batgam men were brought to the *walawwe* as servants in the mid-nineteenth century. The majority of Batgam, the richest and most numerous caste in the community today, can trace their ancestry back to these two *walawwe* servants.

In its heyday the Devideniya *walawwe* probably owned all the paddy land in the Devideniya paddy tract. It appears, however, that by 1869 the process of disintegration had set in. The owner of the Devideniya *walawwe* at that time, Devideniya Banda, although still the single largest paddy-land owner in the community, could lay claim to less than half of the Devideniya paddy tract.[9] Older inhabitants of the contemporary Rangama/Devideniya community attribute the *malawwe*'s ruin to the drunken and immoral behaviour of its Radala occupants. These aristocrats apparently got into debt and settled their debts by giving away their land. Thus the last owner of the Devideniya *malawwe* (Devideniya Nilame) inherited, in the latter part of the nineteenth century, an impoverished and decaying *malawwe*. He completed the financial ruin of the *malawwe* by getting enmeshed in a court case against the British authorities. At his death Devideniya Nilame left no legitimate offspring.[10]

The Grain Tax Assessment Register of 1877 shows that many fields belonging to the Devideniya *malawwe* were either left abandoned or had been acquired by other villagers. Certain low-caste families benefitted from the disintegration of the *malawwe*. Former tenants such as the washerman acquired the fields they had been cultivating. Moreover, Ambakumburalage Ukkuwa, the eldest son of one of the *malawwe*'s Batgam servants, not only obtained a considerable amount of land but also occupied the *malawwe* site.

Thus by the turn of the century no trace was to be found of the Devideniya *malawwe*. Nevertheless Devideniya during the baseline period had no connotations of low-caste status. The memory of the Devideniya *malawwe*, and the fact that the two village *malawwes* were situated in Devideniya, allowed this village to retain the prestige of its past. It was still considered an aristocratic village.

Notwithstanding the dissolution of the Devideniya *malawwe* and the dispersal of its land, the high castes in this community owned a disproportionate amount of land in the baseline period. This, together with the fact that local-level power at the turn of the century was linked to wealth and high-caste status, make it possible to describe the years 1885 to 1910 as a time prior to that in which a significant divergence between the hierarchies of inequality had occurred. In the Rangama/Devideniya community during the baseline period the hierarchies of caste, class and power were not cumulative. But as the following chapters will demonstrate, there was, as in the Kandyan kingdom, a considerable overlap between the occupants of the highest strata of the different hierarchies of stratification.

4   The Caste Hierarchy in the Baseline Period

There are two principal issues involved in examining the social structure of caste. The first is the determination of the caste groups and the way in which they are hierarchically ranked within the society in question.

The second major issue of concern is the investigation of the interaction between the hierarchically defined groups. This chapter shows that in the baseline period the pervasiveness of caste discrimination was not mutually exclusive with a high degree of inter-caste interaction and co-operation.

CASTES IN THE COMMUNITY

In this study castes are defined as groups possessing differential degrees of social honour and prestige. These groups place restrictions on marriage with individuals in other such groups, and membership in them is hereditary, determined by descent from one or both parents already members of a given caste.

The ranking of caste groups in South Asian society has been the subject of numerous studies and a long-standing theoretical debate between the proponents of the 'attributional' and 'interactional' theories of caste ranking. According to the former, a caste is ranked high or low in relation to the criterion of relative purity determined principally by such attributes as occupation and diet.[1] But the ranking of castes on a scale of purity and impurity has been found to be inadequate even in Hindu India, where the purity/pollution concept is strongest. The attribution theory would for example rank meat-eating castes lower than vegetarian castes, although in many communities some of the former may be observed to have a clearly privileged position in inter-caste interaction with some of the latter. In situations where the caste system is associated with discrimination/privilege among the groups, therefore, the structure of inter-caste interaction as

Table 3   *Caste distribution of households 1897*

Names used in the community	Other names in the literature	Traditional occupation	No. of households	% of households
Walawwe	Radala	state officials	2	3.4
Goigama	–	cultivators	19	32.2
Muslim	–	traders	2	3.4
Paṭṭi	Nilamakkārayo	cowherds	9	15.3
Gallat	Navandanna; Kammal Kārayo; Acāri	blacksmiths	6	10.2
Vahumpura; Hakuru	–	juggery makers; cooks	5	8.5
Hēna	Radā	washermen	4	6.8
Batgam; Padu; Dura	Batgam Dura	soldiers; cultivators; menial labourers	11	18.6
Vahal	Padu; Batgam	servants of aristocrats	1	1.7
			59	100.1(a)

Compiled from: High Land Register, Rangama Vasama, Kegalle District, 1897.
(a) Discrepancy is due to rounding.

propounded by Marriott appears to provide a more satisfactory objective criterion by which to rank castes.[2] Marriott himself emphasizes asymmetrical exchange of food and ritual services but it is entirely possible that other forms of asymmetrical exchange may, in a given community, be equally or more significant indicators of caste rank.[3]

Sinhalese caste rules specify a series of asymmetrical relations between castes. These include not only asymmetrical inter-caste transactions in food and services, but also asymmetrical seating arrangements and forms of address. On the basis of older inform-ants' descriptions of inter-caste interactions in this community in the past, it was possible to divide the population of the baseline period into nine groups which could be called castes according to the definition employed in this study (see Table 3).[4] The hierarchy of ranked castes in Table 3 differs in two significant ways from the conventional treatment of caste in Sinhalese society.

Firstly many observers treat three of the groups (Walawwe, Goigama and Paṭṭi) which I have identified as separate castes, as sub-castes of a single large Goigama caste. The significance they attach to categorizing these groups as sub-castes rather than castes is however difficult to understand. For one thing the terms caste and sub-caste, though freely used, are rarely defined precisely.[5] In addition, whilst describing these groups as sub-castes, in practice observers often treat them as separate castes,[6] and recognize them to be endogamous and unequal in status.[7] It appears likely therefore that the variable native usage of the term 'Goigama' to refer both to those who are known exclusively as Goigama as well as those who are known in local areas by some other caste name has unduly influenced such analyses.

In the Rangama/Devideniya community at the turn of the century two groups of people (Walawwe and Paṭṭi) who in certain Sinhalese areas are loosely included under the category Goigama, were strictly endogamous and were, on the basis of asymmetrical relationships, clearly ranked higher and lower respectively than a third group known simply as Goigama. According to the definition of caste employed in this study, therefore, at the turn of the century the Walawwe, Goigama and Paṭṭi constituted three separate castes.

The second significant difference between conventional ana-lyses and the identification of castes presented here lies in the inclusion of the Muslims. Because Muslims are ethnically distinct from the Sinhalese and are adherents of Islam, they are conventionally excluded from the analyses of caste in Sri Lanka. It is my contention, however, that in those situations where Muslims are resident within or in close proximity to Sinhalese villages, their relationship to the caste hierarchy should be empirically determined rather than a priori assumed to be one of exclusion. I have treated the Muslims as a caste group because within and around the Rangama/Devideniya community the Muslims formed (and still do), an endogamous group which can clearly be seen to occupy a rank in the caste hierarchy (see below).

Having identified the caste groups in the community it was not difficult to assign individuals to their appropriate groups. In the baseline period the most unambiguous objective indi-cator of a person's caste was his or her name.[8] The formal name of Kandyan Sinhalese in this community is that used when a person is asked to state his or her full name and that used on government documents. The formal name consists of a *vāsagama* (surname) followed by a personal name. During the baseline period most personal names and all but one *vāsagama* name were caste specific. What follows is a description of each of the nine castes in this community at the turn of the century. This constitutes a necessary first step to an understanding of the operation of the caste system at the baseline period and the way it has changed over the past century.

The Walawwe Caste

In the baseline period the Walawwe caste occupied the highest rank in the community caste hierarchy. *Walawwe* means manor house and Walawwe people are aristocrats. These families were not however known as Radala, a term reserved for the descendants of the famous regional *walawwes* of the Kandyan period, whose owners were important officers of state and who were granted vast tracts of land by the king. In contrast those known as Walawwe people were essentially village aristocrats whose ancestors were probably petty bureaucrats in the Kandyan government. Nevertheless it appears that marriage connections with the Radala people did take place, and that the Walawwe people shared the historical traditions of the Radala.

The *vāsagama* names of the two Walawwe families in the community during the baseline period harked back to a grand past. One *vāsagama* referred to a *walawwe*, whilst the other was a titled *patabändi*[9] name which established connection to an illustrious ancestor. Of the two families one, the Watte Gedera Walawwe, was older, better known, wealthier and said to have had good marriage connections with many famous Radala families including the Devideniya *walawwe*. The other, despite boasting a closer kinship link with the Devideniya *walawwe*, was poorer, and their 'manor' had only recently been established through marriage into the community of an indigent aristocrat from another area.

Even the grander Watte Gedera Walawwe family was not financially capable of maintaining as aristocratic a lifestyle as they may have wished. For instance it was never possible for the head of the *walawwe* to afford the luxury of abstaining from cultivating paddy himself. Nevertheless the memory of their manorial traditions persisted, and during the baseline period these traditions were maintained wherever possible. Their lifestyle differed in two respects from other households in the community. Firstly, the women of this *walawwe* never deigned to step into mud and participate in paddy cultivation. Secondly, the Watte Gedera Walawwe family had attached to it a family of people known in the community as 'slaves' (the Vahal caste in Table 3), who performed a variety of menial tasks and helped in the cultivation of paddy.

The Goigama Caste

The Goigama were second only to the Walawwe people in the caste hierarchy and constituted the solid core of respectable people in the community. The Goigama of the Rangama/Devideniya community did not (and do not) claim to belong to any of the 'respectable' Goigama 'sub-castes' the literature refers to (e.g. Mudali – leaders; Liyanagē – scribes; Kāriyakārage – performers of official duties). Older Goigama simply state that they are 'good people' (*hoṅda minissu*). Although members of all castes in this community engaged in agriculture, the Goigama, as the farmer caste, had the privilege of referring to agriculture as their sole traditional occupation.

With nineteen families, the Goigama were the most numerous caste in this community during the baseline period. All but five families belonged to four principal kin groups and together with the Watte Gedera Walawwe people, constituted the oldest established families in the community. Members of one family – the Ganege Rallage – were the customary incumbents of the Rangama *vihāraya* from as far back as the mid-nineteenth century and possibly earlier. In addition, at the turn of the century bureaucratic posts in the community were monopolized by these four kin groups.

All but one Goigama family had *vāsagama* names that were exclusive to Kandyan Goigama. The Portuguese derivation of the name of one household head – Muthuthanthri Bastiange Elias Fernando – however, clearly indicated his Low Country origin.

Low Country presence in the Kandyan highlands increased

rapidly as a result of British rule. Elias Fernando was one of many Low Country Sinhalese who was drawn to the highlands by the commercial and employment opportunities which were created as a consequence of the British presence. The Grain Tax Assessment Registers show that he was a relatively recent arrival in the Rangama/Devideniya community – between 1869 and 1877 he appears to have bought three–and–a–half acres of paddy land which had formerly belonged to the Devideniya *walawwe*.

To those familiar with Low Country Sinhalese castes, Elias Fernando's name indicates his non-Goigama and probably Karava (fisher) caste status. But most Kandyan villagers are, even today, unfamiliar with the caste system in the Low Country. This, coupled with the difficulty of verifying the status credentials of settlers from far off places, has enabled many Low Country people to assume a higher caste status in the highlands than they possessed in their natal villages. Elias Fernando was the first of many Low Country persons of dubious caste status who successfully 'passed' into the ranks of the Goigama in this community.

The Muslim Caste

The literature on caste in Sinhalese society invariably excludes the Muslims on the grounds that they are a separate ethnic and religious group. Ethnicity and religion are not, however, part of the definition of caste employed in this study and do not therefore, on their own, constitute valid reasons for placing Muslims outside the hierarchy of caste.

Muslims have been resident in Sri Lanka for centuries and, except on the East coast, are not concentrated in Muslim regions but are dispersed throughout the Sinhalese areas of the island. It is these latter Muslim people, most of whom are resident within, or in close proximity to, Sinhalese villages, with whom I am here concerned. Their position with regard to the caste hierarchy has been problematic even to those observers who insist that Muslims are a 'non-caste'. Ryan, for example, claims that Muslims 'are not a caste, for they are socially a distinct people outside the system within which caste relationships are operative', but is constrained by his own empirical observations to go on to state that 'in trading relationships they (Muslims) have been drawn into direct contact with their neighbours, and hence into a position requiring a status relationship . . . inevitably the Moors have acquired the patterns of inter-caste etiquette conventional to their surroundings.'[10]

The exclusion of Muslims resident in Sinhalese areas from the caste hierarchy appears somewhat arbitrary because socially Muslims are *not* distinct from the Sinhalese – they are not marginal to Sinhalese society. Muslim presence in the Kandyan highlands dates back to the time of the Kandyan kingdom. The trading function of the Muslims was recognized by the Kandyan government and they, like all other caste groups, were attached to a state department. Because the majority of Muslims did not hold service lands they were grouped into the *sulan badda* (*sulan* means wind – hence unsettled) within the larger *madige badda* (transport department). In return for living and trading in the Kandyan Provinces the Muslims had to fulfil various obligations. These included selling arecanuts belonging to the crown, providing oxen for transport and supplying the royal stores with salt and dry fish.

Muslim traders in the highlands did not confine their activities to the larger towns and bazaars. The itinerant Muslim trader was a familiar sight in remote villages. Over the centuries Muslims settled into established villages, first along the main trade routes and then in interior villages. They formed a separate endogamous group but have always been in intimate contact with the Sinhalese – in some contemporary highland villages Muslims even have Sinhalese *vāsagama* names.

Muslims bought paddy land and settled down in the Rangama/ Devideniya community in the last quarter of the nineteenth century. Separate religion and customs allowed the two Muslim families in the community during the baseline period to be less obsessed than their Sinhalese neighbours with the finer points of caste etiquette, and uninterested in receiving many of the specialized caste services. Nevertheless their interactions with various caste groups involved asymmetrical relations on the basis of which they could clearly be seen to occupy a distinct position in the community caste hierarchy. Like other castes in the community, Muslims used specific caste-related forms of address and were in turn addressed variously depending on the caste of the speaker (see Appendix II). It appears that all but the Walawwe and Goigama addressed Muslim males by the respectful term mudalali, indicating that the latter occupied an intermediate position in the caste hierarchy – lower than the high castes (Walawwe and Goigama) and higher than the lower castes (all other castes). Investigations into the giving and receiving of food also suggested a rank immediately below the high castes. Religious food taboos, which forbid Muslims to consume pork or shellfish and the flesh of any animal not slaughtered according to Islamic rules, made Muslims reluctant in general to accept food from Sinhalese. When they did, however, Muslims would only eat rice meals cooked in high-caste households, although all the lower castes were prepared to accept food from them. Even today Muslim traders who visit the Rangama/Devideniya community during the clove harvest season observe such commensal restrictions. The purchase of cloves on the 'leasing' system requires the buyer to live in close proximity to the leased clove trees for several days in order to safeguard and harvest the crop (see pp. 118–19). If the clove trees belong to low-caste Sinhalese persons the Muslim traders cook their own food, but when 'leasing' clove trees belonging to high-caste persons, they accept food cooked in the latter's kitchens.

The Paṭṭi Caste

The Paṭṭi people[11] were the highest of the low castes. Their position in the caste hierarchy was reflected in their names. Although they shared a few personal names with the high castes, many of their personal names (e.g. Pinhamy, Siyathuhamy) were, like their *vāsagama* names, not merely exclusively Paṭṭi but also contained elements (e.g. Siyathu) which clearly indicated low-caste status.

The caste occupation of the Paṭṭi during the Kandyan kingdom was cattle herding – Paṭṭi cowherds looked after the cattle of the king and the aristocratic families. It is not improbable that the ancestors of the Paṭṭi in the Rangama/Devideniya community served as cowherds to the Devideniya *walawwe*; the majority of Paṭṭi families still reside west of the Maha Oya, in the area of Rangama which borders Devideniya. (Some contemporary villagers allege that the Paṭṭi are the descendants of slaves of the Devideniya *walawwe*.) During the baseline period, however, the Paṭṭi did not practise their caste occupation and were full-time agriculturalists.

Status Competition between the Gallat and the Vahumpura

Observers of caste during the colonial period ranked the Vahumpura relatively low in the caste hierarchy. Knox (1681) and Davy (1821),[12] for instance, both ranked the Vahumpura lower than the Hēna caste. In this community, however, there was (and is) general agreement that the Vahumpura are superior to the Hēna. This subjective ranking coincides with the lower rank to which the Hēna would be assigned on the basis of the objective criterion of inter-caste interaction (see below).

The Vahumpura of the Rangama/Devideniya community not only claim precedence over the Hēna, but insist that they are also superior to the Gallat – a caste that modern observers of caste in Sri Lanka, like their counterparts in the colonial era, invariably rank higher than the Vahumpura.[13] Within the community, support for the Vahumpura claim to superiority over the Gallat is not widespread – it comes only from the high castes. The Gallat and most of the lower castes have a model of the caste hierarchy which places the Gallat higher than the Vahumpura.

During the baseline period both castes in question practised agriculture as well as their traditional caste occupations. The Gallat fashioned all the agricultural implements (ploughs, knives, axes, etc) used in the community. The Vahumpura made juggery. In addition the Vahumpura provided certain special services to the higher castes. The Vahumpura women cooked in Walawwe and Goigama houses on special occasions, and when the latter went on formal visits (e.g. wedding visits) or informal visits (e.g. to see relatives in another village), a Vahumpura man would carry the box of sweetmeats and/or rice that was presented to the host.

Both of these castes justify their claim to superiority principally by reference to an old Sinhalese description of themselves as

handuru bāgayak (*handuru* is an honorific used by low castes for
the Goigama, and *bāgayak* means half). This description therefore
implies that they are in some sense partially Goigama or possess
some attribute of the Goigama.

On the basis of inter-caste interaction, the objective ranking
of the two competing castes is not in fact difficult to determine. Forms of address between these two castes were (and
are) asymmetrical in a way which indicates the lower status
of the Vahumpura. The latter, like most other lower castes,
address the Gallat by the respectful terms bās unnähē/gurunānse
(M) and upāsikāva (F). Moreover, although the Gallat and
Vahumpura did not exchange services directly, the criterion
of caste service may also be used to rank the two castes. For,
from the observer's point of view, when one of two competing castes is refused a service which is yet granted to the
other, the latter may be judged to be superior. The Gallat,
like the Walawwe and Goigama, received the specialized services of two castes. The Hēna people washed their clothes
and participated in their life crisis rituals, and a caste known
as the Oli[14] (whose traditional occupation was dancing) carried
the rice box for the Gallat when they went on visits out of
the community. Both these castes denied their services to the
Vahumpura.

The status competition between the Gallat and the Vahumpura
illustrates the danger of accepting native models of society
uncritically. Many or even all such views may well be at variance
with the behavioural reality. In this particular case, although the
model of the caste hierarchy held by certain castes does coincide
with the observer's analysis, the Walawwe and Goigama (and
of course the Vahumpura) model does not. The high castes
accept the correctness of the Hēna caste's denial of service
to the Vahumpura, but still insist on the superiority of the
latter over the Gallat on the grounds that a close and trusted
relationship has always existed between themselves and the
Vahumpura. Acceptance of the 'high caste' model of the caste
hierarchy (an all too common feature of theorizing on South Asian
society) would have resulted in a distorted view of the behavioural
realities in this community.

The Hēna Caste

In some regions of Sri Lanka, the performance by the Hēna of their specialized caste services for the Vahumpura clearly indicates the former's inferior status. In the Rangama/Devideniya community the Hēna did not participate at the life crisis rituals of the Vahumpura, but asymmetrical forms of address pointed to their lower status. The Vahumpura addressed the Hēna in the same way as did those castes (including the Walawwe and the Goigama) for whom such services were performed (see Appendix II).

During the baseline period the Hēna engaged in agriculture but members of each of the four households carried out their caste occupation as well. Owing to a process of in and out migration, the internal composition of the other caste groups has varied over the years. The Hēna caste, however, is today, and has been for as long as people can remember, composed of a single kin group whose *vāsagama* name – Heneyalage – was not only caste exclusive but also caste descriptive. At the turn of the century this kin group owned, amongst others, a paddy field called *radā wela* (washerman's field). This field had been cultivated by this kin group continuously from that time in the Kandyan period when the Devideniya *walawwe* was established. The Hēna peoples' association with this community is therefore well established and disputed by no one.

The Batgam Caste

Contemporary Batgam are known by other castes in the community as Padu, or if a more polite term is considered appropriate, Dura[15] people. During the baseline period, however, the caste was most commonly known as Padu. At that time they constituted the second most numerous caste in the community and were superior in status only to the single Vahal family.

The Batgam are not clearly associated with any particular caste occupation. The literature lists their duties in the Kandyan period as including the bearing of palanquins, serving in the king's army and carrying out a variety of menial services.[16] Contemporary Batgam dissociate themselves from these services and claim that their sole occupation in the past was the cultivation of paddy to supply the royal granaries. Although exaggerated, the claim

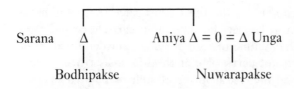

Figure 1   Batgam ancestry

is based on fact. During the Kandyan period the majority of
Paduvas (as the Batgam people were known then) lived in a
special type of royal village known as *batgam* (rice villages)
and were obliged to cultivate certain fields to supply the king's
granary.

The fact that all the Batgam in this community at the turn of
the century shared the same *vāsagama* name (Ambakumburalage)
did not indicate membership of a single kin group. The Ambakumburalage people were made up of two kin groups related only by
virtue of the fact that they were descended from two men, one
of whom had married the widow of the other's brother (see
Figure 1). The two brothers, Sarana and Aniya, first came to
Devideniya in the mid-nineteenth century as servants – part
of the dowry of a rich, aristocratic woman who married into
the Devideniya *walawwe*. Aniya died without offspring and a
man called Unga from a village called Ambakumbura married
Aniya's widow. The contemporary kin groups descended from
Sarana and Unga call themselves Bodhipakse and Nuwarapakse
respectively.

Sarana and his offspring remained closely associated with
the Devideniya *walawwe*, and with its disintegration became
the beneficiaries of some *walawwe* land. One of Sarana's sons
even occupied the old site of the *walawwe*. By the turn of
the century, therefore, the descendants of Sarana were more
prosperous than those of Unga. Nevertheless the latter (the
true Ambakumburalage people) were less marked by the stigma
of having been *walawwe* servants, and it would appear that as
a result of this Sarana's descendants 'borrowed' the *vāsagama*
Ambakumburalage.

The Vahal Caste

Vahal means slave. During the Kandyan period Vahal was not a caste category but rather an economic and legal condition. Surprisingly, according to the literature, most slaves were members of the higher castes. A person did not lose caste status by becoming a slave.[17] In the Kandyan Provinces slaves were household servants of Radala aristocrats and formed part of the lord's retinue. The institution of slavery survived through both Portuguese and Dutch rule, but was abolished by the British in 1844.

The single family categorized as Vahal by all other castes in this community during the baseline period would, in all probability, have described themselves as Padu and been so called by persons outside the community. My treatment of them as a separate caste does not rest on their designation as Vahal. Rather it is because this family belonged to an endogamous group which was distinctly inferior in caste status to the Batgam. Their *vāsagama* names were caste exclusive (e.g. Hulawali Pedige, Horana Pedige, etc.). Today, those who consider themselves 'true' Batgam claim that these people belong to a group traditionally bound to perform for the Batgam such services as removing the leaf on which a person ate, spreading cloths on the ground at funerals and carrying baggage on journeys. Although these claims are difficult to verify, there is no doubt that at the turn of the century 'true' Batgam treated this group with contempt. They refused to accept food from the Vahal family and would have considered intermarriage an infringement of caste endogamy.

The members of the Vahal family in this community were not slaves in any legal sense. They were, however, in a position of servitude to the Watte Gedera Walawwe family and lacked any form of economic independence. The family possessed no land but was given a small plot on which to build a house. (The degree of dependence on the *walawwe* is indicated by the fact that the family's *vāsagama* name referred to this plot of land.) Over and above shelter their master provided them with food and clothing. No wages were paid. Although the alliance was theoretically voluntary, the abject poverty of the Vahal family and the economic conditions of the time gave them no real opportunity of breaking the association with the walawwe.

MANIFESTATIONS OF CASTE INEQUALITY

An observer of Rangama and Devideniya at the turn of the century would not fail to have been struck by the pervasive influence of caste. In the life of each individual caste rules came into operation from the time he or she received a name. *Vāsagama* names were determined by caste, and although personal names were not totally caste bound, the range of their applicability was strictly defined. True the restrictions on names applied equally to the Walawwe and Goigama as it did to the lower castes, but it was a disability only to the latter whose caste names were demeaning and unflattering.

During the baseline period all inter-caste interaction was strictly governed by the rules of caste etiquette. How people addressed each other, sat in each other's company, partook of food and drink, and who they married, was not left to the discretion of the individuals concerned but was prescribed by well-known rules, rules by which the majority of people abided.

The symbols of superiority and inferiority that came into play in inter-caste interaction varied with the context in which the interaction occurred. The chance meeting of two persons of different caste on a footpath for instance would have elicited one or more of a series of gestures (e.g. stepping off the path and giving precedence to the other, removal of headgear, bending the head to one side, touching the back of the head or touching the shawl that villagers wore thrown over their shoulders) on the part of the person of lower caste. Each of these gestures was symbolic of deference. The number of gestures employed varied with the relative rank of the interactors. If the person of higher status was a Walawwe or Goigama person, for example, all these gestures were brought into play and it was necessary for the person of lower status to speak in a cringing, beseeching manner.

Use of a term of address (both the vocative and the second person pronoun) involved the manipulation of complex linguistic patterns. The vocative was exclusively determined by the caste status of speaker and addressee and was (with the exception of the term 'appe' used for young Walawwe people) independent of age considerations (see Appendix II).

Thus, for example, an old Vahumpura woman would call a young Goigama girl 'manike' (jewel) while the latter would address the old woman by her personal name. In the case of the second-person-singular pronoun Sinhalese speakers have a wide choice of hierarchically ranked terms[18] which include:

thō; thopi	– you	(very demeaning)
umba	– you	(familiar if used by parents to children or between friends; demeaning in all other contexts)
oyā	– you	(familiar in the same contexts as umba; disrespectful in all others)
oba; thamuse	– you	(equal but formal)
thamannānse	– you	(elevated, formal)
hāmuduruvo;	– your highness	
oba vahanse		(used also by the laity for Buddhist monks)

Whilst factors such as age, education and job were marginally important, the single most significant determinant of pronoun used in inter-caste interactions in the baseline period was the relative caste status of the interactors.

When the home was the venue of inter-caste interaction other forms of caste etiquette came into play as well. A person visiting the house of an individual of higher caste would not presume to approach the front of the house but would make his way to the rear. The host might, if he felt inclined, take his visitor to the front of the house, but wherever the actual interaction took place the person of low caste would always be seated on an inferior seat. Kandyan houses had at least three types of ranked seats,[19] the status of each of which was directly related to its height. Even the Goigama did not escape discrimination. For the Walawwe people, as keen as everyone else to establish superiority, gave the Goigama a bench rather than a chair to sit on.

Hospitality was governed by caste-based commensal rules which ordained an asymmetrical exchange of food between castes – an individual could accept food and drink from a person of a higher caste but not vice versa. This, combined with the etiquette of seating, meant in effect that only status equals could sit at a table and partake of food together. For a host would not allow a visitor of lower caste than himself the honour of sitting at a table. For instance a Paṭṭi man who accepted a meal from a Goigama house would be served on a banana leaf (so as not to pollute the Goigama crockery) and eat the food sitting on a bench or a low stool. Ironically, the otherwise snobbish Goigama were hardly treated any better when accepting food in a *walawwe*. They were seated on a bench and the food was laid out on a stool (*ätul pat peṭṭiya*).

Asymmetrical food exchanges were also strictly adhered to in the paddy fields. Then, as now, when co-operative labour teams worked on a field, the individual whose field was being worked customarily supplied food and drink for the whole team. But in the baseline period all those of higher caste than the field owner would not even drink tea prepared in the owner's house. They deigned to accept only betel (a masticatory) and coconut water which could be drunk directly from the coconut without the use of a receptacle. Special arrangements were made to have their meals cooked in a nearby caste-fellow's house and brought to the fields.

The exchange of food as a symbol of inequality manifested itself above all on the occasion of weddings. Only close relatives of the bride and groom participated in the principal wedding feast which consisted of a meal of rice with a large variety of curries. Since caste endogamy was strictly enforced and there were no inter-caste marriages during the baseline period, the principal wedding feast was shared only among caste fellows. The expression *apē magul geval valata enne nä* – (they don't attend our wedding house) – indicates the superior or inferior status of the speaker depending on whether he is referring to persons of lower or higher status than himself. Indeed, participation at the wedding feast was perhaps the most significant index of equality in rural Sinhalese society and no caste would compromise its status by allowing inferior castes to share in it. Goigama were excluded from wedding feasts of Walawwe folk just as rigidly as they themselves excluded all those of lower caste status than themselves. The expression of shared status celebrated on the wedding day itself was in stark contrast to the festivities of the preceding days. For the ideal form of these festivities involved the invitation of all the other caste groups, each on a separate day, for a celebration.[20] The castes were invited in order of rank, and the serving of food and drink conformed to the rules of commensality – betel and coconut water for those higher than the host and traditional festival foods such as *kävun* (oil cakes) and *kiri bat* (milk rice) for those lower.

During the baseline period one did not have to observe inter-caste interaction to evidence inequality. For a variety of sumptuary laws prescribed the correct mode of dress and even hair-styles of the various castes. The low-caste Batgam, for instance, had to abide by a number of taboos. Their men could not wear a *koṇḍe* (hair tied in a knot) and Batgam of both sexes could not wear any clothing below the knee or above the waist. Vahumpura people had somewhat more freedom. They were permitted clothing above the waist and their men could wear a *koṇḍe*. Yet their women were not allowed to wear the *osariya* (Kandyan sari). Only the 'high caste' Walawwe and Goigama people had the freedom to dress as they pleased.

At the turn of the century there was near universal conformity to caste-determined modes of behaviour, and caste rules were not compromised by extraneous factors such as a person's education or job. These latter enhanced one's position *vis-à-vis* one's own caste fellows but made little difference in one's interactions with those of higher caste. The case of Bilinda, a Batgam man who was appointed headman of Devideniya in 1912, is interesting in this regard. His job brought with it virtually no attenuation of the disabilities of his caste status except for the fact that some young people of the high castes called him Vidāna mama[21] instead of Bilindajja. He was still not offered a chair in houses of higher castes and whilst he could assume a relatively superior form of dress (a coat) within the confines of his own village, he had to be bare-bodied whenever he approached the Ratemahatmaya (chief native headman) who was always a Radala aristocrat.

Nor was caste etiquette compromised by religious scruples in this community. Although the Rangama *vihāraya* served people of various castes, its incumbency was restricted to a person of high-caste status according to the rules of the Siyam *nikāya* (sect), and to a member of a particular family (Ganege Rallage) according to local custom. Discrimination was also rife among the laity. For instance within the *vihāraya* premises Walawwe and Goigama people would not deign to sit alongside low-caste persons in the preaching hall – a rope was tied across the hall reserving one side for the 'high' and the other side for the 'low' castes. The *vihāraya* was also an arena where commensal restrictions operated. On days when pious lay persons observe *sil* (abide by the eight precepts of

Buddhism), it is considered meritorious for other lay persons to provide refreshments for the devotees, but many people refused to accept any food or drink offered by those of lower caste than themselves. The Walawwe and Goigama people were particularly discriminatory in this regard. They made arrangements to have their food sent from their houses and would make a point of finishing their meal prior to the time of the alms-giving in order to avoid being offered food and drink by low-caste persons.

Caste etiquette and the symbols of superiority/inferiority which it maintained were not uniformly graded along the caste ladder. In general, while each caste tried its best to assert its superiority over those below it, caste etiquette was most fully developed and most strictly adhered to in the interaction between the high-caste Walawwe and Goigama people on the one hand and all the low castes on the other. In certain situations these two high castes did make fine distinctions among the low castes, but by and large, as far as the former were concerned, all the latter were primarily low-caste persons and only secondarily members of specific castes. Although there was inequality in the interactions between the Walawwe and the Goigama people, *vis-à-vis* other castes they together flaunted the privileges of high-caste status to a greater degree than took place between superior and inferior castes further down the caste ladder. In this community during the baseline period these two castes even arrogated to themselves certain privileges over and above those prescribed by conventional caste rules. They insisted, for example, that all other castes should bathe downstream from them and reserved a section of the Maha Oya called Haputhota Wala, after a prominent Goigama family, for their exclusive use.

The Walawwe and Goigama people did not have to put up with any disapproval of their privileges from the British colonial government. On the contrary the majority of British officials accepted the caste system and in certain respects British rule actually enhanced the position of these high castes. An acceptance of the superiority of the high castes and a strong desire to maintain the traditionally stable patterns of social order led the British to retain the caste-based Radala and Goigama dominated bureaucratic structure that had prevailed during the Kandyan kingdom. These considerations also led to members of the high castes being appointed to fill prestigious white-collar jobs (registrars, co-operative managers, school teachers etc.), created during the period of British rule.[22] British policies thus resulted in a situation where low-caste persons, however intelligent, were denied the opportunity of white-collar jobs and the advancement they offered.

In Rangama/Devideniya at the turn of the century not even death could overcome the inequalities of caste. Although cremation is the prescribed Buddhist way of disposing of corpses, here cremation was yet another privilege that the Walawwe and Goigama people reserved for themselves. Low-caste persons had to be satisfied with burial.

INTER-CASTE CO-OPERATION AND COMMUNICATION

The fact that discrimination was rife in the community did not mean that contact between people of different castes was deliberately kept to a minimum. Inter-caste contact was frequent and took place in a variety of formal and informal contexts.

The most formalized kind of contact between castes was based on the performance of traditional caste services. These transactions were not monetized and gratitude was expressed by gifts of rice and coconuts, the size of the gift being entirely at the discretion of the person who received the service.

Much more informal were the inter-caste transactions that took place in the context of paddy cultivation. Co-operative labour teams were, for example, constituted without regard to caste. To the extent that in dispersed communities such as this, recruitment of caste fellows for a task was impractical, multi-caste teams might appear to be a necessary concession to convenience. Yet older informants of today's community insist that it was considered quite natural for people of different castes to work together in the paddy fields, and that it did not require any suppression of a preference for caste exclusiveness.

The ethos of reciprocity leading to inter-caste contact was also demonstrated in the relationship between the Goigama and a Gallat man called Pinchi Appu. Pinchi Appu was important to the community in two ways. He was a skilled blacksmith and a renowned native doctor. In return for the help he rendered the village, persons of all castes, including rich Goigama, helped

Pinchi Appu cultivate his quite considerable paddy holdings. Whilst this was for many the most economical way of repaying Pinchi Appu, rich Goigama had a more convenient alternative. They could have settled their debts through gifts in kind. On their part then, involvement in cultivating Pinchi Appu's fields was purely voluntary and is cited by contemporary Goigama as evidence of the goodwill and camaraderie that existed in the past between different castes.

Despite discrimination, religious rituals and performances were carried out jointly by all the Buddhists in the community regardless of caste. In a certain sense this was hardly surprising given the prevailing circumstances and conditions. For one thing there was only one *viharaya* in the area and whatever its shortcomings all castes had, of necessity, an interest in its maintenance. Secondly domestic religious rituals involved considerable organization and expense[23] and therefore necessitated the participation of a larger number of people than any single caste group at the turn of the century could have supplied. But granted the necessity for intra-community participation, it is nevertheless remarkable that *viharaya* activities, which were dominated by the high castes, and in which certain forms of caste discrimination occurred, were not marred by disputes. Rather they appear to have been occasions when inter-caste co-operation was manifest.

In like manner the asymmetrical nature of commensal rules did not act as a restraint upon social visiting and the acceptance of hospitality, although the venue of the visit was usually the home of the person of superior caste. Ironically, however, in the absence of licensed taverns and their supply of 'caste-free' toddy,[24] the Walawwe and Goigama men who felt it beneath their dignity to manufacture toddy themselves, nevertheless went to low-caste (Batgam) houses to buy and drink toddy. Although the Goigama and Walawwe men carried with them leaf cups to avoid using low-caste crockery, the acceptance of toddy was in theory an infringement of caste rules. But it was winked at by people in the community and the high castes appeared unconcerned by the contrary way in which they scrupulously avoided drinking the tea of the very people from whom they were happy to accept toddy.

Despite the presence of discrimination then, inter-caste contact was frequent and took place in many situations that could not be described as 'unavoidable'. It appears that not only the higher castes, but the lower castes also, voluntarily initiated inter-caste contact in spite of the inherently unequal features of those interactions. Relations between castes were, by all accounts, characterized by goodwill. The evidence suggests that there was in the baseline period a strong ethos of 'community loyalty' and 'vertical solidarity' which is conspicuously absent in contemporary Rangama/Devideniya.

5 The Class Hierarchy in the Baseline Period

Application of the three-dimensional model to the analysis of social stratification shows that class is not a late-twentieth-century development in Rangama/Devideniya. This chapter examines the way in which material inequality created cleavages in this community and structured relations between people at the turn of the century. Rather than neglecting class altogether or analysing it within the framework of caste, recognition of its independent importance as a basis of stratification also makes possible the examination of the interplay between the class and caste hierarchies.

THE ECONOMIC ORGANIZATION OF THE COMMUNITY

In this book the Rangama/Devideniya community has been termed a 'peasant society'. My reasons for so defining it rest on the nature of the community's economic organization, both during the contemporary period and at the turn of the century.

The definition of 'peasant society' has been the source of a long-standing debate. Whilst anthropologists agree that peasant societies are not isolated communities but are to a greater or lesser extent integrated with the wider society, there is less agreement on how best to conceptualize this partial integration. Some perceive the peasant society's inter-relationship with the wider society primarily in cultural terms, as the interaction between the 'great tradition' of the city and the 'little tradition' of the peasant community.[1] The great tradition/little tradition dichotomy is, however, of limited value, since it results in an artificial fragmenting of the cultural system of a people into great and little tradition elements. It is more useful to conceptualize the peasant society's partial integration with the wider society in terms of its economic organization. Peasants are subsistence cultivators who are also involved in the external market economy.

The economy of the Rangama/Devideniya community during the baseline period could, according to this definition, be described as a peasant economy. Although all the inhabitants did engage in subsistence agriculture, they were, in a variety of ways, simultaneously involved with the wider cash economy.

The majority of people in this community participated in an agricultural market by selling some of their crops. The cash they obtained from the sale of agricultural goods was essential to them. For one thing certain basic consumer goods such as salt, cloth and matches were not available in the community but could be procured for cash either from the itinerant Muslim traders or the Muslim shops in Dambawala. Cash was also a necessity because, during British rule, the inhabitants of Rangama/Devideniya, like other rural Kandyans, were increasingly drawn into the wider economy through the colonial tax structure.

In the early part of the baseline period the tax which impinged most heavily on the peasantry was that levied on grain.[2] Apart from the village headman, part of whose remuneration was exemption from the tax, every owner of paddy land was obliged to pay the grain tax. Default on the tax due resulted in the sale of the crop or the land itself. In the Kegalle district, the annual grain tax was payable either in the form of one-fourteenth of the crop or by commutation at the rate of Rs 1.25 per *päla* (⅝ acre). From conversations with older informants it would appear that most people found it more convenient to pay the grain tax in kind. There were, however, other taxes imposed by the British colonial government which did require cash. In the case of the road tax (Rs 1.50 a year), this was because few Kandyans found acceptable the alternative form of payment, which was the performance of six days unpaid labour on roads. Defaulters were sent to 'village prisons', which were in effect labour camps organized by the District Roads Committee, where they were forced to work for 24 days. Escapees from these labour camps were liable, if caught, to a month's stone-breaking in prison.

The tax that most older informants in the contemporary community recall most clearly was the Village Committee tax. This tax was 0.50 cents a year and payable by all persons between the ages of 18 and 40 years. Older informants all insist that many people found it difficult to pay the Village Committee tax and were obliged to perform unpaid labour for the government in recompense. The physical shortage of cash they attribute to the difficulty of finding buyers for agricultural produce at the time, and the low price such goods fetched even when they were sold.

Despite the fact that the Rangama/Devideniya people's involvement with the cash economy of the wider society took place on terms unfavourable to themselves, the community as a whole was relatively prosperous. This was because the community was only partially integrated with the external economy, its relative prosperity stemming from the internal subsistence sector of the economy. Each family produced a large proportion of the food necessary for consumption. In comparison with the contemporary community the population pressure on land was low,[3] and land, though highly valued, had a lower marginal utility at the turn of the century than it does today.

The peasantry of Hatara Korale was prosperous enough to avoid having to seek employment on British plantations. Most British officials recognized this fact and indeed some were even committed to preserving the economic status quo.[4] Rural unemployment was virtually non-existent in this region[5] and even in situations where some economic incentive may have been present, there was, on the part of Kandyan Sinhalese, a cultural prejudice against labouring on foreign estates.

The unavailability of Kandyan labour was serious enough to merit the concern of other less paternalistic colonial officials.[6] In the Rangama/Devideniya community for example, only a few Batgam men felt it worth their while to work as labourers on the British plantations. Their position in the caste hierarchy,[7] and their close proximity to Berawila and Natha Kande estates, probably accounts for this involvement.

The economy of the community which enabled the people of Rangama and Devideniya to be virtually independent of the plantations that surrounded them was primarily agrarian in character. At the turn of the century agricultural land in this region was divided into two basic categories on the basis of physical features – *maḍa iḍam* (literally mud land, i.e. paddy land) and *goḍa iḍam* (high land). The latter was further divided on the basis of cultivation technique into *vatu* (garden land) and *hēn* (chena land).

Hēn (chena land)

Chena land, the least valued type of agricultural land, was forest land surrounding the village, on which swidden agriculture was practised. In this community chena land was used to grow supplementary food such as *kurakkan* and *amu* (types of millet), *bada iriṅgu* (Indian corn), hill paddy, and a variety of vegetables.

During the baseline period it appears that almost all household heads engaged in chena cultivation, since forest land, despite British interference, was still freely available. Apart from privately-owned forest land,[8] peasants in remote areas such as this continually encroached on what was deemed 'crown' forest land. Although there was no shortage of forest land, three reasons militated against the limitless expansion of this type of agriculture. Firstly, chena cultivation was time consuming and laborious. It involved felling trees, clearing and burning the forest, fencing the plot and guarding the crop from wild animals and birds. Secondly, there was no market for chena crops. Thirdly, chena cereals were considered less wholesome and less palatable than rice,[9] and were consumed less through choice than through necessity.

Vatu (garden land)

'Garden land' referred to high land (usually around the house) on which perennial crops were cultivated, with the primary aim of satisfying subsistence needs. Each person tried to grow on garden land as many of the crops that were considered necessary to supplement the staple food – rice. Even a garden of half an acre contained the mandatory coconut, jak, banana and breadfruit trees, kitul palms and as many fruit trees as possible. The 'cultivation' of garden land implied nothing more than the planting of seedlings and nurturing of young plants. Once the plants had matured and started bearing they were neglected, except for the harvesting of the crop in the right season.

Market outlets for jak, breadfruit, mangoes, bananas, mangosteens, lemons, rambutans etc., which grow profusely in the Kegalle district, are rudimentary today and were virtually non-existent in the baseline period. As a result these crops were grown strictly for consumption. Although a coconut or bunch of bananas could occasionally be sold, the only highland crop which could be classified a commercial crop was arecanut.[10] Despite its commercial value, arecanut was not cultivated any more scientifically than other garden crops. Even the smallest extent of garden land contained a few arecanut trees, but older informants insist that there was never any question of expanding arecanut cultivation at the expense of subsistence garden crops. Once planted, arecanut trees reproduced rapidly and richer villagers had whole groves of such trees.

Sinhalese use the raw, mature arecanut along with betel leaves as a masticatory. The trade value of arecanuts, however, has for centuries been the result of the South Indian market for the sun-dried, tender arecanut known as *karunka*. Thus from early times arecanut was an item of inter-coastal trading in the region.[11] The South Indian merchants who monopolized the inter-coastal trade, were supplied with arecanuts by Muslims and Sinhalese of the fisher caste who were the sole buyers of Kandyan arecanut. At the turn of the century this long-standing pattern of arecanut trade continued virtually unchanged, except for the fact that the transactions involved were gradually being conducted via the medium of cash rather than through barter.

Despite the steady demand for arecanuts over the years, the arecanut market has until very recently been a buyers market. In the Kandyan period 'since the trade in Arecanuts was a royal monopoly, the price of the nuts was very low; the villagers being left only with two alternatives, either to sell the nuts to the king's traders at a nominal price or let the nuts rot under the trees.'[12]

The ending of the royal monopoly of the arecanut trade hardly improved matters for the Kandyan peasants. For the marketing of arecanuts at the turn of the nineteenth century remained as poorly developed as it was centuries ago. In isolated villages like Rangama and Devideniya, itinerant Muslim traders still provided the only market outlet for arecanuts. The market was not systematized – the traders visited the villages intermittently, and their numbers remained small enough to preclude any significant competition among them which would have proved beneficial to the sellers.

Maḍa Iḍam (paddy land)

Paddy land refers to the low-lying areas in the valleys and some of the lower terraced slopes of hillsides that are exclusively used for the cultivation of paddy by the 'wet' method. Under this technique paddy fields must have a constant but regulated supply of water during the growth of the crop.[13] Rice grown on paddy land was, and is, the staple food of the Sinhalese. But paddy was not an exclusively subsistence crop. It was a cash crop as well – excess paddy was sold within the community or to itinerant Muslim traders.

At the turn of the century paddy land was unambiguously the most highly-valued type of agricultural land. Paddy land was held in such high esteem because it was the source not only of the staple food but also of power (see pp. 69–71). Over the centuries it had assumed a position of vital importance, and village social life revolved around the paddy cultivation cycle. In order to ensure the proper growth of the crop and a good harvest, Kandyan peasants not only expended more labour on paddy land than on any other type of land, but also engaged in magic, rituals and ceremonies to appeal to gods and appease demons, at each stage of cultivation.

Only one crop of paddy was grown each year during the baseline period. This crop, cultivated during the *maha* season (October/November to March), coincided with the north-east monsoon and was an entirely rain-fed crop. A second (*yala*) crop, coinciding with the south-west monsoon, was planted in some parts of the Kegalle district at the turn of the century. However, the paddy fields in this community were left fallow during the *yala* season, since the rainfall from the south-west monsoon was irregular and often insufficient to irrigate the paddy fields satisfactorily. (The minor irrigation works providing supplementary water which make a *yala* crop feasible today, were constructed well after the baseline period.)

The techniques of paddy cultivation at this time were much as they had been centuries ago in the time of the Kandyan kings. And it does not appear, at least from the testimony of certain British officials, that Kandyan peasants were over-enthusiastic about adopting scientific measures for obtaining higher yields.[14] Mechanization was unknown, and every task was carried out either by bullocks or by manual labour. A time-honoured co-operative labour arrangement known as *attam* was used to carry out labour intensive tasks that needed to be completed within a short space of time. The production of paddy was essentially a preserve of the Sinhalese male, the women's role being limited to weeding, gathering and stacking the paddy after harvesting, and carrying the stalks to the threshing floor.[15] On account of their alleged impurity, women were debarred from even watching the grain being threshed. This process was highly ritualized and included magical practices and appeals to gods for a good yield. In the absence of chemical fertilizers and the high-yielding paddy varieties used today, the yield at the turn of the century was less than half of what it is today. The only fertilizer used consisted of discarded pieces of dry fish which the more enterprising farmers bought in the nearest town or bazaar. The kinds of paddy sown were the relatively low-yielding indigenous varieties which had a long maturation period.

A characteristic feature of paddy land which distinguished it from garden and chena land was the complexity of its tenurial arrangements. In terms of differential rights, an individual's relationship to paddy land took one or more of three basic forms – landlord, owner-cultivator and tenant. Wage labour in paddy cultivation was non-existent, and any person who worked on another's land did so in the capacity of a tenant. Over and above these differential rights to land, there were (and are) to be found distinctive tenurial practices related to the physical features of paddy-land holdings. An individual's paddy-land holding was usually made up of a number of separate parcels (each a part of a larger 'field') which varied in size, location and fertility. These tenurial practices were designed to facilitate economy, convenience and equality among landowners with common interests in a particular field.[16]

THE CLASS HIERARCHY IN RANGAMA/DEVIDENIYA

Demarcation of Classes

Just as it is today, so in the baseline period, the economy of this community was primarily an agrarian one. Land was therefore the most important basis of material inequality. In the baseline period, however, unlike today, there was a close equivalence between ownership of land and its control.

If the 'value' of an asset is considered to be synonymous with its cash or market value, at the turn of the century the population of the Rangama/Devideniya community could best be divided into classes on the basis of ownership of high land. Arecanut, the principal cash crop grown on high land thrived in the Kegalle district better than in any other part of the island; yields were high and in the baseline period arecanut sold for a price that made it more remunerative per acre than paddy land.[17] But according to the definition of class employed in this study, an asset is deemed to be valuable only to the extent that it contributes to the material well-being of the person who has control over it. Based upon this perception of the 'value' of an asset, it appears that differential ownership of paddy land was more significant than high land for the demarcation of class categories in the baseline period.

Despite the higher market value of arecanut, it appears that the Sinhalese universally preferred paddy land and would not have considered expanding high-land cultivation at the expense of paddy land. Contemporary informants claim that those with the wherewithal to buy land invariably opted to purchase paddy land. The unwavering preference for paddy in the face of the pecuniary superiority of arecanut troubled the British, who constantly stated their opinion that in the Sri Lankan context the cultivation of paddy was 'uneconomic'.[18]

This preference of the Sinhalese only appears as a manifestation of peasant irrationality when the 'value' of an asset is equated with its cash or pecuniary value. But such an equation is based on two assumptions, neither of which were valid in the Rangama/Devideniya community at the turn of the century.

Firstly, it assumes the absence of non-material ends which override cash incentives. But such ends were operative in this community. For one thing the high cultural value placed on being self-sufficient in rice made paddy cultivation more honourable and prestigious than other forms of agriculture. This was sufficient reason for those not self-sufficient in rice to buy paddy land when the opportunity arose. For those who had enough paddy land to satisfy consumption needs another non-material goal –

power over tenants – was operative in their desire to invest further in paddy land.

Secondly, even if material advancement was the sole end, equation of the 'value' of an asset with cash value assumes developed trade and market systems and the consequent exchangeability of cash for goods and services. This was not the case, however, in isolated areas in the highlands at the turn of the century. The Rangama/Devideniya community was geographically isolated from, and poorly integrated with, the wider regional and national economies. Poorly-developed trade and markets resulted here in two types of market uncertainty which undermined the pecuniary advantage of arecanut and made paddy a more valuable crop than its strictly cash value would suggest. For one thing the market supply of rice was uncertain, and peasants who were not self-sufficient in rice could not depend on the availability of rice in the local market. Cash was no security against the threat of doing without the staple food, rice. Secondly, there was a considerable degree of insecurity facing those selling high-land crops. The principal demand for arecanut was located in a foreign country and cultivators were vulnerable to market forces beyond their control. While this is true of most agricultural enterprises, rudimentary communications and lack of information concerning the arecanut market made this particularly problematic for Kandyan peasants. Moreover, in the event of a collapse in the arecanut market there was at the time no known or proven alternative high-land cash crop.

In such an economic environment, paddy land was in fact a far more 'valuable' asset than high land. Paddy land was indispensable for material well-being in a way that high land was not. For an individual who had high land, to the exclusion of paddy land, lacked the security of a steady supply of rice and could not be ranked with someone of superior wealth.

It appears, then, that individuals in the Rangama/Devideniya community at the turn of the century could most realistically be categorized into classes on the basis of paddy-land ownership. Information given to me by older informants indicates that degree of self-sufficiency in rice was an important economic basis for structuring relations between people in this community. Accordingly, along a continuum of paddy-land ownership, degree of self-sufficiency in rice may be used to divide the population into classes. Self-sufficiency in rice is here defined as a situation where the rice required by a household in order to maintain what is considered a minimally satisfactory standard of living can be produced from the paddy land owned by the household. (The emphasis on ownership rather than tenancy is intentional and relates to the security of rice supplies.[19])

The quantity of rice required by a household to be self-sufficient has increased over the years despite the fact that the average household size has decreased from six to five persons. For contemporary inhabitants of this community a satisfactory standard of living entails having three meals of rice per day. This requires at least 60 bushels of paddy per year, which under present cultivation techniques can be produced on half an acre of land. Despite a probable preference for such an exclusively rice-based diet, individuals at the turn of the century had, of necessity, to lower their standards. Yields were low and unpredictable (20–30 bushels per acre) and only one crop could be harvested annually. Thus even a household with a relatively large extent of two acres would have been hard pressed to satisfy its full cereal requirements with rice. Rice intake was thus supplemented with other cereals, principally *kurakkan* and hill paddy grown on chena land. Under these circumstances it is plausible to assume that self-sufficiency in rice at the baseline period meant having one full meal of rice per day every day of the year. To meet this minimum rice requirement one acre of paddy land was necessary.

Individuals whose paddy land holdings enabled members of their households to have between one and three rice meals per day are here termed 'middle farmers' (with landholdings of one to three acres of paddy land). All those with less than one acre may be said to have constituted the 'poor' class. In order to meet minimum rice requirements they would have been constrained either to purchase paddy or to work as tenants on others' land. At the other extreme were the 'rich', who would have had sufficient paddy land (over three acres) to ensure each year, not only three meals of rice per day, but also a regular supply of excess paddy that could be sold (see Table 4).

Whilst paddy land was indispensable for material well-being, high land, especially if it contained arecanut, was useful as a source

Table 4   *Classes in the community – baseline period*

Class	Paddy Extent per Household	No. of Households	% of Households	Total Paddy Owned by Class			% of Paddy Owned by Residents
				A	R	P	
Rich	over 3 acres	8	13.6	40	0	10	47.7
Middle Farmers	1–3 acres	17	28.8	33	3	18 ⅓	40.3
Poor	under 1 acre	34 a	57.6	10	0	6 ⅔	12.0
		59	100.0	83	3	35	100.0

Compiled from: Grain Tax Assessment Register, Kegalle District 1888.
a   Seventeen of these households owned no paddy land at all.

of cash. Unlike paddy-land ownership, possession of arecanut trees was not limited to a certain section of the population. It was much more widespread than paddy-land ownership and given the pattern of mixed gardening, arecanut as a source of cash income was available to virtually everyone in the community. According to the High Land Register of 1897, with the exception of a handful of individuals, every household head owned over half an acre of high land.

This does not mean that high-land ownership was undifferentiated. With few exceptions an individual's high-land holdings were commensurate with his class position as defined by paddy-land holdings (see Table 5). A handful of individuals, however, had small paddy-land holdings but relatively large high-land extents. These individuals may be termed 'class marginals' insofar as their

Table 5   *High-land ownership in relation to class – baseline period*

Class	Total High Land Owned by Class			% of all High Land	Average High Land per Household		
	A	R	P		A	R	P
Rich	56	2	00	30.4	7	0	10
Middle Farmer	56	3	00	30.5	3	1	14
Poor	72	3	10	39.1	2	0	22
	186	0	10	100.0			

cash surpluses may have enabled them to overcome the insecurity of not having paddy by buying rice in bulk whenever it was available in the local market. Apart from one Muslim, all the 'class marginals' belonged to the Batgam caste who lived in the higher reaches of the hillsides.

The extensive high-land holdings of these individuals may be explained by the fact that they lived in close proximity to forests, which made it easier for them to clear it and convert it into chena or garden land. During the baseline period, these individuals were probably accumulating their cash to invest in paddy land and did not appear to have any significant impact on the economy of the community. But in the second and third decades of the twentieth century, the cash these 'class marginals' possessed was to enable them to obtain lucrative contract work on British plantations and thereby play a crucial role in the changing pattern of landownership in this community.

Inter-class Relations

Material inequality based on differential ownership of paddy land not only divided the population of this community into three class categories – the rich, the middle-farmers and the poor – but also served as an important basis for structuring relations between these groups. Contemporary inhabitants of this community were able to provide useful information regarding the nature of the interactions between those who possessed different degrees of wealth in the past. Their accounts indicate that the interactions between the different groups were not of the same intensity or frequency.

The 'middle farmers' appear to have had little contact or need for interaction with either those higher or lower than themselves in the class hierarchy. The 'middle farmers' had sufficient paddy land to meet their consumption needs and sufficient high-land cash crops to pay their taxes, buy dry fish, salt, matches and other essential commodities. On the one hand they were largely independent of the 'rich' (except in time of severe crisis), and on the other had little of the surplus wealth which would have encouraged the attentions of the 'poor'. In contrast the interactions between the 'rich' and the 'poor' were frequent.

The relationship between the 'rich' and the 'poor' was by

all accounts cordial and friendly. The attitude of the former towards the latter was one of paternalism and noblesse oblige. At a time when there were virtually no national welfare services, the 'poor', it is claimed, often depended upon the 'rich' for their very survival, and the 'rich' duly played out their role as concerned and sympathetic father figures. For instance the lady of the Watte Gedera Walawwe personally arranged a marriage for her 'slave'. Moreover the concept of noblesse oblige was well internalized by the 'rich'. Rice and coconuts were freely given away to indigent members of the community, and in 'rich' houses food was always prepared for about five extra persons, so that anyone who happened to turn up at meal times would be sure of getting a meal. The generosity of the rich even extended to the gifting of plots of land to those prepared to beg for them. Not surprising then that many contemporary inhabitants of the community claim that in the past many poor people literally lived off the rich.

Nostalgic tales of the generosity of the 'rich', whilst not false, do not tell the whole story. For the material benefits and security provided to the 'poor' were not bestowed on charitable or humanitarian grounds. It is interesting to observe, for instance, that rice and coconuts were never distributed on a regular basis to the 'poor'. Rather they were handed out in small quantities and to receive them a 'poor' person had to initiate an interaction with a 'rich' person in which the former invariably played a role of subservience. In return for material favours the 'rich' demanded and received a price – subordination and compliance. In short, the other side of the coin of paternalism and noblesse oblige was that of power over economic dependants.

THE INTERPLAY OF CASTE AND CLASS

Although much has been written about the relation between caste and power especially in relation to modern democratic politics, understanding of the interplay between caste and class at the local level has been inhibited because the caste bias of many researchers has led them to treat class as a function of caste or analyse it within a caste framework.

A comparison of the cleavages created by caste and class in this community shows that to assume that class was simply a

Table 6   *Class categories in relation to caste*

| | | Classes | | |
		Rich	Middle Farmer	Poor
	Walawwe	1	1	
	Goigama	4	9	6
	Muslim		2	
	Paṭṭi			9
Castes	Gallat	2		4
	Vahumpura		1	4
	Hēna		3	1
	Batgam	1	1	9
	Vahal			1
	Total	8	17	34

manifestation of caste would be severely to distort the behavioural reality at the turn of this century. If wealth was a function of caste, then at the very least one would expect to find that the eight 'rich' people in the community belonged to the high castes, the seventeen 'middle farmers' were predominantly those of intermediate caste status, and that the lowest castes would be heavily concentrated among the ranks of the 'poor'. The actual distribution of class categories in relation to caste, however, (see Table 6) shows that it would be impossible to make a case for the causal primacy of caste at the turn of the century. Each class was composed of members of a variety of castes and there were several noteworthy discrepancies between the hierarchies of wealth and caste status. For instance six of the nineteen Goigama families belonged to the 'poor' class, while one Batgam family was in the highest strata of the class hierarchy.

The head of this single 'rich' Batgam household was Ambakumburalage Ukkuwa, the eldest son of the Devideniya *walawwe* servant Sarana (p. 42). Ukkuwa was not a 'class marginal'. He owned four acres of paddy land and was securely in the ranks of the 'rich'. His wealth in paddy can be explained by two factors. The first was his close connection with the Devideniya *walawwe*, the decline of which proved particularly beneficial for him. Secondly Ukkuwa was one of the few men in the community who had thought it worth his while to work on the neighbouring

Table 7   *Walawwe, Goigama and Batgam ownership of high land*

Caste	No. of Households	% of Households	Extent			% of Total Extent
			A	R	P	
Walawwe	2	3.4	11	0	00	5.9
Goigama	19	32.2	79	1	10	42.6
Batgam	11	18.6	34	3	00	18.6

Berawila estate. By the end of the nineteenth century he had, in contrast to fellow Batgam who were casual labourers on the estates, achieved the responsible and more remunerative job of *kankāni* (overseer), and had secured for his second son a job as a watcher on Berawila estate.

Ukkuwa Kankaniya notwithstanding, the Batgam as a whole could not be described as prosperous even by the end of the baseline period.[20] Nevertheless Ukkuwa Kankaniya was a precursor of, and instrumental in, the development of future Batgam prosperity. For in this community he was a pioneer in establishing connections and good relations with the British planters, and laid the foundations for a long and profitable liaison between the British and the Batgam people of this community in the years ahead.

The significance of the rise of Batgam prosperity and the concomitant impoverishment of many Walawwe and Goigama individuals in the decades after the baseline period, can best be understood in terms of the position of these three castes in relation to landownership at the turn of the century (see Tables 7 and 8). It is clear that during the baseline period the 'high castes' were superior to the Batgam with regard to both high-land and paddy-land ownership.

The Walawwe and Goigama people together made up 35.6 per cent of the households of this community but owned 48.5 per cent of the high land. Moreover, they had maintained this superior position despite the loss of chena land to the British crown during the course of the nineteenth century. Although, as Roberts has pointed out, the extent to which village chena lands were appropriated by the British has been exaggerated in the literature,[21] there is no doubt that legislative enactments did

Table 8   *Walawwe, Goigama and Batgam ownership of paddy land*

Caste	No. of Households	% of Households	Extent A	R	P	% of Total Paddy Land Owned by Residents
Walawwe	2	3.4	5	0	30	6.2
Goigama	19	32.2	41	1	10	49.2
Batgam	11	18.6	10	3	10	12.8

result in the decrease of chena land. And in this community it was the long-established families who had extensive claims to forest land, often without legally binding deeds, that lost the most land. For example, after the Waste Lands Ordinance of 1897, which set up the machinery for the systematic survey and proclamation of government claims to land, 13 acres of what was described as 'the only forest in the village' was appropriated by the crown. The grounds for appropriation were that the Goigama claimants (Haputhota Rallage and Ganege Rallage families) could not substantiate their claim with adequate documentary proof.[22]

In the case of paddy land, the disproportionate ownership by the 'high castes' was even more marked. In 1888 the Walawwe and Goigama caste groups owned 55 per cent of the paddy land owned by residents, whereas the Batgam owned only 10 acres. The large extents of paddy land owned by the 'high castes' probably meant that during the baseline period those Goigama of the 'poor' class who were tenants would have rented paddy land from high-caste landlords. Their contemporary counterparts are less fortunate. The rapid increase in low-caste ownership of land in the intervening years has led to the exacerbation of conflicts of wealth and status, because many indigent Goigama are today tenants and labourers of low-caste individuals.

Application of the three-dimensional model to the analysis of social stratification has shown that during the baseline period this community could not simply be described as a caste-based society. Caste did constitute an important basis of stratification, but it was not the only, or even the 'basic' form of structured inequality. Material inequality also stratified this community at the turn of the century and divided people into ranked groups.

The separate analysis of the class hierarchy has made possible an understanding of the way inequalities of wealth were, at the turn of the century, related to the other dimensions of stratification. On the one hand, although the high castes owned a disproportionate amount of land, it has been shown that class position was not a manifestation of caste status. On the other hand, the examination of inter-class interaction suggests that there was an intimate relationship between class and power. This relationship will be explored in greater detail in the following chapter, which is concerned with the power hierarchy in the Rangama/Devideniya community during the baseline period.

6   The Power Hierarchy in the Baseline Period

Power in the Rangama/Devideniya community during the baseline period was intimately linked with wealth and with birth status. This does not imply any necessary functional relationship between class and caste on the one hand, and power on the other. In contemporary Rangama and Devideniya, for instance, power is not even related to, let alone a function of, birth status, and its connection to wealth has been considerably weakened. The advantage of adopting a three-dimensional model of social stratification is that without positing any necessary relationship between the three dimensions of inequality, it makes possible the exploration of the contingent relationships between caste, class and power that prevailed at the turn of the century. Such a theoretical framework, which involves the conceptual and analytical separation of the three hierarchies, not only avoids the pitfalls of the 'dominant caste' model, but also reveals that in the baseline period the relationship between power and class was quite dissimilar to that between power and caste The interplay between power and caste was a more complex one, dependent upon the intervention of extra-community factors.

POWER AS A FUNCTION OF CLASS

The relationship between the 'rich' and the 'poor' in the Rangama/Devideniya community during the baseline period was not an exclusively economic relationship. It was also a power relationship.

It was their ability, in the absence of public welfare services, to dispense or withhold essential material goods that allowed the 'rich' to assume a position of power *vis-à-vis* the 'poor'. Whilst landed wealth in general enabled the 'rich' to secure the subordination of the 'poor', it was with regard to paddy land that the idea of 'land-is-to-rule' was particularly relevant. For the power of the 'rich' was most clearly evidenced in their role as landlords.

It is, however, important to bear in mind two points with regard to the power of the landlord. Firstly, the categories landlord and tenant were not synonymous with the class categories 'rich' and 'poor' – many of the 'rich' were also owner-cultivators and not all of the 'poor' were tenants. Secondly, the relationship between landlord and tenant was not invariably one of power – often brothers or father and son stood in that relationship. What is significant is that during the baseline period the landlord–tenant relationship had within it the potential of a power relationship, a potential that was most fully realized when the landlord was interacting with a poor tenant who was not a member of his immediate nuclear family (power *was* exercised over tenants who were nephews, cousins, etc.).

Basically the landlord's power rested in his ability to deny the tenant access to a paddy field. Those tenants who belonged to the 'poor' class in this community possessed no bargaining strength in their relationship with the landlords. The large number of aspiring tenants resulted in a competition for tenancy rights which precluded the possibility of any collective action against the landlord(s). Even had the tenants been able, collectively, to withhold their services, they would still have suffered the loss of a vital source of subsistence, whereas the non-cultivation of a field for one season did not represent a financial disaster for a 'rich' landlord.

During the baseline period there was no security of tenure. All tenancy contracts were valid for one year only, although they could be renewed. Who among the competitors for a tenancy actually obtained cultivation rights to a field depended in part on who paid the highest *madaran* (tenancy fee). The system of *madaran* payment resembled bidding at an auction. Each candidate for tenancy approached the landlord with his bid (a sum of cash) and a sheaf of betal. Other things being equal the highest bidder secured cultivation rights. Some degree of certainty in tenurial rights might have prevailed if *madaran* alone was operative in determining who obtained access to rented paddy land. But another factor – the landlord's opinion of the applicant's reliability and compliance – was an equally important determinant. However high his *madaran*, an individual with a reputation for recalcitrance had no hope of obtaining land to rent. Moreover a tenant who incurred his landlord's displeasure faced certain eviction at the end of the annual contract.

Thus tenants had little choice but to accept a role of subservience. Over and above the paddy cultivation duties outlined in the tenancy contract, the tenant was obliged to perform a myriad of other customarily ordained services. These included working without pay in the landlord's house and in the fields that the landlord cultivated himself; showing respect to the landlord by visiting his house with a tribute at the Sinhalese new year; and on special occasions worshipping the landlord and presenting him with a sheaf of betel leaves.

THE RELATIONSHIP BETWEEN POWER AND CASTE

Wealth was not the sole basis of power in this community in the baseline period. The highest stratum in the hierarchy of power (i.e. those with the ability to impose their will on the greatest number of people) consisted of two minor bureaucrats whose position depended as much on superior caste status as it did on landed wealth. These bureaucrats were the Vel Vidane and the Aracci.

The Vel Vidane was the irrigation headman. Following the Irrigation Ordinance of 1856, irrigation headmen were appointed in all parts of the Kegalle district, even though they were not strictly necessary in communities like Rangama/Devideniya where there were no irrigation works of any significance, and the single paddy crop was entirely rain-fed.

The post of Vel Vidane was, ideally, meant to be filled by election – the voters being the field owners. Theoretically then, among those who owned paddy land, caste and wealth need have had no bearing on who obtained this post. However, as British administrators were to discover, the procedure of election to office was alien to rural Sinhalese. Time and again field owners failed to turn up for elections and when they did they declined to make the selection themselves.[1] Thus the Assistant Government Agents inevitably ended up appointing 'suitable' persons for the posts. And given colonial attitudes it was not surprising that in mixed-caste villages a 'high caste' person was always appointed Vel Vidane.

This community was no exception. The post of Vel Vidane was always held by a rich member of one or other of the four established Goigama kin groups. During much of the baseline period, Ganege Rallage Ranhamy held the post of Vel Vidane. His office gave G.R. Ranhamy, already a rich man, an opportunity to increase the number of his economic dependants (i.e. tenants). For the Vel Vidane was entitled to a payment called *huvandiram* (one sixty-fourth of the crop of each field under his jurisdiction) which enabled him, if he so wished, to rent out more of his own land or invest the proceeds in more paddy land. Although the Vel Vidane in this community had little irrigation to supervise, he was a powerful figure because his duties included settling paddy-land disputes and appearing as a witness when these disputes were taken to court.

The Vel Vidane's bureaucratic colleague in this community was the Aracci – minor headman. Like the Vel Vidane the Aracci was not paid a fixed salary. Until 1892 he was exempted from the grain tax. After the abolition of the grain tax the Aracci's remuneration consisted of a share of the fines in cases he prosecuted in connection with his police duties, and a variety of rewards and commissions for travel, good work, etc. In addition Araccis were always given preference when government contracts for small public works were under consideration. Although the remuneration the Aracci received for his services was less than that of the Vel Vidane, the Aracci was without doubt the more powerful of the two bureaucrats. For administrative purposes each inhabitant of a province belonged to a series of expanding jurisdictional areas (see Figure 2). The post of Aracci was a powerful one because at a time when specialized government departments had no local field representative, the Aracci was the general, all-purpose administrator of the smallest, regular administrative unit – the *vasama*, which usually consisted of a group of villages.

The administrative hierarchy was made up of British Government Agents and Assistant Government Agents and under them a series of 'native headmen'. This system of 'native headmen'

Administrative Unit	Name of Unit	Bureaucrat
Province	Sabaragamuva	Government Agent
District	Kegalle	Assistant Government Agent
Division	Paranakuru Korale	Ratemahatmaya (chief headman)
Pattuwa	Tumpalata Pattuwa West	Korala
Vasama	Rangama	Aracci (minor headman)

Figure 2   Administrative location of the community – baseline period

was structurally similar to the provincial bureaucracy in the Kandyan kingdom. In appointing native headmen the British maintained the caste-based nature of the system and hence its bias in favour of the Radala and Goigama castes. Persons of castes lower than the Goigama were not, in the Kegalle district, allowed to aspire to any of the regular administrative posts outlined in Figure 2. Their bureaucratic careers were limited to achieving subordinate headmanships of those exclusively low-caste villages, found within larger *vasama* units, which were allowed to have their own headmen.[2]

The antiquated 'native headmen' system was retained primarily on account of its convenience to the ruling power. The British were scrupulous in observing caste etiquette in the administrative system. Low-caste village headmen were known by specific caste-associated titles (e.g. Vidāna Duraya (Batgam); Vidāna Hēnaya (Hēna); Vidāna Dēvaya (Vahumpura) etc.), and native headmen were required to abide by a caste-based dress code.[3] In administrative appointments great store was laid on the possession of long family traditions of service in the Kandyan or British bureaucracies.[4] Some British officials even took steps to maintain the honour of old, respected Kandyan families. In one instance the punishment for an offence was lessened in order to avoid the 'stigma it would have cast' on the family, and in another an administrative appointment was granted to 'retrieve the good name' of a family.[5] Minor headmen were appointed by the Assistant Government Agent on the recommendation of the Ratemahatmaya, and in the Kegalle district at the turn of the century it would have been inconceivable for the headman of a *vasama* to belong to a low caste. Thus, like the Vel Vidane, the three men who occupied the post of Aracci of the Rangama *vasama* during the baseline period came from the old, established Goigama families. Two of the three men were brothers, the older of whom held the Aracciship continuously for twenty-one years from 1880 to 1901.

The Power of the Rangama Aracci

The power the Rangama Aracci exercised over persons in his *vasama* derived from his role as broker in controlling the channels of communication between the local community and wider regional and national levels. Apart from the Vel Vidane, the Aracci was the sole point of government authority in this community. In contrast to the Vel Vidane's limited area of jurisdiction (paddy cultivation) and single-stranded link with the outside, the Aracci, as a general purpose administrator, had numerous extra-community connections and was the principal intermediary between the Sinhalese peasants on the one hand and the British colonial government on the other.

Under British rule the duties of the Aracci were many and varied and impinged upon virtually every aspect of the lives of the inhabitants of his *vasama*. They included assisting surveyors and pointing out the boundaries of villagers' land; collecting taxes; reporting illicit felling; assisting in the suppression of the illicit trade in liquor; and carrying out police work. The latter involved reporting cases of crime, arresting criminals, giving evidence in courts, serving summons, executing warrants and even conducting prosecutions.[6] The extent of the Aracci's police duties and the degree of discretion he was allowed in carrying them out was perhaps the single most important factor which enabled the Aracci to exercise his will over the inhabitants of this community.

British rule enhanced the power of minor headmen not only by increasing the range of their duties but also by rendering obsolete a time-honoured institution, the *gamsabhāva*. During the Kandyan period the *gamsabhāva* (village council composed of the principal men of a village) was convened periodically to arbitrate disputes, and served to mitigate the power of the headman. But this indigenous judicial body was undermined by the British presence and fell into disuse with the introduction of a new legal system for the whole island in 1833. The revival of the *gamsabhāva* in connection with paddy cultivation and irrigation in 1856, and the extension of its powers with the establishment of village committees (organizations which carried out public works) and village tribunals (local courts) in 1871, did not affect the power of minor headmen. For despite their name, village committees and village tribunals were not village based. The area of their jurisdiction was large – Paranakuru Korale for example, which comprised 27 *vasamas* and over 200 villages, was served by one village tribunal and two village committees. These institutions were a source of power to the Ratemahatmaya who presided over them, but had virtually no impact on local-level power hierarchies.

Despite the presence of local courts, therefore, dispute settlement in the Rangama *vasama* was a preserve of the Aracci and was carried out in his house. According to older informants, in most cases the disputants accepted his verdict. If any opposition was expressed, the Aracci did not hesitate to use physical force to gain compliance with his wishes. In using such extra-judicial measures the Rangama Aracci acted in the confidence that he would not be reprimanded by the Assistant Government Agent. On the contrary there was tacit approval of such action by British officials who felt it was 'necessary for the due maintenance of his [the headman's] dignity' and was an example of 'headmen thinking for themselves'.[7]

During the baseline period, therefore, the Rangama Aracci was in no uncertain terms the 'boss' of the community. He was feared and obeyed. He was not, however, simply a village thug. For if a 'leader' is a power holder who is respected and admired and whose power is relatively permanent, then the Rangama Aracci was also certainly a 'leader'. The power and influence of the Aracci was even felt by British planters in the vicinity of the community. For instance Mr Mant, manager of Natha Kande estate, considered H.R. Mudianse, Aracci of the Rangama *vasama* for twenty-one years, to be such a threat that he went so far as to trump up charges against him in order to have him discredited and removed from office. In the event, Mr Mant failed to do so.[8]

The relationship between power and caste in the baseline period was not exhausted by the power wielded by the high-caste Aracci and Vel Vidane. Power was latent in the relationship between *all* high-caste and low-caste persons. High-caste persons in the Rangama/Devideniya community possessed power by virtue of the fact that they were indirect beneficiaries of the negative sanctions at the disposal of their caste fellows – the Vel Vidane and the Aracci. Since a breach of caste etiquette, or defiance by a low-caste person towards a high-caste person, threatened their own privileged position, it was in the interest of these superordinate power holders to support their caste fellows in any confrontation with the lower castes. Thus, although the relationship of power was not so directly discernible in the relationships between castes as it was in the case of classes, the higher castes could still be seen to have had power over the lower ones.

THE INTERPLAY OF POWER, CASTE AND CLASS

The nature of power in the Rangama/Devideniya community at the turn of the century resulted in a situation where the relationships embodied in the power hierarchy were in many ways replicated in the hierarchies of class and caste. For the higher strata identifiable in the class and caste hierarchies also possessed power over certain of the lower strata in these hierarchies.

With respect to the relationship between material inequalities and inequalities of power, a point of general applicability may be noted. That is to say, where the group ranked highest on the class scale possesses a monopoly of a highly-valued resource – particularly one which also has high cultural value – then there is likely to be a close connection between the class and power hierarchies. This can be observed in the context of the Rangama/Devideniya community, where the 'poor' were economically dependent on the 'rich' people's superior control of paddy land and other resources – a control which bestowed upon the latter direct power over the former.

Just as the rich had power over the poor, high-caste persons at the turn of the century had power over those of inferior birth. One of the primary advantages of the three-dimensional model is that it avoids caste bias in the analysis of social stratification and thus ensures that the power possessed by the high castes is not interpreted in terms of the 'dominant caste' concept. The concept of the 'dominant caste' is of dubious value as an analytical tool because it carries with it certain implications and assumptions which can often distort the analysis of power. For one thing it implies that the caste categorized as dominant has a monopoly of power in the community. In this community at the turn of the century, however, this was clearly not the case, as rich people, regardless of their caste, possessed power over their economic dependants. Secondly, the 'dominant caste' concept assumes that all members of the dominant caste possess an approximately similar degree of power. But in Rangama and Devideniya the vast majority of high-caste persons possessed power only indirectly, in so far as they were backed by the two powerful village bureaucrats. Finally, and perhaps most importantly, the 'dominant caste' concept implies that the power of the caste possessing it is locally rooted in such factors as numerical, economic or ritual status superiority. But the basis of high-caste power in the Rangama/Devideniya community was not so much a derivative of any local factor but rather of factors to be found beyond the bounds of the community, at the regional and national levels.

The three-dimensional model has a second advantage in the analysis of power in that it allows for understanding the complexity of the interdependence between the various hierarchies. Under more conventional models such relationships are often merged into an artificial and ultimately misleading uniformity. But despite the similarities in the interplay between power and class on the one hand, and power and caste on the other (i.e. higher strata in both class and caste hierarchies possessed power), these were in fact distinctly different relationships.

In the case of the interplay between power and class, power was the direct result of the possession of landed – primarily paddy – wealth. The ability to influence the actions of others unambiguously derived from the fact and extent of land ownership. Thus the relationship between power and class in the baseline period was a functional one which was encompassed within the local community.

The situation is very different with respect to the interplay of power and caste. Power was clearly not a function of caste in so far as superior birth status on its own did not entail the ability to influence the actions of others. Those of superior birth in Rangama and Devideniya possessed power only because of the impingement of extra-community factors – primarily the Radala and Goigama-based 'native headmen' system. The concentration of power in high-caste hands was beneficial to the colonial government, because rewarding those of superior birth with power continued a long-standing and accepted tradition of local government which in turn promoted overall political stability. Thus it was ascriptive politics motivated by self-interest at the centre, which caused the coincidence of caste and power at the periphery.

The analysis of power demonstrates the fact that the interplay between the three dimensions of inequality at the local level cannot be understood in isolation from developments at the regional and national levels. As we shall see, the introduction of redistributive policies by national governments radically undermined the causal connection between wealth and power in this community, and when the dictates of electoral politics rendered advantageous the abolition of the headmen system, the link between caste and power was severed altogether.

7 The Ideology of Stratification During the Baseline Period

The examination of the social structure of stratification in the past three chapters shows that the Rangama/Devideniya community during the baseline period could not be understood simply as a caste-based society. An individual's class position was not determined by his position in the caste hierarchy, and although power was linked with both class and caste, high-caste status, in contrast to wealth, was only a necessary but not a sufficient condition for achieving power. Wealth and power were not therefore manifestations of caste in the baseline period. A comparison of the three dimensions of social stratification did show, however, that there was considerable overlap between the members of the higher strata of the three hierarchies.

This chapter examines the ideology of stratification in the Rangama/Devideniya community at the turn of the century. Examination of the cultural realm of stratification at an earlier period is inevitably less exhaustive than that of social structure. Not only is there less archival material to supplement the information provided by older informants; it is also the case that such informants have less difficulty in disentangling past and present patterns of behaviour than they do their past and present attitudes.

Using the three dimensional model in the analysis of ideology, this chapter shows that Sinhalese notions of stratification in the baseline period were not confined to caste but also included perceptions of power and material inequality. Within each dimension a further analytical distinction is made between the descriptive and evaluative components of ideology. The descriptive component contains the 'native' definition of a particular type of inequality and a theory of how society is structured with respect to it. The evaluative component comprises the 'native' judgement of the structure's legitimacy or illegitimacy.

In this chapter I also seek to emphasize the extent to which ideological consensus prevailed in this community at the turn of the century, largely as a result of the widespread acceptance of the Buddhist karmic theory of causation. All inhabitants shared, and approved of, the same ideologies of caste, class and power regardless of their positions in the hierarchies of inequality. The higher strata of this society therefore not only enjoyed superiority of wealth, social honour and power, but also exercised 'hegemony' over the lower strata.

THE DESCRIPTIVE COMPONENT OF THE IDEOLOGY OF STRATIFICATION

Caste

Louis Dumont is the principal proponent of the now widespread view that the underlying basis of caste is the Hindu ideology of purity and pollution. According to Dumont, 'caste proper' may be said to exist only in the presence of an ideology of hierarchy based on the opposition of purity and pollution, along with the separation of status and power and the subordination of the latter, as expressed in the Brahmin/Kshatriya relationship.[1] Although Yalman's work on caste ideology in Sri Lanka[2] lays similar stress on notions of purity and pollution, most other scholars have observed a marked absence of such notions both among the Sinhalese and the Tamils.[3]

My own observations on caste ideology in the Rangama/Devideniya community showed that people's understanding of the differences between castes was to some extent associated with notions of differential degrees of purity and pollution. But the inhabitants of this community most readily understood caste inequality in terms of a division of labour ordained by a king in ancient times – the differences between castes, they felt, stemmed from the division of the population into various occupational groups. Conversations with older informants suggest that the perception of castes as occupational groups may have been stronger in the past than it is today. This is hardly surprising. Caste occupations were widely practised in the baseline period, whereas in the contemporary community the relationship between caste and occupation is highly attenuated. The attitudes of older informants also indicate that in the baseline period caste differences were perceived as necessarily implying privileges for those ranked higher, and discrimination against those ranked lower, in the hierarchy of birth status.

The inhabitants of Rangama/Devideniya in the baseline period regarded the caste hierarchy to be a Sinhalese hierarchy. People may have disagreed as to whether the Vahumpura or the Gallat were ranked higher, but then, as now, there was general agreement that Muslims were not part of the hierarchy of birth status.

Class

In examining conceptions of material inequality it is important to distinguish 'class ideology' from 'class consciousness'. 'Class ideology' refers to the totality of cultural perceptions with regard to material inequality – both descriptive and evaluative components. 'Class consciousness' on the other hand, is an awareness of one's position in the hierarchy, and a desire to act with other members of one's strata to further common interests. 'Class consciousness' is not an invariable part of 'class ideology'. It is a phenomenon which may or may not be associated with the evaluative component of 'class ideology'.

There is little to suggest that the lower classes at the turn of the century possessed 'class consciousness' (see next section). Nevertheless the people of Rangama/Devideniya in the baseline period did have an ideology of class.

For the Sinhalese rice is more than a staple food. It is considered the most superior and, for many, simply the only proper food. The question 'have you had a meal?' is in Sinhalese 'have you eaten rice' (*bat kālada?*). At the turn of the century paddy-land ownership was regarded as the ultimate measure of a person's wealth. Even today in circumstances of vastly improved markets, there is a bias against money if it is not accompanied by the ownership of paddy land. People often say of a moneyed man with no paddy land – 'What is one to do with money? Does he have paddy? Does he have rice?'[4] The cultural value attached to paddy land influenced the perception of class hierarchy in the baseline period. Class strata were depicted in terms of landlords and tenants – the higher stratum owned the paddy land, the lower stratum cultivated it.

Power

Examination of the descriptive component of the ideology of power demonstrates that a close ideational relationship prevailed between the different dimensions of stratification. This ideational relationship was in many ways similar to what Obeyesekere has described as the 'ideology of feudalism' – an ideology which postulates a congruence between notions of status, wealth and power.[5] Contrary to Dumont's representation of Hindu ideology,[6] in Sinhalese ideology no single conception of inequality assumed a super-ordinate position in relation to the others – rather each implied the other. In the baseline period power was perceived as a derivative of wealth, high caste status, and office (*dhanaya, kulaya, nilaya*). The information of older informants suggests moreover that a power holder was thought of as a leader in possession of a following (*pirisa*) whose members obeyed his commands (*anata kīkaru venava*).

THE EVALUATIVE COMPONENT OF THE IDEOLOGY OF STRATIFICATION

The descriptive component does not exhaust the ideologies of caste, class and power. In any given society the 'native' evaluation of inequality as just or unjust, legitimate or illegitimate, constitutes an integral part of the cultural concepts of inequality. Indeed the degree of ideological consensus that prevails in a society cannot be ascertained outside of an examination of the evaluative component of ideology.

In this book, 'ideological consensus' will be said to prevail only in those situations where common recognition by members of a society regarding the hierarchical structure of their society is accompanied by an acceptance of the legitimacy of that structure. Consensus on the ideologies of inequality implies that the lower strata accept the legitimacy of systems which are advantageous to the higher strata. It will be argued here that in the Rangama/Devideniya community in the baseline period, the perceptions of hierarchy described in the previous section were not only common to almost all inhabitants, but were also considered legitimate by them. In other words it is possible to show that the higher strata in this community manifested their supremacy in the two ways outlined by Gramsci – 'domination' or 'coercion' and 'intellectual and moral leadership' (predominance of ideas and values). This latter type of supremacy ('hegemony') being obtained by consent rather than force.[7]

Older inhabitants of contemporary Rangama/Devideniya assert that despite the pervasiveness of inequality and discrimination in the past, the relationship between rich and poor, the powerful and the powerless, the high castes and the low castes, was not characterized by bitterness, rancour and antagonism, as is the case today. It appears therefore that there was, at the very least, overt acceptance by the lower strata of ideologies that were unflattering and disadvantageous to themselves.

To observe the lower strata's acceptance of unjust systems may not in itself, however, constitute evidence that they believe in the legitimacy of such systems. It is possible to argue that social harmony in stratified societies does not imply 'consensus on the legitimacy of systems of oppression' but rather an 'agreement on who has the power, and when and under what circumstances and with what effect it is likely to be used.[8] That is to say, overt acceptance of unjust systems may simply demonstrate a highly self-conscious and self-interested form of play acting in situations where to exhibit resentment or antagonism would entail unacceptable consequences. The evidence from Rangama/Devideniya, however, does not support the contention that the lower strata's acceptance of inequality was simply a ruse to protect themselves against the threat of coercive action. On the contrary it appears that the attitudes of the lower strata contained an acceptance both of the legitimacy of the systems of inequality as a whole, and of the inferior positions that they occupied within them.

Older informants assert that in the past villagers willingly accepted the decisions of the power holders. This is one piece of evidence which suggests that Sinhalese villagers at the turn of the century regarded as legitimate the power wielded by high-caste, wealthy, state officials, More significant perhaps is the fact that villagers of that period appeared reluctant to change the bases of power even when the opportunity to do so presented itself. In the election of Vel Vidanes, for instance, field owners, who were entitled to vote, rarely turned up for elections. When they did, they exhibited a disinclination to use their votes as a means of selecting a candidate of their own preference for this powerful bureaucratic position. An Assistant Government Agent supervising the election of Vel Vidanes wrote in desperation – 'These elections as a selection by the suffrage of the people are extremely unreal. The electors seem to assume that I personally am in favour of the particular candidate whom I name first. And the whole of the votes are generally given for the first man on the list. I tried putting the last man first and found the same thing. He was assumed to be my candidate and got all the votes'.[9] The behaviour of the voters in Vel Vidane elections suggests that Sinhalese villagers during the baseline period considered wealth and high-caste status appropriate bases of power, and regarded as alien and unacceptable the notion that power could be obtained by popular election.

In respect of caste also, there is evidence to show that ideological consensus prevailed in the baseline period. The attitudes of certain contemporary low-caste persons in the community are significant in this regard. The ideology of caste has long been repudiated (in theory if not in practice) by national governments, and the high castes in the contemporary community lack any type of coercive power. Nevertheless, some of the middle-aged, and all older, low-caste persons in Rangama/Devideniya continue, at the risk of annoying their educated offspring, to abide by the rules of caste etiquette in their interactions with those of higher caste. They would not, for example, wish those of higher caste to accept food from them, since they feel 'it is not right to pollute good people' (*hoňda minissu iňdul karana eka hari nä*). Moreover they conform to caste etiquette even in their interactions with economic dependants. My landlady for instance, a middle-aged Vahumpura woman from one of the richest households in the community, addresses a tenant of Walawwe origin by the honorific 'bandara mahatmaya', and her Goigama labourers by the honorific 'ralahamy'. These contemporary attitudes suggest that in the baseline period not only the high castes, but also the low castes, accepted as legitimate the ranking of people on the basis of birth status, and the asymmetrical patterns of inter-caste interaction which favoured the higher castes.

The attitudes of tenants in the contemporary community indicate that much the same was true of conceptions of class in the baseline period. Today, over thirty years after the passage of the Paddy Lands Act which legally reduced the landlord's share to one-fourth of the crop, all but a handful of tenants continue to give the landlords the customary half-share of the crop. This provision of the Act has been widely rejected principally because it is contrary to long-standing standards of morality. Many tenants insist that they continue to give up half the crop because the landlord is, after all, the owner of the field. These tenants appear to be uncomfortable with the proposition that one could own a field and receive only a quarter of its yield. Some claim that it is tantamount to stealing to take more than half the crop from a field one does not own. These strongly-held notions of the inviolability of private property in the late twentieth century make it plausible to assume that poor people at the turn of the century did not regard the hierarchy of material inequality and the wide disparities in land ownership as unjust or oppressive.

Analysis of the evaluative component of ideology thus demonstrates that to describe the baseline period as a situation in which ideological consensus prevailed is not to indulge in a synecdochic representation of the cultural conceptions of this community. The attitudes of elderly informants of the lower strata, just as much as that of the higher strata, suggest that almost all inhabitants of Rangama/Devideniya at the turn of the century subscribed to, and accepted as legitimate, ideologies which benefited the higher strata.

The higher strata of Rangama/Devideniya may thus be seen as having exercised 'hegemony' over the lower strata. Ideas and conceptions of inequality which suited them were widespread throughout the community. According to Gramsci 'hegemony' as opposed to 'domination' is obtained by consent and exercised through 'the ensemble of educational, religious and associational institutions'.[10] The evidence from Rangama/Devideniya supports Gramsci's view of the way 'hegemony' is established. For the people of this community were adherents of a religion in which ideas of inequality and hierarchy were pervasive, and which, moreover, proffered a powerful explanation and justification of social inequality.

Inequality and Hierarchy in Buddhism

The consensus of ideologies of inequality prevailing in this community at the turn of the century is not surprising when we take into consideration the fact that the Sinhalese are adherents of Buddhism. The worldview of people in Buddhist countries is pervaded by hierarchy and inequality. Kirsch has shown that, in Thailand, karma and the belief in rebirth results in a moral hierarchy – a conception of intrinsic inequalities in individual moral value due to differential balance of merit and demerit.[11] In Sinhalese Buddhism (which, like Buddhism in other countries, goes beyond doctrinal orthodoxy and incorporates a variety of popular cults),[12] hierarchy and inequality can be observed in four distinct areas – each of the three sects of the Buddhist monkhood in Sri Lanka is hierarchically organized; the Sinhalese Buddhist pantheon consists of a power hierarchy (Figure 3);[13] all Sinhalese Buddhists see themselves as fitting into a pan-Sinhalese hierarchy of piety and religious virtuosity (Figure 4); and Sinhalese Buddhist theory ranks all karmic bound creatures in a hierarchy of karmic excellence (Figure 5).

It would be erroneous to assume that hierarchy in Sinhalese Buddhism is present *despite* the egalitarianism of doctrinal Theravada Buddhism. Although certain aspects of Buddhism show it bo be antithetical to caste,[14] doctrinal Buddhism's denunciation of caste is not categorical or universal. Many passages in the Theravada scriptures are indicative of an attitude where the caste system is not considered necessary or justifiable, but is nevertheless accepted as an inevitable part of Indian society. Moreover denial of birth status as an index of superiority/inferiority was often not so much a repudiation of the caste system *per se*, but of the super-ordinate position of the Brahmins within the system.

Far from being an egalitarian philosophy, inequality is central to the worldview of doctrinal Buddhism. Doctrinal Theravada Buddhism ranks all human beings in a moral hierarchy of spiritual liberation. This hierarchy consists, in order of moral excellence, of monks, kings and householders.

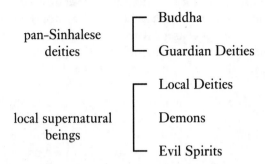

Figure 3   The Sinhalese Buddhist pantheon

Tāpasa (hermit monks)
Ordinary monks
Upāsaka (elderly laymen who renounce the world)
Ordinary laymen

Figure 4   Hierarchy of religious virtuosity

Gods
Human Beings
Animals
Evil Spirits and Demons

Figure 5   Hierarchy of karmic excellence

It is the theory of causation proffered by doctrinal Buddhism, and the extent to which it was accepted, that is most significant with regard to understanding the attitudes of the lower strata in the Rangama/Devideniya community during the baseline period. The fact that all old people in the contemporary community without exception adhere to the karmic theory of causation, indicates that there was widespread acceptance of the theory at the turn of the century. The karmic theory of causation is possibly the most satisfactory religious theory yet evolved to justify inequality, and this appears to have afforded a strong underlying basis for the ideological consensus that characterized the cultural conceptions of stratification during the baseline period. According to karmic theory, the condition of one's present life is determined by the accumulation of merit and demerit earned in one's past lives. Individuals are not rich, high caste or powerful by virtue of an accident of birth. Rather such individuals deserve their fortunate position in society because they have achieved it by accumulated good karma in their past lives. Karma thus conditions its adherents to a worldview in which inequality occupies a fundamental position and is deemed a necessary and inevitable part of existence itself.

THE INTERPLAY OF IDEOLOGY AND SOCIAL STRUCTURE

Part I of this study has examined the social structure and ideology of stratification which prevailed in the Rangama/Devideniya community at the turn of the century. The analytical separation of the social and cultural realms facilitates investigation of the relationship between action and idea rather than assuming causal priority for either, or a necessary correspondence between them.

A comparison of the behavioural and ideational aspects of stratification in the Rangama/Devideniya community during the baseline period shows that there was no uni-directional causal influence between ideology and behaviour. Rather the social and cultural realms reacted upon each other, the one influencing the other.

At the turn of the century the behavioural relationship between landlord and tenant was a function of certain ideational features. Landlords were able to translate material superiority (i.e. paddy land) into power over tenants only because the latter desired to cultivate paddy. At a time when forest land was available for the cultivation of alternative types of food, people still wished to cultivate paddy land and voluntarily placed themselves in positions of subordination *vis-à-vis* the landlord because of the unassailable cultural conviction that rice was the superior food. But the influence was not solely in the direction of action being shaped by ideas. For in turn the power relationship between landlord and tenant acted on ideology by enhancing the value of paddy land as the vehicle for bestowing power upon its owner.

ideas	*action*	*ideas*
rice valued as superior food $\longrightarrow$	people wish to become tenants; power relationship between landlord and tenant $\longrightarrow$	value of paddy land enhanced as source of power

Separate analysis of the social and cultural realms also shows that there is no necessary correspondence between them. At any particular point in time people's ideas about inequalities in their society may be quite different from the behavioural reality which the observer uncovers. In this community during the baseline period, people's perceptions of the ranked groups based on birth status and wealth were at variance with the hierarchies of caste and class as they manifested themselves at the level of behaviour.

In the dimension of caste, for example, the lack of 'fit' between behaviour and ideology is evident with regard to Muslims. At the level of social structure Muslims formed an endogamous status group, and their interaction with Sinhalese castes involved asymmetrical relations as ordained by caste rules. Yet at the level of ideology Muslims were generally regarded as being outside the hierarchy of birth status. Likewise in the dimension of class there was a lack of correspondence between the class categories perceived by the Rangama/Devideniya people and the cleavages created by material inequality in the society. Notions of class revolved around the landlord–tenant relationship. But the inhabitants of this community did not fit simply into landlord and tenant classes. Not only was there a class of relatively wealthy 'middle farmers' but also, as pointed out earlier, the 'rich' and the 'poor' were not exclusively landlords and tenants respectively.

In contrast to the ideology of caste and class, however, the ideology of power at the turn of the century did correspond closely with the structure of the local-level power hierarchy. The perception of power as a function of wealth, high-caste status and office, 'matched' the power wielded by local bureaucrats, and to a lesser extent landlords. Moreover during the baseline period, both at the level of social structure and at the level of ideology, the relationship between the power elite and the powerless took the form of that between leaders and followers.

The close correspondence between the ideology and social structure of power and the lack of such correspondence in the dimensions of caste and class assume significance when we turn our attention to contemporary stratification. For although in the realm of behaviour the power hierarchy has undergone radical change, the people's definition of power, owing perhaps to the close fit that existed between action and ideology in the baseline period, has remained virtually unchanged over the past century. Ironically this has today resulted in a perception of power which diverges sharply from the contemporary power structure in this community.

Part II

Contemporary Stratification

8   The Contemporary Community

Part I of this study was concerned with the analysis of stratification in Rangama/Devideniya during what I have termed the baseline period (1885–1910). Part II examines the contemporary structure and ideology of stratification in this community and the changes that have taken place in the intervening years.

These intervening years witnessed the ending of British colonial rule in Sri Lanka. It was also a period in which a general improvement in the living standards of most rural people occurred. This was particularly true of the post-independence decades. For the inhabitants of the Rangama/Devideniya community, minor irrigation works, agricultural diversification, the spread of government institutions and welfare provision, the establishment of schools and hospitals and the development of transport and communication have all contributed towards a more comfortable and secure life.

The benefits of these developments have, however, been somewhat offset by the fact that the population of this community has almost trebled over the past century. Demographic change in Rangama and Devideniya has not only been the result of internal expansion of families in the community but also of a considerable degree of in and out migration. Many landless families have migrated to settlement schemes in the dry zone, whilst others have migrated to towns and cities in search of employment. In-migration has taken place through the purchase of land by outsiders and through settlement on government allotments. The latter, known as 'colonies', are a standard feature of contemporary rural Sri Lanka, and consist of plots of government land (one quarter to two acres) granted to landless or land-poor families. Of the 42 settler families, 25 (approximately 10 per cent of the total number of households in the community) are outsiders who have received government allotments under one or other of the four village expansion schemes that have been developed within the community since 1938.

Table 9   *Increase in cultivated land since baseline*

| | Baseline | | | 1979/80 | | | |
	A	R	P	A	R	P	% increase
Paddy land	103	1	15	116	1	30	12.6
High land	188	2	10	336	3	25	78.6

The large increase in population has not been matched by a similar increase in the extent of cultivated land (see Table 9). Rice remains the staple food, but despite the aswedumization (process of creating a paddy field) of all available land, the increase in paddy land has been a mere 12.6 per cent. This has not, however, resulted in a decrease in the quantity of paddy produced relative to population because of improvements in productivity. Improved cultivation techniques, new high-yielding seed varieties, and minor irrigation works which make double cropping feasible, have meant that the community as a whole produces perhaps more paddy relative to population than at the turn of the century. Paddy-land owners have prospered, but since paddy land is unequally distributed, the imbalance between increase in population and paddy land has resulted in rural unemployment and an increase in the number of land-poor and landless families.

The increase in cultivated high land is greater than that of paddy land. There are two reasons for the 78.6 per cent increase in high-land acreage: firstly the conversion of forest land to the cultivation of new and profitable cash crops such as rubber, coffee and spices; secondly the cultivation of high-land crops on government land (usually parts of plantations) which has been allocated to poor families under village expansion schemes.[1]

Whilst village forest land has been gradually converted to high land on which cash crops are grown, the reverse process has taken place in large sections of the Berawila and Natha Kande plantations. Rubber replaced tea as the major crop on these plantations soon after the baseline period, and as a result these plantations profited handsomely during the rubber boom in the early decades of this century. After the British relinquished control, however, the plantations suffered a decline. Ownership passed through the hands of a series of Sri Lankan capitalists who failed to replant the rubber and allowed large sections of the plantations to revert to jungle. All but 100 acres of the two plantations were acquired by the government under the Land Reform Acts of the 1970s. For all that, in 1980 less than half of a total of 650 acres was under intensive cultivation. Apart from 150 acres of minor cash crops, Natha Kande is a timber forest, and with the exception of a similar extent under rubber and mixed high-land crops, Berawila estate consists of old rubber trees and encroaching secondary forest.

During the period of fieldwork there was no electricity or gas supply to the community.[2] Firewood – the only fuel used for cooking – was gathered by village women from the surrounding forests. Nor was there tap water. The majority of villagers use well water for drinking and cooking purposes and use the waters of the Maha Oya and other smaller streams for bathing. Lighting is primarily by kerosene oil lamps. For the purchase of kerosene and a variety of other consumer goods, villagers use bazaars or locally-based government co-operative stores.

Although the Rangama/Devideniya community is isolated by the standards of many Low Country villages, its communications with the outside have greatly improved since the baseline period. Inhabitants of the community no longer have to wade through rivers and streams to reach bazaars. Causeways have been built across the Maha Oya, Kuda Oya and Moragammana Ela and both villages are connected to Dambawala by motorable roads along which buses of the Ceylon Transport Board run once a day to Devideniya and six times a day to Rangama. The introduction of public transport has been a great boon to the people of this community, given the paucity of private transport. There are only three motor vehicles in the community and bullock carts and bicycles are rarely seen since the majority of public thoroughfares leading off the two motorable roads are narrow footpaths. The existence of two motorable roads and the introduction of buses have made the northern population centres relatively accessible to villagers, except when the low-lying causeways are flooded during the monsoons. Although the accessibility of bazaars has meant that villagers no longer depend on itinerant Muslim traders for the purchase of consumer goods, itinerant Muslim middlemen remain a feature of community life because they provide the most important market outlet for spices.

Dambawala, the closest bazaar, is still provincial (one cannot buy a newspaper there) but has expanded since the baseline period. It consists of a series of single-storey structures lining the road. These 'buildings' house a variety of enterprises – retail shops selling groceries and household items, tea kiosks, two barber salons, a private dispensary, a handful of trading stores (operated by middlemen who buy rubber and spices from villagers) and a timber store. Dambawala also boasts an English tutory, a one-room shack on the bank of the Maha Oya – the Kremlin Academy of English. During the baseline period, the only two shops in Dambawala were owned and operated by Muslims. Today, however, the Muslims no longer have a monopoly over trading and retail activities in this area. In contemporary Dambawala Muslims are involved in only seven of the eighteen commercial establishments.

A gradual out-migration of Muslims from this area has resulted in a decrease in the Muslim population in the Rangama/Devideniya community. Today the single Muslim household constitutes the numerically smallest caste in the community. The three largest castes are the Batgam, the Goigama and the Vahumpura. The numerical preponderance within the Rangama/Devideniya community of these three castes reflects the general caste distribution in the Kegalle district as well as in the Sabaragamuva province as a whole, where the Batgam and Vahumpura together are almost as numerous as the Goigama.[3] Indeed the Batgam concentration in certain areas of the Kegalle district led to the creation of a new electorate by the Delimitation Commission of 1976, with the aim of enabling this low caste to have better representation in the national legislature. In the 1977 general election the Kegalle district was thus divided into nine electorates of which one was the Naranhana electorate within which Rangama/Devideniya is situated.

For administrative purposes the Rangama/Devideniya community is still within the Kegalle administrative district as it was under colonial rule. But in the years preceding independence and the decades following it, the structure of the provincial administration has undergone major changes. At the time of my field work the province was not a significant administrative unit[4] and the area of jurisdiction of the Government Agent was, as it still is today, the district (see Figure 6). After 1946, moreover,

Administrative Unit	Name of Unit	Bureaucrat
District	Kegalle	Government Agent
Division	Naranhena	Asst. Government Agent
Vasama	Rangama	Grama Sevaka

Figure 6 Administrative location of contemporary Rangama/Devideniya

Radala Ratemahatmayas (chief native headmen under the British) were gradually phased out. Their functions were taken over by civil servants known as Divisional Revenue Officers (now called Assistant Government Agents). The latter's area of jurisdiction is in general smaller than that of the Ratemahatmaya. During the baseline period for instance, the Kegalle district was divided into four Ratemahatmaya divisions. Today the Kegalle district has ten Assistant Government Agent divisions, one of which is Naranhena.

Below the divisional level there is today a single administrative level – the *vasama*. A *vasama* is made up of one or more villages and contains a population of approximately 2,000–4,000 persons. Following the abolition in 1963 of caste-based minor headmanships (Araccis, Vidāna Durayas, etc), a salaried official known as a Grama Sevaka administers each *vasama*. The Rangama/Devideniya community belongs to the Rangama vasama.[5] In contrast to the Rangama Araccis at the turn of the century who were members of the old, established Goigama families in the community, every Grama Sevaka who has served in the Rangama *vasama* has been an outsider belonging to the Batgam caste.

Because the old administrative unit known as the pattuwa and the office of Korala no longer exist, the Rangama Grama Sevaka's immediate superior is the Assistant Government Agent of Naranhena, whose office is located at Doragala, a town four miles north of Dambawala. In Doragala also are situated the principal government services for the region – the hospital, police station and Agrarian Services Centre.

Government institutions in Sri Lanka are not, however, confined to provincial towns, and their spread into remote villages is remarkable by the standards of third-world countries, including many of those which are 'richer' than Sri Lanka. Within the Rangama/Devideniya community, for instance, there are three schools (one of which prepares students for the GCE Ordinary level examination), two co-operative stores, a sub-post office, a resident midwife and a dispensary with a resident apothecary. The neglect of the rural population, characteristic of so much of British colonial rule, has been replaced by the much greater solicitousness of national governments to village needs, which has done much to raise the security and quality of life of the contemporary inhabitants of Rangama and Devideniya.

9 The Contemporary Caste Hierarchy

Many studies of South Asian society have tended to identify the caste hierarchy with the behavioural effects often empirically associated with it: inequalities in dress and forms of address, asymmetrical exchange of caste services and of food, and so on. But if an adequate comprehension of caste is to be achieved it is imperative to recognize that there is no necessary connection between unequal birth status on the one hand and social privileges/disadvantages on the other. It will be argued in this chapter that despite the attenuation of high-caste privileges in contemporary Rangama and Devideniya, caste is as pervasive in this community today as it was at the turn of the century.

THE DECLINE OF HIGH-CASTE PRIVILEGE

An observer familiar with the caste structure in this community during the baseline period would no doubt find remarkable the relatively small degree to which, today, inequalities of birth give rise to inequalities of opportunity and privilege. There are several reasons for the decline in high-caste privileges, among them the increased commercialization of the Rangama/Devideniya community; advancement in literacy and educational attainments; and more generally the greater welfare and egalitarian orientation of national, as opposed to British colonial, governments.

Residential exclusivity was one of the first privileges that high castes had to surrender. (As will be shown in Chapter 10, in the contemporary period 'high caste' becomes the equivalent of the Goigama caste and accordingly for the rest of the chapter 'high caste' and Goigama will be used interchangeably.) At the turn of the century the lower castes occupied separate clusters of dwellings such that the houses of the high castes were physically separate from those of the lower. But two types of migration, beginning as early as the 1930s, radically altered this residential pattern. Firstly, poor families from outside the community were granted allotments of 'crown' land under government village expansion schemes. Secondly, rich Batgam individuals from Devideniya, and to a lesser extent Vahumpura from Galewala, bought land in Rangama and settled on that land. Thus contemporary Goigama in this community are constrained to live cheek by jowl with the lower castes.

Parity in dress was achieved much later. In the Naranhena region, for instance, as recently as 1947, Batgam in mixed-caste villages were conforming to the caste-prescribed dress code which allowed them clothing only between the waist and knee. The standard of dress achieved by the contemporary lower casts in this community is therefore remarkable. A trained eye may notice that none of the few old men who still wear *koṇḍa* belong to the very low castes, and that only Goigama women wear blouses with puffed sleeves. But these are exceptions to the rule of uniformity in dress. In contemporary Rangama and Devideniya caste-based sumptuary laws are defunct. The young have virtually abandoned Sinhalese forms of dress in favour of Western styles, and as in the case of their more conservative elders, the minor differences in dress observable reflect differences of wealth not caste.

The dissociation of name from caste was, like dress, a relatively late development. Under British rule registrars were always drawn from the higher castes and frequently used their position to thwart those lower-caste persons who wished to flout the caste-based naming system.[1] In post-independence years there were many changes in names but, unlike those of dress, these changes did not lead to uniformity of nomenclature. The degree of change was directly related to the lowness of the caste in the hierarchy. For instance all castes have shed old-fashioned personal names in favour of popular names such as Wasantha (M) and Kusuma (F). But whilst the Goigama rigorously maintain the high-caste Banda (prince) and Manike (jewel) suffixes,[2] the lower castes have adopted popular names precisely to get away from caste-associated personal names which are today regarded as demeaning and embarrassing.[3] Name changing has been most extensive among the lowest castes who have gone so far as the change their *vāsagama* names more than once since the baseline period. The following two examples demonstrate the way in which the names in a Hēna and a Batgam family have changed with each generation:

(i) *Hēna*

AGE	NAME (*vāsagama* name shown in italic)	COMMENTS
Dead	*Heneyalage* Kuda Henaya	Both names are caste-associated
50	*Vidana Heneyalage* John	Personal name is neutral, anglicized. *Vāsagama* name is caste-associated but grandiose – reference to an ancestor who was a headman.
13	Kumari *Vithanage*	Personal name is high caste, meaning princess. *Vāsagama* name is not caste-associated – simply refers to headmanship.

(ii) *Batgam*

AGE	NAME	COMMENTS
Dead	*Ambakumburalage* Ranhotiya	Both names are caste-associated.
80	*Nuwarapaksage* Kiri Duraya	Personal name is caste-associated. *Vāsagama* name is grandiose (means loyal to Kandy) but is non-Goigama.
50	*Nuwarapaksage* Gunatileka	Personal name is neutral, used by many castes including Goigama.
15	Anura *Gunatileka*	Both names are not caste-associated.

Thus, though there is still some caste-based differentiation in names, the stigmatizing aspects of the old naming system have all but disappeared.

Concomitant with the dissociation of caste and name has been an attenuation of caste-determined forms of address. Today the age, education and profession of the addressee influence the vocative in ways that would have been inconceivable in the past. Firstly the term 'mahatmaya' (a respectful title for a person of some education) is often used today in conjunction with the personal name or the job of the addressee (e.g. manager mahatmaya; overseer mahatmaya) in preference to the caste-associated vocative. Some low-caste persons even bestow this title on illiterate Goigama as a way of avoiding the honorific 'ralahamy'.[4] Secondly the term mudalali (a polite term for those engaged in trade) has been greatly extended and has lost its caste-association. In the baseline period the term mudalali was only used by low-caste persons when addressing Muslim males. Today the Goigama also address Muslims as mudalali instead of the less polite 'thambi' or 'nana' employed in the past. Moreover the term is generally used today as a vocative for a member of any caste who is engaged in business or commercial activity. Thirdly, a considerable number of young people in the community address older persons who are of lower caste than themselves by the terms *māma* (MB) and *nënda* (FZ). These terms clearly connote the lower status of the addressee (actual kinsmen are addressed by the variants *māmandi/nëndamma*) but are considered more polite than the use of an older person's personal name as a vocative.

The tendency to dissociate caste from forms of address is so great that the second person singular pronoun with its numerous hierarchical forms is used far less frequently in the community today. Many people replace it by the vocative in conversation.

The decrease in discrimination in inter-caste interaction goes beyond the liberalization of forms of address to affect even those most potent symbols of caste inequality – seating arrangements and commensal restrictions.

Although rising standards of living have introduced a super-ordinate member to the hierarchy of seats (the armchair), infractions of seating etiquette are frequent today. During the baseline period a low-caste person would not have presumed ot sit on a chair except in the company of his caste fellows, and neither educational or occupational achievement compromized caste etiquette in seating arrangements. As recently as 1930 the Goigama Vel Vidane of Rangama was obliged to sit on a bench in Walawwe houses. But the contemporary Batgam Grama Sevaka of the Rangama *vasama* is offered an armchair whenever he visits a Goigama house. In official gatherings and public meetings low-caste persons are often seen sitting on chairs in the presence of the Goigama.

It is these occasions also that most commonly witness the relaxation of caste rules concerning the exchange of food and drink. Although commensal restrictions remain a symbol of caste superiority/inferiority and are observed in outline by most people, the dictates of education and official position are often seen to override traditional caste rules. Whatever their private opinions on the matter of commensal restrictions, Goigama teachers and officials abide by the liberal codes espoused by the modern state on public occasions, and partake of food and drink with low castes sometimes even on low-caste premises.

It is in the occupational sphere, however, that the decrease in the disabilities of low-caste status are most evident. There are two reasons for this – firstly the attenuation or commercialization of caste occupations and secondly the democratization of white-collar jobs.

There is no smithy in the community today, for the single Gallat man who practises his caste occupation works in Kegalle. The relinquishment of their specialization by the Gallat has inconvenienced all members of this community. The Vahumpura's break with caste service on the other hand has uniquely affected the Goigama. With the exception of a few Vahumpura families who consent to provide their traditional services to those Goigama families with whom they have had a long association, Rangama Vahumpura refuse to carry out their caste services. To avoid carrying boxes of sweetmeats and rice themselves, the Goigama have to recruit Vahumpura from neighbouring villages or sometimes even be satisfied with a non-Vahumpura accompanying them on journeys. The nature of the interaction has changed from that of caste obligation to a purely commercial transaction. Payment is in cash and is stipulated by the employee prior to performance of the service.

The commercialization of what were once caste duties has been carried furthest by the Hēna. The Rangama Hēna represent an interesting case of a caste that has retained a monopoly of its traditional occupation while simultaneously flouting caste rules in refusing to discriminate as to the caste of the recipients of its services. Two Hēna families in Rangama compete with a mud and wattle 'laundry' set up on the banks of the Maha Oya in Dambawala by washermen from outside the community. For the payment of cash, a person of any caste may have his or her clothes washed and ironed by any of these establishments. The only concession the Goigama receive is a collection and delivery service. Although overtly the Hēna still follow caste rules in denying their services to certain low castes at life crisis rituals, my landlady, a Vahumpura, cited at least one instance where a substantial 'under the table' cash inducement was sufficient to overcome these restrictions.

For the low castes the break with traditional caste occupations has been reinforced by their entry into the white-collar job market. The growing representation of low-caste persons in white-collar jobs can be attributed to the advent of free education (from primary school through university) and to the fact that qualification for such jobs now rests on educational attainment and/or political connection (see Chapter 11) rather than high-caste status. Although in rural areas the majority of senior posts in schools, co-operatives, the administration and the police are still occupied by high-caste persons, this reflects not current inequalities but rather the after-effects of British policy which favoured high castes. The job privileges of the high castes have been gradually undermined in post-independence years. The achievements of the lower castes in this community are remarkable – a Hēna man holds the most lucrative and prestigious white-collar job, all three university graduates in the community are Batgam as are the three students currently in university, and since 1963 every Grama Sevaka of the Rangama *vasama* has been a Batgam. In Rangama and Devideniya therefore it may be safely predicted that any vestige of the privileges enjoyed by the Goigama in the sphere of education and occupation will disappear completely in the near future.

The Decay of Caste?

The achievements of the low castes in this community and the dramatic decrease in high-caste privileges might lead one to conclude that caste in this community is no longer important as a basis for structuring relationships. It is important, however, to avoid such a simplistic conclusion. The decline of high-caste privilege and the attenuation of discrimination does not entail the disappearance of inequalities of birth status. It is not the attenuation of unequal birth status that differentiates the contemporary community from Rangama and Devideniya in the baseline period. Rather it is the way in which inequalities of birth status now find expression in non-conventional behaviour patterns as opposed to the system of unequal privileges of an earlier era.

ANTAGONISTIC BEHAVIOURAL EXPRESSIONS OF CASTE INEQUALITY

In contemporary Rangama and Devideniya antagonistic behavioural expressions of caste inequality take the form of caste conflict and caste competition. Conflict and competition between castes are not, however, the result of disagreement over unequal caste privileges. On the contrary they are largely derivative of the democratization and modernization of rural society.

Caste Conflict

Given low-caste acceptance during the baseline period of the legitimacy of the caste system and its prevailing behavioural concomitants, it is hardly surprising that caste conflict was at the time extremely uncommon. Today, however, much of the violence that occurs in the community takes the form of caste conflict.

During my sixteen months in the community the worst incidence of violence took place in the 'disturbances' of April 1979. These disturbances are worth recounting here in detail because they reveal significant aspects of the nature of caste conflict in the community.

The initial incident giving rise to the disturbance centred on an argument over irrigation water between a middle-aged Goigama man and a young Batgam man (KDK). During the course of the argument KDK slapped the Goigama man. That night a group of 15 to 20 Goigama youth marched to KDK's house, shouted insults at the Batgam and attacked KDK. A few nights later the house of a Gallat family who were away visiting relatives in another village was robbed and burned. Six Goigama youths were arrested and questioned by the police. They were released the following day. It soon became common knowledge that it was in fact KDK who had committed the crime and who had sent his friends to inform the police that the Goigama youths were responsible. The motive supplied by KDK was that the Goigama were expressing their anger over the liaison between a Goigama youth and the daughter of the Gallat family in question. When the Gallat family returned home, however, they charged KDK with the crime. KDK was arrested by the police but released soon after, by all accounts as a result of the intervention of B. Jayasena, a rich Batgam in the community who is a close relative of the Member of Parliament (MP)[5] for Naranhena.

The April disturbances reveal several important aspects of the nature of caste-based conflict. Firstly they show that the decrease in high-caste privileges has not come about by mutual consent – the Goigama are opposed to the democratization of privilege which is a feature of life in the Rangama/Devideniya community today.[6] Secondly the disturbances demonstrate the way in which the low castes unite with each other in a confrontation with the Goigama. Most of the low castes in the community supported KDK. They claimed that the Goigama youths had no right to attack KDK and that the original fight should have been treated simply as an interpersonal conflict and should not have provoked caste retaliation. Thirdly the prominent part played by young members of the community in the violence points to the perpetuation rather than attenuation of caste antagonism in the future. Finally the motive supplied by KDK's friends demonstrates the degree of opposition to inter-caste marriages that exists on the part of the higher of the two castes concerned.

The acceptance by the police of this motive as sufficient to detain the Goigama youths for questioning is not surprising. For inter-caste marriages are increasingly becoming a source of violence in these highland communities.[7] At the turn of the century inter-caste marriages were relatively rare, since the vast majority of marriages were arranged by parents. In modern Sri Lanka the greater freedom enjoyed by young people has led to an increasing number of marriages based on romantic love, some inevitably across caste lines. The intense opposition to inter-caste marriages by the relatives of the spouse of higher caste arises not only because of the breach of caste endogamy but also because the stigma of a low-caste union jeopardizes the chance of arranging a 'good' marriage for siblings and even cousins of the errant individual. And when threats, pleas, sorcery and violence have proved unsuccessful in preventing an inter-caste union, the penalty paid by the spouse of higher caste is exile from family and caste fellows and almost exclusive association thenceforth with lower-caste in-laws.

Caste Competition

Like caste conflict, caste competition is a largely non-conventional behaviour pattern. In the baseline period the only evidence of caste competition was the rivalry between the Gallat and the Vahumpura for precedence in the caste hierarchy, and was thus contained within the system of birth status. Contemporary caste competition, however, operates in new arenas – ironically within those very institutions of the modern state which liberal planners hoped would be caste free.

Voluntary organizations represent a type of modern institution which has, in large part due to caste competition, been unable to function in rural areas. Since independence, a variety of voluntary organizations (e.g. the Village Development Society, the Farmers' Society, etc.) have been instituted in rural areas, but the experiment in local participation has in Rangama and Devideniya and in many other communities been a failure. Villagers are cynical about the aims of these organizations and unenthusiastic because of the poor results achieved by them. The poor results themselves, however, are a result of the lack of co-operation and unity in rural communities. Most government-sponsored voluntary organizations are politicized (see Chapter 11) and split along party lines. In mixed-caste villages such as Rangama, caste competition adds a further dimension of disunity in the face of which many organizations cease to function. The Rangama

Village Development Society[8] is a case in point. After the 1977 elections the United National Party (UNP) government abolished all village development societies and decreed that they were to be reconstituted. The new 'elected' (see Chapter 11) president of the Rangama society happened to belong to the Batgam caste. The Goigama of Rangama, who constitute over 40 per cent of the village population, were bitterly opposed to a low-caste person holding office and refused to have anything to do with the organization. The Batgam president told me that a not insignificant part of the problem centred around their opposition to him occupying a superior seat on the dais at meetings. It is not surprising that the only voluntary organization to function in any sense in Rangama –the Funeral Aid Society[9] – is completely dominated by the Goigama.

In the case of voluntary organizations it was simply assumed by planners that popular participation would promote caste unity. By contrast, the reform of the provincial bureaucracy was primarily a political device used by the Sri Lanka Freedom Party to strip 'headmen' – most of whom were stalwart UNP supporters – of their power. Nevertheless the administrators who were responsible for introducing the reform expected the new system to be more effective in reducing the force of caste in rural society. Merit was to replace high-caste status and wealth as the basis of office.

The most significant reform of the bureaucracy as far as local communities were concerned was the abolition of minor headmanships in 1963 and the appointment of salaried officials (Grama Sevakas) to administer *vasamas*.

The reform of the provincial bureaucracy cannot be said to have been an unqualified success. It was successful insofar as it brought low-caste men into positions of authority on a hitherto unprecedented scale. But the reform contradicted a long-standing tradition of high-caste connection with the bureaucracy and hence fostered caste competition whenever a low-caste Grama Sevaka was appointed to a *vasama* which contained a considerable number of high-caste residents.

Grama Sevakas themselves often exacerbate caste competition by their preference for working with their own caste fellows. In 1975, for instance, when Grama Sevakas were instructed to form crime prevention societies to patrol each *vasama*, the Batgam

Grama Sevaka of Rangama made sure that the Rangama society was almost exclusively Batgam. Because of their close involvement with caste fellows all three Grama Sevakas of Rangama are alleged to have favoured the Batgam in the community – a fact resented by non-Batgam.

In addition to routine administrative work, the Grama Sevaka is expected to advise and guide the inhabitants of his *vasama* to develop their villages and improve their living standards. The extent to which a Grama Sevaka carries out these extra-administrative functions is entirely dependent on his caste and the caste of the villagers under his jurisdiction. The present Rangama Grama Sevaka's relationship with Devideniya, for instance, is qualitatively different from that with Rangama. The Batgam inhabitants of Devideniya co-operate with the Grama Sevaka; the Goigama in Rangama do not.

The Grama Sevaka is treated as a VIP in all Devideniya village activities. He spends a disproportionate amount of his time there and on his own initiative organized a sports club for the Devideniya youth. In contrast the Rangama Goigama, whilst according him a degree of respect which is expedient in interpersonal interaction, are quite dismissive of him in collective activities. They often fail to invite him for village functions and even when he turns up uninvited (as he often does) they do not accord him a position of prominence. The Batgam Grama Sevaka is not, in other words, allowed to assume an important role in Rangama affairs because the Goigama resent his appointment and frustrate his attempts to assume a leadership role.

The bureaucratic reforms have thus benefited the lower castes but at the same time have given rise to inter-caste competition. The introduction of competitive party politics – perhaps the foremost institution of liberal democracy – has had much the same effect. The lower castes have benefited from competitive party politics insofar as it has been electorally expedient for parliamentary candidates to be sympathetic to their interests. At the same time, however, electoral politics has been infiltrated by caste, and serves as an important arena for caste competition.

The only two parties that have an impact in the Naranhena area are the UNP and the Sri Lanka Freedom Party (SLFP). The former is popularly regarded as the party of the aristocracy whilst the latter is looked upon as the party that is more interested in the welfare of the low castes. Hence in parliamentary, village council and even local co-operative society elections the majority of committed party supporters in Rangama (a predominantly Goigama village) vote for the UNP, whereas in Devideniya (a predominately Batgam village) they vote for the SLFP. The non-committed in both villages vote principally on caste lines irrespective of party – Goigama voting for Goigama candidates[10] and low castes voting for low caste candidates. The voting pattern in this community is thus inspired by competition between the Goigama and the low castes.

In the 1977 general election both parties tried to neutralize the effects of caste competition in voting by fielding candidates of the same caste, usually from the numerically preponderant caste in each constituency. Whilst this served to lessen the influence of caste in voting choice, it did not reduce the caste pressure which is brought to bear on elected representatives after the election, or the caste favouritism that often results from such pressure. This favouritism may be extensive since rural MPs have considerable power and are in a position to bestow a large number of favours on their constituents.

Caste favouritism by the MP in this area is often seen to take the form of protection from the police. Rural MPs possess *de facto* power to instruct the inspector (the chief officer of the local police station) to release an individual from police custody. (The release of KDK was apparently the result of a caste appeal.) Such interference in the workings of the police force has resulted in the perpetuation of the connection between caste and the forces of law and order, despite radical changes in the recruitment procedures and composition of the national police since the baseline period.[11] The difference lies only in the fact that the high-caste bias of the past has been replaced in the Naranhena area by police discrimination in favour of the Batgam even though the inspector is a Goigama and proud of his caste status. Police favouritism for the Batgam is resented by all other castes in the region and has had the effect of making certain senior Goigama police officers increasingly caste conscious. Where they can get away with it without antagonizing the MP, it appears that they take every opportunity to favour their own caste fellows.[12] This again is a forceful illustration of the way in which developments favouring a low-caste group engender antagonism between castes.

If caste inequality expressed itself only in antagonistic behaviour, the argument could be made that the behavioural effects of caste inequality are highly attenuated in contemporary Rangama and Devideniya. Caste conflict and caste competition do not constitute day-to-day features of community life. They are sporadic, non-routine behaviour patterns which bear no comparison with the pervasiveness of caste etiquette and caste privileges/disabilities in this community during the baseline period. But the presence of non-antagonistic behavioural expressions of caste inequality in contemporary Rangama and Devideniya render such an argument untenable. For caste inequalities today structure behaviour to no less a degree than in the past through the institution of caste segregation.

Caste segregation in this community is not a consequence of Goigama exclusiveness and does not simply result in a bifurcation of the community into low-caste and high-caste groups. The different low castes have no more contact with each other than do the Goigama with all the other castes. Nor is it the case that segregation results from the attempt of each caste to maintain separation from all those beneath it in the caste hierarchy. With regard to any two caste groups the initiation of, or the desire for separation is not a preserve of the higher caste. A Vahumpura individual, for example, is eager to minimize contact not only with the Batgam and Hēna but also with the Goigama. Caste segregation in contemporary Rangama/Devideniya is therefore not a case of discrimination by one caste against another lower than itself in the hierarchy.

In contrast with the situation in the baseline period, inter-caste interaction rarely takes place for reasons of sociability in the community today. True, men of different castes do occasionally meet in tea kiosks, but spending one's time drinking tea and chatting in boutiques is often looked upon askance and many men do not indulge in this pastime. Social visiting in each other's houses on the other hand is hardly ever indulged in across caste lines. Most schoolchildren in the community, for instance, have never been inside the houses of those classmates who belong to different castes. Adults go to the house of a non-caste fellow only for a specific economic reason – i.e. to conclude a commercial transaction or to discuss a particular agricultural issue.

Despite the numerous economic links that prevail between members of different castes, agriculture has not escaped the impact of caste segregation. Certain types of inter-caste contact are unavoidable – as, for example, when landlord and tenant or landowner and labourer belong to different castes. Every effort is made, however, to keep non-essential contact to a minimum in agricultural activities. The mixed caste *attam* teams of the baseline period, for instance, are a rarity today. Even in the process of transplanting, which is often carried out by young schoolgirls, there is a marked preference for co-operative labour teams to be caste exclusive.

For a considerable number of Vahumpura and Batgam persons resident in Rangama, exclusive association with caste fellows has resulted in more frequent and intense extra-village interaction for purposes of sociability than intra-village interaction. These persons (or their parents) migrated to Rangama from neighbouring West Galewala and Devideniya respectively and they maintain close ties with their ancestral villages. For these people association with caste fellows from neighbouring villages has been so close that it has resulted in identification with those villages. Approximately half the Rangama Vahumpura[13] and an equal proportion of Rangama Batgam consider themselves West Galewala and Devideniya people respectively.

The caste segregation of many Rangama Vahumpura and Batgam even extends to the religious sphere. During the baseline period all castes in the community worshipped at the Rangama *vihāraya*. In the 1940s, however, two new *vihāra* were built in the area – one in Devideniya and one in West Galewala. Both *vihāra* were financed by the people of these villages and significantly neither belongs to the Siam *nikāya* which restricts ordination to the Goigama. The establishment of these *vihāra* have enabled the majority of Batgam and Vahumpura of this community to maintain a high degree of caste segregation.

The monks of the three *vihāra*, far from trying to unite the laity, are at odds with each other and are not above exacerbating caste disunity to further their own ends. None of these *vihāra* are endowed with large grants of land, and the material comfort of the monks as well as the prosperity of the *vihāra* rests on lay donations and support. Each monk therefore competes with the others to get as many devotees and donees as possible. The Rangama monk resents the new *vihāra* because he feels that they are responsible for the loss of a congregation (and its material support) that is rightfully his. His relationship with the Batgam monk of the Devideniya *vihāraya* is strained and that with the Berava (drummer) caste monk of West Galewala is directly hostile. Accusations and counter-accusations are common and the Galewala monk berates those Vahumpura from Rangama who support the Rangama *vihāraya* for their folly in associating with a *vihāraya* whose monk perpetuates aristocratic values.

Caste segregation also characterizes domestic religious rituals which indeed may be seen as epitomizing the separation of castes in this community. In contrast to the situation in the baseline period where *pinkam* brought together all members of the community in a spirit of co-operation and goodwill, *pinkam* in Goigama, Vahumpura and Batgam houses are performed without inter-caste co-operation.[14] Each of these castes is now large enough to provide the organization and finances necessary for a *pinkama* and only caste fellows are asked to help in providing the breakfast and luncheon feasts for the monks. Likewise only caste fellows attend the all-night *pirit* chant.

Whilst caste exclusiveness denies members of other castes the privilege of participating directly in the ritual, the fiction that all are welcome to gain merit is nevertheless maintained through the ingenious institution of a voluntary public appeal. In order to allow non-caste fellows to contribute towards the ritual a tray of betel leaves and a book are left in a village shop prior to the ritual. Hence any criticism that caste segregation is being applied to religious affairs is forestalled. All who wish to gain merit from the ritual are enabled to do so by placing a donation on the tray and recording the amount given in the book. In this way merit can be gained by all without compromising the caste-exclusiveness of those participating in the ritual.

Caste segregation in contemporary Rangama and Devideniya is a direct result of the conjunction of inequalities of birth status on the one hand and the liberalization of caste etiquette on the other. In the baseline period caste etiquette served as the governing principle of inter-caste interaction. The undermining of caste rules has meant that today every inter-caste interaction is characterized by a degree of uncertainty. In the absence of an accepted, regularized pattern in inter-caste interaction each individual runs the risk of being insulted – the higher by the lower flouting caste etiquette, and the lower by the higher maintaining it. Such risks are avoided by caste segregation. Uncertainty regarding form of address, for instance, led to the termination of interaction between two girls – one a Goigama the other a Batgam. The Batgam girl was not willing to address the other by the caste honorific 'manike', but knew that usage of the personal name would have incurred the displeasure of the Goigama girl. The latter, for her part, avoided the Batgam girl for fear of being insulted by being so addressed. This is a good example of the way in which caste segregation is used as a device to avoid the risk of being insulted by those of a lower or a higher caste than oneself.

Analysis of caste in this community thus shows that the liberal ideologies and welfare policies of the modern state have succeeded in eroding the privileges of high caste status but not in eradicating inequalities of birth status. Caste segregation is less obvious, and, to some, less discomforting than caste discrimination, but is nevertheless evidence that inequalities of birth status remain today, as they were at the turn of the century, a significant basis for structuring behaviour in rural society.

10 The Contemporary Class Hierarchy

Between 1910 and 1950 a large amount of high-caste land entered the land market and passed into the hands of low-caste individuals. This chapter shows that assertions such as 'the caste hierarchy is upset through acquisition of large holdings by persons of low caste',[1] and 'the spread of capitalist relations and associated modern legislation have undermined the traditional caste system; . . . socio-economic class . . . increasingly determines collective behaviour',[2] do not further the understanding of class nor that of caste. The three-dimensional model allows for a quite different interpretation of contemporary stratification in Rangama/Devideniya because the class hierarchy is analysed outside the shadow of a supposedly decaying caste system.

The relational quality of the three-dimensional model avoids the 'class replaces caste' interpretation of social change. It leads instead to an examination of the changes in the class hierarchy over the past century and the way in which they have served to change the nature of the relationship between class and the hierarchies of caste and power. The increasing divergence between the groups forming the hierarchies of class and caste consequent to the increase in low-caste land control, far from 'upsetting' the caste system, has led to the reinforcement of the salience of birth status. And other major changes in the class hierarchy, such as the disinclination of the rich to bestow largesse, and the decreased level of dependence of the rural poor upon the landed elite, are related to a fundamental change that has occurred in the relationship between wealth and power since the baseline period.

THE AGRICULTURAL SECTOR OF THE LOCAL ECONOMY

The economy of the contemporary Rangama/Devideniya community is predominantly agricultural. Although the number of inhabitants employed in non-agricultural occupations is propor-

Table 10   *Principal source of income of household heads*

Nature of Principal Source of Income	Number of Households	%
Agricultural	183	77.5
Agricultural and non-agricultural yielding equal income	16	6.8
Non-agricultural	37	15.7
	236	100.0

tionately higher than in the baseline period, agriculture (the cultivation of land directly or indirectly) constitutes the principal occupation (i.e. major source of income) of the vast majority of household heads[3] (see Table 10).

Agricultural land in the Rangama/Devideniya community is still divided into two basic categories – paddy land and high land. High-land cultivation has, however, undergone a major change. Mixed crops are grown on *vatu* (gardens) in much the same manner as in the baseline period, but chena cultivation has been entirely replaced by the scientific cultivation of a perennial cash crop – rubber. During the baseline period high land was more remunerative but paddy land, for a variety of reasons, was more 'valuable' (see pp. 59–60). In contemporary Rangama/Devideniya, however, paddy land, garden land and rubber land are not only equally remunerative but are also equally valuable. Improvements in trade and markets, as well as the diversification of high-land crops, have reduced the market uncertainties that undermined the pecuniary value of the single high-land cash crop in the baseline period. At the same time, paddy land has become more remunerative because of increased yields and national price supports.

In order to understand the economic organization of agrarian Sinhalese communities it is important to draw attention to the ways in which the spatial aspects and management of landholdings in Sinhalese villages differ from those of the Western 'farm'. One should note firstly that the land belonging to a single household is not usually contiguous. There exists a basic spatial differentiation between high land and paddy land. In addition a household's high land is itself commonly divided into separate parcels and its paddy land almost invariably so.

Another distinguishing feature is that the legal owner of an extent of land often cannot point to a specific geographic area as defining the boundaries of his landholding. This is because Sinhalese land ownership often implies ownership of a *share* in a particular property which itself is left physically undivided, either in order to avoid uneconomical cultivation units or in order to ensure equality for co-owners of a property characterized by differential fertility. Originally share owners of a property were siblings or close kinsmen, but today shares have changed hands many times and co-owners may be non-kinsmen or even outsiders with no kinship connection to people in the community.

The tenurial arrangements associated with the presence of undivided property and shareowners makes for a third distinction with the Western 'farm'. In Sinhalese villages the extent of land an individual cultivates and/or receives an income from is not co-extensive with the extent he owns, and usually varies from year to year on a cyclical pattern.

These distinctions will become clearer in the following more detailed examination of the different types of agriculture practised in contemporary Rangama/Devideniya.

High Land Cultivation – Garden Land

Of the two types of high land, garden land is more widely distributed among the inhabitants of this community than rubber land. An individual will turn to rubber cultivation only if he has at least a quarter of an acre of garden land. Since houses are built on garden land, a minimum of 20 perches (one-eighth acre) of a household's garden land is non-income yielding. Nevertheless all but 27 households (11.4 per cent) possess some income-yielding garden land.

All garden land is owner cultivated and, although share ownership in undivided property is present, this only applies on very small extents of land which are deemed too small to warrant division. The management of shares in such cases is uncomplicated. Share owners are usually close relatives and, apart from the unusual case, have an amicable arrangement whereby the share owner who resides on the land enjoys the produce of it. The resident share owner may occasionally give some of the produce on an informal basis to other share owners resident in the village. Non resident co-owners are interested in the land only to the extent that the resident owner is not allowed to change the character of the land (by felling trees, digging clay for making bricks etc) without prior permission.

An individual with only a quarter acre of garden land would still choose to plant subsistence crops such as coconut, jak, breadfruit, bananas and other fruit trees[4] rather than cash crops. This is not due to any failure to appreciate the value of cash crops but the result of a desire for security and a disinclination to get completely involved with the market economy. Those who have more than a quarter of an acre grow a variety of cash crops – pepper, coffee, cocoa, cloves and cardamom, in addition to the long-standing arecanut. The sharp rise in the price of cloves (from Rs 1.50/lb in 1964 to Rs 75.00/lb in 1979) has made it the most profitable garden cash crop. In 1979/80 an acre of mixed-crop garden land could yield a net income of between Rs 2,500 and Rs 4,000 per annum.

Despite the diversification of cash crops and the increased profitability of garden land, however, garden cultivation is still carried out as unscientifically as it was in the baseline period – various crops are scattered haphazardly in the garden and no fertiliser is applied.

The producer of garden cash crops enjoys far more favourable market conditions than he did in the baseline period. This is not primarily due to government initiative – despite official enthusiasm for the cultivation of these export crops there have, for example, been no attempts to set up government collection centres. Nevertheless, the producer does now have a variety of options in choosing where to sell his produce, in sharp contrast to the buyers' market of earlier days (see p. 56). There are today three middlemen operating in the Dambawala bazaar to whom the smallholders can sell their produce. Those with relatively large extents (over ¼ acre) of any one crop can take advantage of a 'leasing' system under which they sell their crop by leasing their land for a fixed sum during the period in which the crop is harvested. Here too there is healthy competition among the buyers. For example, prior to the clove harvesting season as many as 20 traders examine various garden plots and place their 'bids' with the owner.

The leasing system itself is of considerable benefit to the seller because it transfers the risks involved in harvesting to the trader. Both pepper and cloves, for example, require drying after harvesting, and in the absence of special smoke rooms, rainy weather could ruin these crops. If a crop is leased, however, the trader is responsible for safeguarding, harvesting, drying and transporting the crop. Moreover the buyer's 'bid' is based on an estimate of the yield, which is sometimes lower than expected.

High Land Cultivation – Rubber

The Kegalle district has the largest absolute acreage of rubber in the island. In the Naranhena area rubber is grown on plantations[5] as well as on peasant holdings. Rubber holdings in the Rangama/Devideniya community are larger than garden holdings (the smallest holding is half an acre and three residents own over 10 acres), but are less widely distributed. Only 59 households possess rubber land. Seventeen of these have old low-yielding rubber trees amidst secondary forest, whilst the remaining 42 households own higher-yielding grafted rubber trees. An acre of grafted rubber in peak condition could yield a net income of up to Rs 6,000 a year in 1979/80. The yield of rubber trees does, however, vary with age, and the standard range of income obtained from an acre of rubber in this community was between Rs 2,313 and Rs 4,879.[6]

Rubber cultivation is far more labour intensive than garden cultivation, and unlike paddy cultivation the labour requirements are not seasonal. Mature rubber trees are tapped every day of the year, except on days when there is heavy rain. The regularity of the labour requirement for rubber cultivation makes it difficult for the landowner to combine this with a non-agricultural occupation. Thus rubber tappers are employed not only by those who own large extents of rubber but also by those smallholders who have regular non-agricultural employment. Over a third of those who own grafted rubber trees employ rubber tappers. The latter are employed either on the basis of a fixed sum per pound of rubber tapped or on the basis of sharing the yield.[7] From the landowner's point of view the former is the more profitable – 60–90 cents per pound – whereas under the sharing system the landowner may pay the tapper up to Rs 1.70 per pound. It is only the larger rubber owners (owning over 1½ acres) who can find employees willing to work on the fixed sum per pound system, since on smaller extents the yield is too small to obtain a reasonable daily wage (i.e. Rs 8–10). Hence the larger the extent, the less the landowner has to pay the rubber tapper per pound of rubber, and consequently the greater the profits.

In contrast to the lack of government involvement in the marketing of garden crops, state participation in rubber marketing is well developed. A producer may sell rubber in one of three stages. Unprocessed latex can be sold to two government purchasing centres situated at some distance from the community. If transport were made available or the centres situated closer, selling latex would be a profitable way for producers to market their rubber. In 1979–80 latex sold for just 0.30 cents less than Grade I quality sheet rubber, and by selling latex the producer avoids the costs and materials required to process latex into rubber sheets, many of which do not eventually reach Grade I standard. As it stands, however, this alternative is inconvenient because it involves carrying heavy pails of latex for three to four miles: private traders in Dambawala do not buy latex. Most producers in the Rangama/Devideniya community therefore process the latex into solid sheets and sell them (either before or after drying) to traders in Dambawala, or at a slightly higher price to the government purchasing centre at Naranhena.

Paddy Cultivation

Although the increase in cultivated extent has not been large, paddy production in this community has increased appreciably since the baseline period. As a result of improved infrastructure and cultivation techniques, the annual yield per acre is 300 per cent greater than at the turn of the century. In 1938 a dam was constructed across the Maha Oya, and in subsequent years many of the streams and rivulets which feed the Maha Oya were also dammed. These minor irrigation works not only made double cropping feasible but also brought an improvement in the Maha crop (principally rain fed) by enabling the regulation of water to the fields. Higher yields were also obtained by replacing the broadcast sowing of the past with the nursery sowing and transplanting method.

Cultivators do not question these benefits but are ambivalent about the recent adoption of NHYV seeds and the usage of chemical fertilisers and pesticides. Older villagers grumble that the new varieties are tasteless and are unwholesome because of the chemicals used in the production process. Despite these reservations, however, modern cultivation techniques are used by all and the average yield per acre is 60 bushels. At Rs 40 per bushel, an acre of paddy yielded a net income of Rs 3,272 a year for an owner-cultivator.[8]

Although both garden and rubber land have the potential to yield greater returns than paddy land, the latter has several advantages of its own. Firstly, rice being the staple food of Sri Lankans, national government legislation has since 1948 protected paddy prices from world market fluctuations.[9] Secondly, with the development of irrigation the output of paddy land is more predictable than that of high land. Rubber trees must be replanted at intervals and the yield decreases as the trees get old. Moreover clove trees can in certain years, for no accountable reason, produce a very small crop. Finally, paddy land bestows creditworthiness on those who have access to it. Not only is paddy land the most suitable type of agricultural land to be mortgaged or leased (see note 18), but creditors are more willing to lend small amounts of money to those with access to paddy land because they are sure that they can recover their loan in paddy at harvest time.

Household paddy-land holdings vary between one-sixteenth of an acre and seven acres. One-hundred-and-six households (44.9 per cent) have no access to paddy land. Perhaps due to the relative scarcity of paddy land and the desire to have access to it, even in the capacity of a tenant, the tenurial arrangements developed over the years on paddy land are more complex than those on high land. Two basic types of tenurial systems are used in the Rangama/Devideniya paddy tract:

– tenurial systems based on share ownership of undivided property;

– tenurial systems based on tenancy agreements.

Tenurial systems based on share ownership of undivided property

Rights in paddy land shares of even minute extents (one-sixteenth of an acre) are rigorously asserted, and the cultivation of undivided fields with share owners is governed by two long-standing tenurial patterns[10] which result in highly equitable but also highly complicated working arrangements between the share owners. The operation of the more common pattern, *taṭṭumāru*,[11] in contemporary rural society has, however, frequently been misunderstood by scholars and planners alike. *Taṭṭumāru* is employed in the Rangama/Devideniya community when share owners of a field deem it 'uneconomical' to cultivate their shares simultaneously. Each owner takes it in turn to obtain cultivation rights to the whole field for a year. The frequency with which cultivation rights are obtained depends upon the size of each person's share. Thus if there are five share owners, each with an equal share, each cultivates the entire field once in five years. But if A owns half the field, and B and C own a quarter each, A works the field for two years then B and C for one year each, and then A again for two years.

When this system originated centuries ago it is likely that 'uneconomic' shares meant shares of the field which were physically too small to warrant cultivation simultaneously. It is erroneous to conclude from this, however, that contemporary participants of the *taṭṭumāru* system are necessarily poor and are involved in cultivating small extents. Though the system remains, the conditions under which it operates have changed. Firstly, with the emergence of a land market, shares have changed hands many times and today's share owners are not necessarily the inheritors of ancestral property that has been passed down through the generations, getting progressively more divided along the way. Secondly, not all shares involved in *taṭṭumāru* today are the result of past *taṭṭumāru* arrangements. Some paddy fields were, and are, left undivided in order to ensure equality of fertility among the inheritors, and these shares may be quite large.

In the contemporary Rangama/Devideniya community what is

considered an 'uneconomic' share is entirely relative and depends not only upon the actual extent of the share, but also upon whether the share owner has other parcels of paddy land, and if so on their location in the paddy tract. For instance, a farmer who owns fairly large shares in three fields dispersed in various parts of the paddy tract at some distance from each other, may feel that it is more economical (from a labour saving point of view) to cultivate one or all of these shares on a *taṭṭumāru* basis with other share owners, rather than having to carry out cultivation every year in three different locations. Indeed in the Rangama/Devideniya paddy tract, certain large paddy land owners cultivate shares as large as half an acre on the *taṭṭumāru* basis. Conversely many poor people still consider it economical to cultivate their single one-eighth acre share each year without engaging in *taṭṭumāru* because they need the regular (if small) supply of paddy that their single share yields.

Tenurial systems based on tenancy agreements

A second type of tenurial arrangements results from the presence of tenancy on paddy land. Two types of crop-sharing tenancy are practised in the community, the most common being the *anda* system under which landlord and tenant share the crop. In Rangama/Devideniya 53 per cent of the paddy tract is cultivated by *anda* tenants. Seed paddy is bought by either the landlord or the tenant, and is recovered at harvest time with a 50 per cent interest. The costs of fertilizer and pesticides are borne equally by both parties. All other money costs (buffalo hire, food for *attam* labour teams, etc.) are the tenant's responsibility and are not recoverable at the crop division.

The second form of tenancy is the *karu anda* or *kūttu anda* system. Here the tenant carries out half the cultivation tasks (either those involving buffalos or those involving manual labour) and receives in return a quarter of the crop.

The Paddy Lands Act (PLA) of 1958 radically altered the structure and organization of tenancy-based tenurial arrangements in paddy land. The Act had as its principal aims the provision of security of tenure for the *anda* tenant (*karu anda* tenants were not covered by the Act) and the prevention of exploitation by the landlord. Tenants who can prove that they have worked a particular plot for 1½ years continuously are granted permanent cultivation rights, irrespective of subsequent changes in the ownership of the land. These tenants are given the power to nominate a successor, sell, transfer or gift their rights to any other person. The vast majority of tenants in the Rangama/Devideniya paddy tract today have obtained security of tenancy under the Act. Landlords can dispossess them only if it is proven to the agricultural authorities that the tenant is not maintaining a reasonable standard of production, or if the landlord wishes to cultivate the field with his own labour.

In addition to security of tenure the PLA improved the tenant's position by proscribing the levy of a tenancy fee (*madaran*) as well as the landlord's imposition of extra services on the tenant. The latter include the obligation to transport the landlord's share of the crop from the threshing floor to the latter's granary.

Most tenants in this community however, do not avail themselves of that provision in the Act which reduces the landlord's share of the crop to a quarter, or 15 bushels per acre, whichever is less. A handful of tenants whom the landlords have tried unsuccessfully to evict take three-quarters of the crop and a few others secrete some of the grain from the threshing floor during the night before the landlord comes for the crop division.[12] Apart from these, however, all tenants continue to give the landlord the traditional half share of the crop.

Whilst the PLA has been favourable to those tenants who were fortunate enough to obtain security of tenure, it has also resulted in a large number of families being permanently excluded from paddy cultivation. Firstly, with the Act impending, many tenants who had cultivated the same field for a number of years were evicted. Landlords managed to 'break' their fields (*kumburu käduva*) from tenant control by taking over cultivation themselves, changing tenants every season, or moving tenants around their various fields, thereby denying the latter a chance to prove continuous cultivation of a field – the necessary requirement under the Act to be registered as an *anda* tenant. Some landlords evicted their more gullible tenants by using their fields to borrow money on the usufructuary system. Here the creditor obtains usufructuary right of the field until the principal is returned, the yield constituting the interest. Tenants were told that they would regain cultivation rights once the debt was repaid but had by then lost tenancy rights by giving up cultivation.

Secondly, a large number of former tenants were displaced from the land because of the abolition of the free market in tenancies. By bestowing security of tenure the PLA created a privileged group of tenants who gained permanent cultivation rights over certain fields by denying all others access to these fields. In a situation where the demand for tenancies outstripped the supply of rentable land, the former *madaran* system enabled tenancy rights to be distributed among a greater number of families. By making tenancies more accessible to non-owners of paddy land, the *madaran* system promoted greater equality among the latter.

Thirdly, although all but a handful of paddy-land holdings are still cultivated by owner-cultivators or tenants, there is today a preference for cultivation with hired labour or contract labour[13] rather than with tenants on newly acquired fields. For those paddy-land owners disinclined to cultivate their fields with their own labour, the PLA has created a disincentive to rent their land. Landlords resent the permanent cultivation rights that tenants gain over what they consider their freehold property, and most would, if they could, evict those of their tenants who are not close kinsmen. If landowners do rent their land today they ensure that the tenants cannot get registered under the Act, by paying the acreage tax and buying the fertiliser and pesticides themselves. Most, however, choose not to take this risk, and if they cannot or do not wish to cultivate their fields with their own labour, use hired labour or employ a contractor. In this way, too, the supply of available tenancies has remained stagnant, to the detriment of those who do not own paddy land and have not gained secure tenancies.

THE CLASSES IN CONTEMPORARY RANGAMA/DEVIDENIYA

The economy of contemporary Rangama/Devideniya is predominately agricultural and, as in the baseline period, it is differential control of the land that creates cleavages of wealth and material well-being in the community. However, the demarcation of class categories is a far more complex matter than it was at the turn of the century primarily because control of land can no longer be equated with ownership of land.

According to Marxist convention, and indeed according to the conventions of many other types of political economists, when class is analysed according to differential control of land, the categories 'landlord', 'owner-cultivator', 'tenant' and 'labourer' are used to demarcate class groups. Each category is commonly held to exhibit 'greater' control over land and hence the four groups are assumed to be ranked in order of decreasing superiority. However, for the reasons given below, this framework is seriously inadequate for the purposes of demarcating agrarian classes in rural Sri Lanka.

Control over land is relevant for the purpose of demarcating classes only insofar as it is taken to mean control over the product or income yielding potential of the land. Such control is gained when there is secure expectation of a regular stream of income from a given parcel of land. The conventional analysis of class makes an unwarranted assumption that there is a necessary and simple correspondence between types of right to land (i.e. the categories landlord, owner-cultivator, tenant and labourer) and the extensiveness of control over income-yielding land. However, empirical analysis of the ways that such control is actually gained in contemporary Rangama/Devideniya reveals that such a correspondence simply does not apply in this situation.

In the contemporary community there are three major ways of securing a guaranteed stake in the produce of a parcel of land. These ways, although resembling in some particulars the conventional categories, do not together form a system of super-ordinate and subordinate levels of land control. Rather they are each equally effective ways of gaining control over the land's yield. The degree of control any individual possesses rests not on the fact of having one type of control rather than another but on the extent of land controlled under any combination of each of the three ways – owner management, tenancy agreement, mortgage and lease.

Owner Management

Owner management may be said to be present when an individual carries out production on his land with his own or hired labour. In both cases the owner of the land gains control over the product. (For the purpose of demarcating classes, hired labourers cannot be said to control a part of the product of the land upon which they labour because there is no recognized contract guaranteeing the labourer a fixed proportion of the yield. Surplus labour in the community[14] makes the work conditions of the hired labourer very insecure.)

Tenancy Agreement

As a result of the PLA, contemporary landlords do not have exclusive control over the product of their paddy land which is cultivated by tenants. During the baseline period landlords did have such control – a landlord could decide whether or not he wanted a parcel of land cultivated on a tenancy basis, and if so who the tenant would be. Today, however, tenants protected by the Act have a permanent, virtually inalienable right to a proportion of the product of the land they cultivate. In net terms this proportion is one-third, since the crop is shared but the tenants bear 80 per cent of the money costs of cultivation.[15] Contemporary landlords in the Rangama/Devideniya community therefore have effectively lost control permanently of one-third of the income-yielding potential of paddy lands cultivated by their tenants. Since tenants are secure in the expectation of one-third of the net product of the land they cultivate, in this study control over tenanted land will be considered as being divided between landlord and tenant – the tenant[16] having control of one-third and the landlord of two-thirds of the extent of such land. In other words, if an owner-cultivator, a landlord and a tenant all controlled two-thirds of an acre, one would be referring to a situation where the owner-cultivator owned and cultivated two-thirds of an acre, the landlord owned one acre, and the tenant cultivated two acres.

Mortgage and Lease

In the Rangama/Devideniya community land is mortgaged or leased in order to borrow money. The individual in the superior financial position (i.e. the creditor) is thus the mortgagee or the lessee. When money is borrowed on 'conditional mortgage', a piece of land is held as security for a loan which must be paid back with interest within a limited time. If these conditions are not met the land becomes the freehold property of the creditor.

Most borrowers however wish to avoid the risk of losing free-hold title to their land and therefore prefer either to lease their land or engage in a 'usufructuary mortgage'. In both these credit transactions the creditor obtains temporary use of the borrower's land. In the former case the yield compensates for the principal plus interest. Under 'usufructuary mortgage' the yield constitutes the interest until the loan is paid back. Rural poor who feel they will not be able to obtain money to pay back a loan are forced to lease out their land. Lessees who obtain use of the land over long, pre-defined periods therefore may be said to gain control over such land, since they are secure in the expectation of receiving a regular income from that land. Other borrowers engage in 'usufructuary mortgages' in the hope that they will be able to repay the debt and reclaim their land. But since the financial position of the rural poor makes it difficult for them to redeem their debts, the mortgagee in these cases gains relatively permanent control over these lands.

This review of the forms of control over the product of land high-lights the shortcomings of conventional agrarian class categories in the analysis of class in contemporary Rangama/Devideniya. For one thing the categories 'landlord', 'owner-cultivator', 'tenant', etc bear no necessary relation to classes defined in terms of wealth and material well-being. In practice many tenants in Rangama/Devideniya with security of tenure over relatively large extents of land, are economically better off than certain 'small scale' owner-cultivators. To assume that all 'tenants' are exploited individuals distorts the contemporary reality where tenants with security control one-third of the land they cultivate and in fact constitute a relatively privileged group. Moreover, as applied to the Rangama/Devideniya community, several incongruities would arise if one were to insist on retaining the conventional categories.

For example, some of the richest men would be excluded from the highest class (landlords/rentiers) since they are frequently owner-cultivators and sometimes even cultivate certain plots as tenants. Conversely certain poor people who, owing to age or ill health, are constrained to cultivate their smallholding through a tenancy agreement, would be included in the ranks of the highest class.

Rather than pigeonholing people into the conventional categories, the inhabitants of contemporary Rangama/Devideniya are better divided into classes on the basis of the sum of their control of income-yielding garden land,[17] rubber land and paddy land (gained through owner management and/or tenancy agreement and/or lease and usufructuary mortgage).[18] Along a continuum of land control it is differential degrees of economic dependence which create cleavages within the community and determine behaviour patterns. On this basis it is possible to divide the inhabitants of contemporary Rangama/Devideniya into four classes – the 'very poor', the 'poor', the 'middle farmers' and the 'rich' (see Table 11).

The 'very poor' constitute the largest class. Each of the 'very poor' households controls less than half an acre of land, the product of which (even when supplemented by welfare provisions) does not afford them a bare subsistence (see below). In order to subsist, therefore, they are economically dependent upon the wealthier members of the community – particularly the 'rich'.

The 'poor' are distinguished from the 'very poor' because the land they control (half to two acres) does allow them to eke out a bare subsistence with the help of government welfare. For those at the lower end of the scale of land control (around half an acre), subsistence means little more than the ability to have some food to eat. Their diet is restricted to rice supplemented by leaves which grow wild on garden land, jak and breadfruit in season, and occasionally coconut. (Quite apart from meat and fish, even vegetables are a luxury for the indigent.) Many 'poor' households find it difficult to maintain even their modest level of living throughout the year and are liable to suffer sudden declines in living standards because they have few reserves to see them through an illness or a bad harvest. Nevertheless the extent of land these households control (albeit modest in absolute terms) affords them the security of expectation of a future stream of income

Table 11 *Contemporary classes*

Class	Income-yielding Land/Household (acres)[a]	No. of Households	% of Households	Total Income-yielding Land Controlled			% of Income-yielding Land
				A	R	P	
Rich	over 4 acres	18	7.6	216	0	1	52.74
Middle Farmers	over 2–4	32	13.6	91	1	9	22.29
Poor	½–2 acres	78	33.1	78	3	25	19.27
Very Poor	under ½ acre	108	45.7	23	1	13	5.70
		236	100.0	409	2	8	100.00

[a] Acres refer to land CONTROLLED not owned.

which distinguishes them from the 'very poor' and makes them less dependent on the upper classes of Rangama/Devideniya.

The lifestyle of the 'middle farmers' epitomizes, by village standards, the 'comfortable life'. Controlling two to four acres of income-yielding land, they live in tile-roofed (i.e. non-thatched) houses, possess radios and sewing machines, and their meals consist of rice and vegetables and frequently even dried fish. The 'middle farmers' are economically independent and are secure in the knowledge that only a major disaster could threaten their standard of living.

Relatively speaking, the 'rich' live a life of luxury. They reside in large, often two-storey, houses and three 'rich' households own the ultimate status symbol – the car. Many (though by no means all) choose not to work on the land themselves. Not only are the 'rich' economically independent, but the land they control gives them a regular surplus of income over and above the requirements for a 'comfortable life' in the style of the 'middle farmer'. This surplus is seldom devoted to productive investment outside of land purchase. Apart from two rubber-rolling machines, two rice mills, a bakery and in a few cases, purchase of real estate (shops in Dambawala), all 'rich' people in the contemporary community have used their surplus income on conspicuous consumption or invested it in landholdings. As a result landed wealth in this community is highly concentrated. The eighteen 'rich' households control over half of all land controlled by residents – each controls on average 12 acres.

The Class Marginals

Since the baseline period there has been a significant increase in the proportion of inhabitants engaged in non-agricultural occupations. At the turn of the century these were restricted to caste occupations. Today 154 people are engaged (either exclusively or in addition to agriculture) in a wide variety of non-agricultural occupations. Approximately one-third of these are, by the standards of the village, 'higher-income' jobs (over Rs 300 per month), whereas the others are 'lower-income' jobs either in the sense that they give irregular employment or in the sense that they are poorly paid (see Table 12).

Table 12   *Non-agricultural occupations*

Occupation	No. of Persons	
Teacher	16	
Clerk	12	
Co-operative Manager	4	
Bureaucrat	4	
Post Office Official	2	
Serviceman	3	'Higher Income'
Estate Conductor	2	
Nurse	1	
Ayurvedic Physician	1	
Small Industry	4	
Wholesale Trader (middleman)	2	
Itinerant Trader	12	
Shop Assistant	13	
Domestic Servant	9	
Wood Sawer	9	
Timber Trader	6	
Carpenter	4	
Mason	4	'Lower Income'
Washerman	3	
Native Doctor	4	
Retail Trader (small scale)	3	
Tea Kiosk owner	2	
Transport Worker	3	
Waiter	4	
Watcher	5	
Other	22	
Total:	154	

Table 13   *Non-agricultural occupations of adults in relation to class*

	Class (No. of Adults)			
	Rich	Middle Farmer	Poor	Very Poor
Higher Income	10	9	11	9
Lower Income	–	–	22	36

In general the non-agricultural occupations of adults[19] are commensurate with their class position defined in terms of land control (see Table 13). By this I mean that the additional income, though reinforcing their class position, is not sufficient to take them (and their households) into a lifestyle and degree of economic independence characteristic of a higher class. However, as can be seen from Table 13, 20 adults owning two acres or less (i.e. from the 'poor' and 'very poor' classes) are engaged in 'higher income' jobs. (These 20 adults comprise only 13 households because they include among their number seven married couples.) By virtue of these occupations, gained principally through education and to a lesser degree through commercial enterprise, these 13 households have achieved a standard of living akin to that of the 'middle farmer' and have overcome the economic limitations of their low degree of land control. These persons could therefore be considered the 'class marginals' of contemporary Rangama/Devideniya.

The investment choices of these class marginals demonstrate the salience of agriculture in the economy of rural Sinhalese communities. Contemporary 'class marginals' have an overriding preference when it comes to spending their surplus income – purchase of agricultural lands. In doing so they ensure that their marginal class position will in time become obsolete because eventually the extent of their land control will be commensurate with their lifestyle and degree of economic independence. In other words by converting surplus income into land control, 'class marginals' gradually become fully-fledged members of the agrarian class hierarchy defined in terms of land control. The 'class marginals' of the baseline period achieved just this. As will be shown below, they withheld investment in land temporarily to take advantage of the quick profits contract work offered, but subsequently invested heavily in agricultural land. Their descendants are not 'class marginals'. They are securely in the ranks of the 'rich' of Rangama/Devideniya by virtue of controlling large extents of land.

INTER-CLASS RELATIONS – THE DECLINE OF NOBLESSE OBLIGE

In Sri Lanka the interest of national governments and national-level voluntary organizations in the socio-economic development of the rural poor has not been matched by similar enthusiasm on the part of the upper classes in local communities. In the Naranhena region there are no locally sponsored welfare associations, and even when externally sponsored ones are introduced into local communities, the upper classes are not prepared to put aside differences of caste and politics in order to bring about improvements that would largely benefit the poorer classes.

Local institutions in which there is a cross-class participation, far from helping the disadvantaged, often benefit the upper classes at the expense of the less well-off. For instance the *attam* system of co-operative labour exchange (in which both large and small farmers participate) may at first glance be seen as a demonstration of the unity of the village community. Perhaps as a result of this, observers frequently fail to realize that the system is biased in favour of the large farmer. Contrary to the findings of certain authors,[20] empirical investigation in Rangama/Devideniya showed that although the exchange is similar in the tasks performed, no exact equivalence of labour hours is exchanged. What is exchanged is help in a task (harvesting, threshing, etc.), regardless of how long it takes. The system is more informal and flexible than has generally been recognized. If for instance B and C have helped A to harvest his field and the harvesting of each of their fields falls on the same day, A can fulfil his *attam* obligation by working part of the day on B's field and part on C's field. However, since no equivalence of labour hours enters the system, it can also be seriously disadvantageous to the small farmer. For example if A, who has a half-acre plot, and B, who has a one-acre plot exchange labour on an *attam* basis, A will contribute more labour hours on B's plot than B does on A's. Small farmers often get more *attam* helpers than they need and lose out not only because they are obliged to return the help, but also because custom dictates that *attam* teams be provided with an elaborate meal. The cost of feeding *attam* teams in fact constitutes the largest item of expense in the productive process for small farmers (see Appendix VI).

It is not, however, only 'traditional' institutions that favour the well-off. A recent innovation – the *ästom* – also works to the disadvantage of the poorer classes. A corruption of the English phrase 'at home', the *ästom* is basically a celebration (wedding, girl's first menstruation, etc) where a host provides food for guests. After partaking of the host's hospitality, the guests, having given the host a sum of money, record their names in a book. Usually the host receives, in total, more in cash than he spends on his outlay for food and drink. The *ästom* is thus a way of mobilizing credit. Similar institutions have been noted in other peasant societies but little attention has been paid to the obvious inequity that is inherent in this institution. For the well-off the *ästom* is a useful institution for obtaining money on credit, which is usually returned when the guests in turn have their *ästom*. But the poor participate in *ästom* only as guests. Lacking the resources to be hosts of *ästom*, they give sums of money to the wealthy which they do not ever recover.

The relationship characterized by cordiality and goodwill between the 'rich' and the 'poor' in the baseline period has been replaced by one which is distant and strained. The deterioration of this relationship has, however, little to do with institutions such as the *attam* or the *ästom*, which are normatively sanctioned by all. Good relations between 'rich' and 'poor' prevailed in the baseline period despite the prevalence of *attam* labour exchange; and participation in *ästom* is, after all, strictly voluntary.

It is rather the disinclination of the 'rich' people to distribute some of their wealth to help the needy that causes the uneasy relationship between the wealthy and the indigent. The landed elite of contemporary Rangama/Devideniya have jettisoned the ideals of *noblesse oblige* and patronage which were adhered to by their counterparts at the turn of the century.

Whereas in the baseline period it was not unusual for the landed elite to donate small parcels of land to indigent supplicants, today, by contrast, the wealthy in the community use their role as moneylenders to gain control of borrowers' land. The failure of institutional sources[21] to meet the credit requirements of the rural poor obliges many of the latter to approach a 'rich' person (and less frequently a 'middle farmer') in order to borrow money. Village moneylenders today, however, are only prepared to lend money if the credit transaction involves a piece of land either as security on a 'conditional mortgage' or for use on a 'usufructuary mortgage' or lease. They will, for instance, lend to those with access to paddy land, small sums that can be recovered at harvest time, but will not accede to a request for a sum which is too large to be recovered from the paddy harvest of the borrower, but too small to warrant the use of land in the credit transaction.

Whilst 'middle farmers' are as unsympathetic as the rich when they conduct credit transactions, unlike the 'rich' their relationship with the indigent has not changed appreciably since the baseline period. As in the baseline period the 'middle farmers' have less economic interaction both with the lower classes and with the 'rich' than each of those groups have with each other. 'Middle farmers' are well-off; but they do not have the degree of surplus that would enable them, were they so inclined, to make an appreciable difference to the well-being of the poor. The 'rich' *do*. Indeed in the baseline period their largesse went a long way in alleviating the hardships of the needy.

The rich people in contemporary Rangama/Devideniya, however, behave towards the poor in a way markedly different from that of their predecessors. A short stay in this community will serve to confirm that far from being solicitous about the welfare of their poorer fellow villagers, the 'rich' are remarkably tight-fisted even when asked to contribute to local projects such as drama groups, temple festivals etc. Nor is it the case that they are generous towards those members of the lower classes who are employed by them. Whilst agreeing in theory that Rs 10 is a fair daily wage for a casual labourer, many 'rich' people paid between Rs 6 and Rs 8 for a day's work. (Compare this with the Rs 8–16 a day that the state paid labourers in this area.) By constant refusal, the three car owners have established the fact that their cars are not available to take a sick person to hospital, even for payment. They do not give lifts to neighbours they see walking home from Dambawala – one car owner has gone so far as to remove the rear seat of his car to preclude this possibility.

Contemporary 'rich' people have few scruples about causing financial hardship to the indigent if it is necessary to further their own self-interest. For instance, at the time when electricity was being introduced to Rangama village, a group of rich men bribed the linesman from the electricity board in order to divert the state-sponsored line off the main road and past their houses. In the process the perennial crops of several lower-class households were earmarked for destruction to make way for the electricity line.

Nor are the 'rich' above taking deliberate action to thwart the welfare of the lower classes. In 1934 Nuwarapakse Mudalali (one of the richest men in the community today) obtained a contract from the British government to construct a road to Devideniya, and arranged for the road to be built up to his house. Recent plans to extend the road towards the centre of the village, which would bring great benefits to the rest of the villagers, have been vehemently opposed by him.

The 'rich' are exclusive and aloof. They maintain a distance from everyone in the community including the 'middle farmers'. Often their only non-economic contacts with the 'non-rich' occur at weddings and funerals. Their own wedding day feasts tend to be not only caste exclusive but also class exclusive. The rich Goigama Haputhota kin group, for instance, restrict their wedding feast to a small circle of rich and prosperous Goigama. All other Goigama (as well as those who can claim Walawwe ancestry) are invited to an *ästom* on an earlier day. The Haputhotas' excuse for this exclusion is the difficulty of organizing a feast for a large crowd. Non-rich Goigama, however, know that the real reason is that a small guest list makes possible a more elaborate feast – *badu vädi*, *pirisa adu* (literally 'more things, less people').

This self-imposed isolation of the rich is accompanied by a greater degree of contact with the outside. Many have family members and relatives living in towns and cities with whom visits are frequently exchanged. Contacts are also maintained if possible with regionally important personages who reside outside the community, such as bureaucrats, politicians, police officials etc.

The outward orientation of the 'rich', the spread of capitalism, and technological improvements in agriculture, have often been cited as the causes of the breakdown of traditional systems of redistribution and sharing within the local community.[22] The diachronic analysis of social stratification in the Rangama/Devideniya community, however, shows that the withdrawal of largesse on the part of the 'rich' is a more complex phenomenon which may be fully understood only in terms of the changes that have taken place both within the class hierarchy and in the interplay between the class and power hierarchies.

The cessation of the flow of material benefits from the 'rich' to the indigent in this community is closely related to another

Table 14   *Means through which 'poor' households have gained land control*

Means of gaining land control	No. of households
Inherited ownership	30
Security of tenure under PLA	22
Government land allotments	19
Land ownership through income from white-collar jobs (i.e. through free education)	7
	78

change that has taken place in the sphere of inter-class relations – the decreasing dependence of the rural poor on the upper classes. This is not to say that the 'rich' have no economic dependants. Fifty household heads (46.2 per cent) of the 'very poor' class have occupations (casual labourer, rubber tapper, *karu anda* tenant, servant) which make them economically dependent on their 'rich' employers. A few 'rich' families even keep certain 'very poor' households in a state of servitude by maintaining a relationship of permanent debt. The 'rich' expect, and still receive, on the occasion of a celebration, illness or *pinkama*, the gratuitous labour of those 'very poor' households that are employed by them on a regular (though not of course permanent) basis.

Nevertheless it is significant that included in the class structure of contemporary Rangama/Devideniya are 78 households who belong to a class (the 'poor') whose members though indigent are distinguished from the 'very poor' primarily because of their greater degree of economic independence. Only 30 households in this class control land which they have inherited (see Table 14). This draws attention to the fact that in rural Sri Lanka the greater degree of interaction between rural communities and the wider society should not be viewed only in terms of 'outward orientation' of the 'rich' but also in terms of the improved economic conditions of the rural poor as a result of the solicitousness of national governments. In the absence of this solicitousness, the bulk of those who constitute the 'poor' class in Rangama/Devideniya would have been in the 'very poor' class and consequently economically dependent on the landed elite. As it stands, however, economic dependence upon the 'rich' has been decreasing over the past three decades. Government redistributive policies and welfare legislation[23] have enabled 48 households (over 60 per cent of the 'poor' class) to gain control over sufficient land (½–2 acres) to meet subsistence needs.

In general it is safe to predict that the trend towards the decreasing dependence of the indigent upon the landed elite in local communities will continue into the future. Contrary to the assertion that the 1972 land reforms 'virtually preserved the status quo in the traditional peasant agricultural sector'[24], the Acts *did* affect the economic structure of this community and their full impact is yet to be realized. For whilst it is true that the 'rich' and 'middle farmers' were not affected by confiscation of land,[25] and that certain redistributive schemes in this region were unsuccessful,[26] the acquisition of Berawila and Natha Kande estates improved the economic position of many households of the lowest class and removed them from the orbit of dependence upon the upper classes.

A variety of schemes became operative in the sections of Berawila and Natha Kande which came under the control of the Land Reform Commission. Firstly, 54 acres of Berawila estate were divided into one-acre blocks and distributed to land-poor or landless families. Secondly, the presence of a timber forest on Natha Kande (which the former owner had planted for his matchbox factory) led to the construction of a pencil factory in the Naranhena electorate, in which some members of the community obtained employment. Thirdly, the transport of timber from Natha Kande to the factory required the construction of a motorable road through Devideniya and this too provided employment for many villagers. Perhaps most importantly, large sections of both estates, which were run as collective farms under the former SLFP government, were handed over to the National Agricultural Diversification and Settlement Authority (NADSA) by the UNP government in 1978. NADSA is a pioneer statutory organization whose policy is the planting of non-traditional cash crops with hired labour and the distribution of the land to these labourers once the land becomes income yielding. In 1979/80 NADSA employed 33 labourers in Berawila and 62 in Natha Kande from the villages in the area. All these labourers will receive an acre and a half of garden land as soon as the crops reach maturity. Although the distribution of land will not be entirely equitable (in the Rangama/Devideniya community, four 'middle farmers' will receive land), the majority of future recipients belong to the lower classes. Eleven 'very poor' households, for instance, will receive land, and when they do will join the ranks of the 'poor' class.

The changed (and changing) economic circumstances of the rural poor have occasioned a new assertiveness on the part of the lower classes. Writing of the 'depressed peasantry' in 1951, the Kandyan Peasantry Commission wrote that: 'the anda cultivator became a virtual slave of the paddy owner . . . even at elections the anda cultivator had to vote according to the dictates of his landlord'.[27] Today, however, the 'poor' (and increasing numbers of the 'very poor') do not readily comply with the wishes of the 'rich', and indeed often actively oppose them. For instance, during my stay in the community, the Assistant Government Agent and the Electricity Board were inundated with petitions protesting against the bribery of the linesman and the illegal diversion of the electricity line. These petitions were, in part at least, responsible for the temporary stoppage of the project and the transfer of the linesman. When work on the project was resumed, the line was constructed along the main road and not past the 'rich' people's houses.

The lack of subservience on the part of many lower-class people has resulted in an attenuation of the functional relationship between wealth and power that prevailed in the baseline period. Rich people in the baseline period were not disinterested benefactors. *Noblesse oblige* was not motivated by humanitarian concern for the needy; rather it was maintained because it brought with it power over economic dependants. The goodwill that prevailed between 'rich' and 'poor' at the turn of the century was therefore the result of a reciprocal relationship in which the 'poor' received material benefits from the 'rich' in return for compliance with their wishes. In a situation where the 'rich' receive decreasing compliance, it is not difficult to understand their lack of sympathy for the poor, and their disinclination to help their fellow villagers. The system of redistribution within this community has broken down because wealth no longer brings with it the subservience

Table 15   *Class categories in relation to caste 1979–80*

	Castes (no. of Households)						
Class	Goigama	Muslim	Paṭṭi	Gallat	Vahumpura	Hēna	Batgam	Vahal
Rich	5				1		12	
Middle Farmer	10	1	1		8	1	10	1
Poor	24		5	1	9	2	34	3
Very Poor	28		4	5	13	4	54	

of the indigent and the landed elite therefore have no incentive to distribute their surplus wealth.

THE INTERPLAY OF CASTE AND CLASS – RISING LOW-CASTE PROSPERITY

One of the most interesting changes that has taken place in the social stratification of this community since the baseline period has been the impoverishment of many high-caste families and the emergence of certain low-caste persons as prominent members of the hierarchy of wealth. At the turn of the century the Walawwe and Goigama owned a disproportionate extent of land in this community and five of the eight rich people came from within their ranks. During the intervening years, however, this landed elite[28] suffered economic decline just as their predecessors – the famous aristocrats of Devideniya *walawwe* – had done in the nineteenth century. Several high-caste families became impoverished through indebtedness and the foreclosure of mortgages. The land they lost was gained almost exclusively by a select group of Batgam individuals from Devideniya.

The class composition of contemporary Rangama/Devideniya considered in relation to caste is given in Tables 15 and 16. These tables, when compared with the situation in the baseline period (p. 65), underline the degree to which the economic decline of many high-caste households has been matched by the rise of low-caste Batgam families into the ranks of the 'rich'. Apart from

Table 16   *Goigama and Batgam castes as a proportion of total number of households and 'rich' households*

	No. of Households in Community	% of Households in Community	No. of 'Rich' Households	% of 'Rich' Households
Goigama	67	28.4	5	27.8
Batgam	110	46.6	12	66.7

the Batgam there has only been one other low-caste household – a single Vahumpura household – which has gained entry into the landed elite.

It is sometimes suggested that where financial success is achieved by groups of low status, this is likely to be the result of their greater willingness to invest their energies in 'non-traditional' lines of enterprise – trade and commerce. High-status groups, under this view, are held to be at a competitive disadvantage because of their disdain for this kind of activity.

Since the baseline period many Sinhalese villagers in this region have started up their own trading and business enterprises with the result that the ethnic monopoly over trade and marketing that used to prevail has gradually disappeared. Formerly only Muslims engaged in itinerant trade and the two shops in Dambawala were owned and operated by Muslims. Today Muslims are still influential in the larger bazaars, as well as in the buying of spices in outlying villages;[29] but since the 1930s successful competition in the retail business from Sinhalese entrepreneurs as well as government co-operative stores, has led to an out-migration of Muslims from small, predominantly Sinhalese villages. Of the commercial establishments in Dambawala, Muslims now own only seven and of this number operate only three. The remaining four are rented to Sinhalese entrepreneurs.

The Sinhalese entrepreneurs in the Dambawala bazaar have come from many villages in this area – Rangama, Devideniya, Moragammana, Kathugoda, Rukthotuwa and Nugapitiya. Many have established themselves in the retail business, whilst a few have successfully entered the wholesale trade. Others have set up tea kiosks. In the Rangama/Devideniya community itself, a handful of individuals have even set up small industrial enterprises.

Table 17   *Established commercial enterprises and caste of entrepreneurs*

	Dambawala		Rangama		Devideniya	
	No.	Caste	No.	Caste	No.	Caste
Timber Depot	1	Goigama				
Wholesale Traders (middlemen)	3	2 Goigama 1 Muslim				
Groceries and/or vegetables	7	4 Goigama 3 Batgam	1	Hēna		
General Store (medicines, cloth)	1	Batgam				
Tea Kiosks	4	2 Muslim 1 Goigama 1 Batgam			2	Batgam
Groceries/vegetables/ tea kiosk/small scale middleman			2	Goigama Vahumpura	1	Batgam
Betal sellers	2	Goigama Batgam				
Rubber Rolling					1	Batgam
Rice Hulling			2	Goigama Vahumpura		
Coir Industry			1	Goigama		
Bakery			1	Goigama		
TOTALS:	18		7		4	

The willingness of Sinhalese villagers to invest in locally-based business initiatives does not, however, go very far in explaining the rise to economic prosperity of low-caste individuals in the community. In the first place, as Table 17 shows, entrepreneurial activity has by no means been limited to the low castes – Goigama are involved in all types of commercial enterprise. In the second place, there is no reason to suppose that entrepreneurial activity has led to economic success. Many of the established concerns listed in Table 17 are small-scale enterprises which yield, at best, a very small profit. And in Rangama/Devideniya, the non-established entrepreneurs outnumber those with a fixed point of operation. These persons are itinerant traders and middlemen. Some walk considerable distances to tea plantations at higher elevations, taking small quantities of rice, coconuts, arecanuts, jak seeds etc, which they purchase in the village, to sell to Tamil estate labourers. Others buy fruit or small quantities of spices, and sell these to larger traders in bazaars. The itinerant traders are distinguished by the fact that they engage in their enterprises irregularly and operate on a very small capital base. None of them fall into the 'rich' or even the 'middle farmer' class.

In fact in the Rangama/Devideniya community there has only been one low caste individual – a Vahumpura – who has entered the ranks of the 'rich' through engaging in locally based commercial enterprise. Welikumburalage Dewaya's career is a rags-to-riches story. The unschooled son of a land-poor peasant, Dewaya started his trading activities in 1918 by buying *oṭṭupāluva* (the congealed latex left over on rubber trees after tapping) from village children. By 1947, Devapriya Mudalali, as he was by then known, owned a two-storey retail shop in Rangama, a car, a lorry, a large tile-roofed house and over 20 acres of land. His offspring, however, did not carry on his trading business. Two of his three daughters have married and left the community. The youngest has contracted a *binna* marriage (as is common in rich families with no sons) and manages her (and her sisters') landholdings. She rents her father's shop to the government, which uses it as a co-operative store.

The major economic success story of the community, however, has been the great gains in land ownership achieved by certain members of the Batgam caste in the first half of this century. Their success had nothing to do with any supposed greater propensity to engage in commerce; nor was it a result, as in Welikumburalage Dewaya's case, of seizing the advantage of investment opportunities presented in the peasant economy. Batgam prosperity has depended rather on a unique piece of historical good fortune – the special relationship they developed with the plantation sector at a time when there was a boom for rubber in the world economy.

Interaction between the British plantations and inhabitants of this community intensified between 1910 and 1930 due to the introduction of rubber[30] as a major plantation crop. During this period the impact of World War I, and the development of the motor car industry, led to a sharp increase in the demand for (and the price of) rubber on the world market. This demand resulted in the extension of rubber cultivation not only on existing estates but also on new plantations.[31] In the second decade of this century, rubber replaced tea as the principal crop on Berawila and Natha Kande. Although these plantations had resident Tamil labourers, their number was insufficient to meet the increased labour requirements that resulted from the extension of rubber cultivation. Planters therefore felt it expedient to give out 'piece work' contracts to Sinhalese for such tasks as clearing the jungle, fencing, planting rubber trees, building rock stone bunds, constructing store rooms etc.

It was the Batgam who benefited from the economic opportunities that such contract work offered. The reason for this did *not* lie in the disinclination of other caste groups to carry out contract work for the British. For example, the Goigama Rangama Aracci was in 1925 constructing a school in Galewala for the British provincial government.[32] And indeed the only non-Batgam to secure a contract on Berawila and Natha Kande estates was a Goigama carpenter from Kadugannawa.[33] The reason lay rather in the accident of Devideniya's proximity to these plantations, and the long association many Batgam (particularly Ukkuwa Kankaniya, pp. 65–6) had with the British planters as a result of this proximity.

The association of the Batgam with the British plantations meant that planters looked first to known Batgam individuals in Devideniya when contracting out work to be done on the plantations. To become a contractor an individual had to have a minimum reserve of cash – the contractor had to pay his labourers from his own funds whilst the job was in progress since planters only paid the contract fee after completion of the task. Although there were a number of others in the community with sufficient cash to become contractors (the Rangama Aracci even owned a motor bus), none the less a relatively high proportion of those with sufficient cash to take on contract work were Batgam caste members. This was in part due to the fact that the Batgam had among their ranks 'class marginals' whose large arecanut groves provided them with cash surpluses. But it was also in large part due to the Batgam's special relationship with the plantation sector, which enabled them to secure all the well-paying, non-labouring jobs, such as overseer and watcher, on these estates. Hence it was the Batgam caste's close contact with the planters which gave them a competitive edge in securing contract work.

Of approximately eight Batgam who secured contract work, three were particularly successful. Their careers are worth sketching in brief because they demonstrate the extent to which Batgam economic prosperity was linked to the favoured relationship they had with the British planters as a result of Devideniya's proximity to the Berawila and Natha Kande estates.

Rana was an orphan who worked as a cattle keeper in the house of Ukkuwa Kankaniya's son. The latter, who was a watcher on Berawila estate, obtained for Rana a job as overseer on the same estate around 1912. When Buthmallawa estate (75 acres, situated east of Rangama) was first planted with rubber in 1918, Rana, on the recommendation of his English employer on Berawila, secured most of the contract work. He established a reputation as an efficient worker among the planters in the region, and during his career as a contractor worked on six plantations, some of which were situated at a considerable distance from the community.

Another successful Batgam contractor was Ambakumburalage Sethuwa, who, like Rana, first worked as an overseer on Berawila. By 1920 he was established as a contractor and had also been appointed Vidāna Duraya (Batgam village headman) of Devideniya. Sethuwa had only one daughter, who married in *binna* her cross-cousin (also called Sethuwa) from a nearby village. Her husband (later known as Nuwarapakse Mudalali or 'Mister President' because of the office he held in various village organizations) continued the tradition of contract work. Sethuwa *Bās* (carpenter, mason) as the planters called him, carefully cultivated his relationship with the latter, and it was due to his contacts with the planters that he was able, in 1934–5, to obtain the highly profitable government contract to construct a motorable road to Devideniya.

Rising Batgam prosperity in the first half of this century was signalled most clearly in the greatly increased extent of their land holdings. Today Ukkuwa Kankaniya's descendants, and the offspring of Rana and Nuwarapakse Mudalali, are securely amongst the landed elite in the Rangama/Devideniya community. Despite the fact that Batgam landowners lost control of almost 10 per cent

Table 18   *Caste distribution of Rangama/Devideniya paddy land and high land controlled by residents*

Caste	No. of House holds	% of House holds	Paddy Land A	R	P	% of Paddy	High Land A	R	P	% of High
Batgam	110	46.6	60	0	19	62.2	196	2	25	62.8
Goigama	67	28.4	23	1	30	24.3	70	2	10	22.5
Vahumpura	31	13.1	6	2	25	6.9	28	2	30	9.2
Patti	10	4.2	3	1	11	3.4	4	1	20	1.4
Hēna	7	3.0		3	15	0.9	3	0	00	1.0
Gallat	6	2.5		1	10	0.3	2	3	00	0.9
Vahal	4	1.7	1	0	35	1.3	3	2	00	1.1
Muslim	1	0.4		2	18	0.6	3	2	00	1.1
TOTALS:	236	99.9	96	2	03	99.9	313	0	05	100.0

of the Rangama/Devideniya paddy tract to tenants after the Paddy Lands Act, of land controlled by residents[34] contemporary Batgam control over 62 per cent of paddy land and a similar proportion of high land (see Table 18).

The Effects of Increased Low-caste Land Control

The change in the pattern of land control has had far-reaching effects on the caste composition of this community.

Firstly, it has had an impact on the demography of Rangama/ Devideniya. The Batgam, who constituted only 18.6 per cent of the population in the baseline period, are today the largest caste in the community. The Goigama population on the other hand (even with the incorporation of the Walawwe – see below) has decreased from 32.2 per cent to 28.4 per cent. Impoverishment has led many Goigama to migrate out of the community. By contrast Batgam migration, where it has taken place, has largely been an intra-community matter – many Batgam left Devideniya and took up residence on the land they had purchased in Rangama.

The effects of Goigama out-migration in the first half of this century may be seen by comparing the increase in the number of households of the four oldest Goigama kin groups and the two principal Batgam kin groups (see Table 19).

Table 19   *Increase in number of households of six kin groups since baseline period*

	Kin Group	Number of Households in Baseline period	Number of Households Today	% Increase
Goigama	Jayawardena Rallage	4	12	200
	Haputhota Rallage	5	10	100
	Ganege Rallage	3	4	33.3
	Ukgoda Rallage	3	2	0
Batgam	Nuwarapaksage	4	22	450
	Bodhipaksage	6	28	366

Changes in the pattern of land control have also resulted in the 'disappearance' of one of the community's prominent castes – the Walawwe. The economic decline of the village aristocrats during the first half of this century stands in marked contrast to the growing prosperity of the other caste group resident in Devideniya – the Batgam. The descendants of the lesser-known *walawwe* have been reduced to living on a government allotment. The grander Watte Gedera Walawwe family has not fared much better. In the 1930s the head of this *walawwe* got heavily indebted trying to outdo himself in celebrating his marriage to a Radala woman from the regionally famous Asmadala *walawwe*. Today far from having 'slave' dependants[35] he is forced to work on the land of low-caste persons. The descendants of both *walawwes* are now in the ranks of the 'poor' class. Rising Batgam prosperity and the impoverishment of the two village *walawwes* meant that Devideniya began to be looked upon not as the ancestral village of local aristocrats but as the home of prominent Batgam. As a result the Walawwe people, soon after the baseline period, disassociated themselves from Megoda Devideniya[36] and increasingly identified themselves and their residences as part of the predominantly Goigama village of Rangama. At the same time their impoverishment made it increasingly difficult for them to contract suitable marriages with caste folk in far off regions. Such changes have therefore made it impossible for the Walawwe as a caste to employ the device crucial to the preservation of caste identity – the ostracism of caste members who choose to marry into the caste beneath them. The attractions of 'romantic love' have made themselves felt in the community but the Walawwe's ability to dissociate themselves from those of their caste who marry Goigama has correspondingly decreased. So although Walawwe descendants often claim status superiority over the Goigama, these claims are no more than aristocratic pretensions of a bygone era. For the Walawwe no longer constitute an endogamous status group. The repeated intermarriages with the Goigama that now occur cannot be described as inter-caste marriages; they take place within a larger group that maintains marriage and commensal restrictions with members of other castes.

Low-caste control of land has thus had far-reaching effects on the caste composition of this community. It has not, however, led to an attenuation of the caste system. On the contrary, the marked divergence created between the hierarchies of wealth and status has reinforced inequalities of birth status and increased their salience as a basis for structuring behaviour.

There was not, of course, complete overlap between caste and class even in the baseline period, but the changes in the pattern of land control has greatly increased the number of individuals with discrepant positions on these two scales of inequality. The issue is not just one of the increasing extent to which the hierarchies diverge, however, but also of the intensity with which it is felt. There were, for example, indigent Goigama in the baseline period who worked as tenants. But since the majority of rich landowners in that period were high caste, few of them would have suffered the indignity, as many do today, of working as tenants and labourers on low-caste land. Even for those who did, the general conformity to caste etiquette would have ensured that they were treated with a modicum of respect. The same is not always true today. A few 'rich' Batgam are aggressively domineering in their dealings with their Goigama labourers (and to a lesser extent tenants), and often, for instance, try to humiliate them by offering them meals.

Far from lessening the impact of caste, the fact of high castes working on low-caste land has increased the salience of birth status in the structuring of behaviour between groups.

The majority of Goigama who work on low-caste land try to minimize their interaction with their economic superiors and have become ultra-fastidious about commensal restrictions, often not even accepting a cup of tea from their employers or landlords. The extent of this fastidiousness may be gauged by the attitude of a Goigama labourer of my Vahumpura landlady, who was suspiciously disapproving of the occasional exchange of cooked food that took place between us (a common practice among Sinhalese neighbours).

Although landed wealth has enabled 'rich' low castes to mitigate some of the disabilities of their low-caste status (they are not for example addressed in a demeaning manner or offered 'degrading' seats), the tension between the claims of status and wealth is no less uncomfortable for them than it is for their high-caste tenants and labourers. The relatively luxurious life they lead, and the recognition they receive from important personages outside the community, make it harder for them than for their poor caste fellows to come to terms with caste discrimination or even the possibility of it. They therefore display marked sensitivity even to minor forms of discrimination, such as the preference of Goigama to sit amongst their own caste fellows at religious festivals.

The result of these tensions is that the low-caste 'rich', both Batgam and Vahumpura families, are eager to minimize their interactions with persons of higher caste than themselves and to maintain caste segregation. The effects are manifest not only in individual interaction, but also in the organization of voluntary community activities. 'Rich' Batgam and Vahumpura households have distanced themselves from Rangama village affairs and have chosen to involve themselves exclusively in the activities of their own low caste ancestral villages. They have, for example, sponsored the construction of separate *vihāra* in Devideniya and West Galewala in the 1940s. They prefer, even if they happen to live in Rangama, to join voluntary organizations (e.g. funeral societies) in these latter villages rather than in Rangama. The difficulties that arise when low-caste persons do attempt to achieve important positions in voluntary organizations in Rangama is well illustrated in the example of the Batgam president of the Rangama Village Development Society (p. 108).

Wealthy low castes tend to seek recognition and advancement

not at the local level but at the regional and national levels. Two of the richest men in this community in the 1950s and 1960s (Nuwarapakse Mudalali, a Batgam, and Devapriya Mudalali, a Vahumpura) donated large sums of money to nationally famous religious institutions in Kandy and Anuradhapura. Many are also active in regional politics. During the SLFP government of 1970–7, low-caste persons from this community served on the Naranhena Agricultural Productivity Committee[37] and one was even chairman of the Peace Council.[38]

It is interesting to note that the only Rangama based institution in which wealthy low castes were active and influential – the Rangama Cultivation Committee – was not a voluntary organization. Involvement in the cultivation committee and the election of its members was not 'open' to anyone in the community. From its inception in 1958 until 1973 (when members were politically appointed), cultivation committee members were elected by paddy 'cultivators'. Thus the Batgam, who owned approximately 70 per cent of the Rangama/Devideniya paddy tract, were able to dominate the Rangama Cultivation Committee. The chairmen of this committee were always 'rich' Batgam, as was its first administrative secretary.

Cultivation committees are now defunct. In the absence of such an institution in which they were (because of their superior land control) assured of influence, the Batgam tendency to conduct local affairs in isolation from their high-caste neighbours in Rangama has become even more pronounced.

Increased low-caste ownership of land has not only promoted caste segregation but has also exacerbated hostility between the two castes most involved, the Batgam and the Goigama; hostility which is not limited to rich Batgam on the one hand and poor Goigama on the other. The class difference between members of these castes are of negligible importance when it comes to slandering the members of the other caste. Batgam, even those without any land of their own, grumble that they are treated badly by people who eat off their land (*apēma kāla, apata dos kiyanavā*). The Batgam also resent the fact that owing to the PLA they have lost control of a large extent of paddy land to Goigama tenants. It is no secret that Bodhipaksage Piyasinghe, a Batgam, the first administrative secretary of the Rangama Cultivation

Committee (which was set up with the aim of safeguarding tenancy rights) helped some of his fellow Batgam landlords to evict their Goigama tenants. Goigama for their part never tire of pointing out that Batgam land represents ill-gotten gain. According to the Goigama the trust the British planters placed in Batgam watchers, contractors and overseers was misplaced – although they act like lords now (*oya thän raja karāta*), Batgam are nothing more than descendants of Walawwe slaves who got rich by robbing the British planters.

The analysis of social stratification in the Rangama/Devideniya community thus far has shown the way in which extra-local forces have impinged upon the local-level class hierarchy, and brought about changes in the interplay between class and the hierarchies of caste and power. The rising international demand for rubber and the impact on the plantation sector brought prosperity to the low-caste Batgam, but led ultimately to a reinforcement rather than an attenuation of birth status inequalities. The effects of national redistributive and welfare policies on the other hand have made themselves felt mainly in the interaction between the hierarchies of wealth and power. Wealth as a basis of local-level power has not only been undermined by national legislation but has also, as will be seen in the next chapter, been superseded by new bases of power that have emerged as a result of the development of democracy and competitive party politics in Sri Lanka.

11 The Contemporary Power Hierarchy

The transition from British colonial rule to independent government and the development of democracy in India and Sri Lanka, have had a major impact on the local-level power hierarchies of these two South Asian countries. A proper understanding of the local-level changes that have taken place in South Asian democracies during the twentieth century has, however, been inhibited by the weaknesses present in the analytical frameworks of many observers. The assumption that the pre-independence period was characterized by static community power structures, and the failure to distinguish between power and leadership, has led many to regard the impact of democratic politics in terms of the overturning of a 'traditional' structure and the emergence of new leaders.

The diachronic analysis of power in the Rangama/Devideniya community shows that although radical changes have occurred in recent decades, change is not an exclusively post-independence phenomenon. The pre-independence power hierarchy in this community was not a static, unchanging structure. The significance of the impact of democracy and national party politics on local-level power structures does not therefore lie in the fact that a 'traditional' power structure has been changed. Nor does it lie in the fact that new local leaders have emerged. It is important, as this chapter demonstrates, to make clear the distinction between power and leadership. For far from the emergence of new leaders, one of the most significant aspects of the development of democracy in South Asia lies precisely in the fact that it has led to the demise of village leaders.

THE MYTH OF THE 'TRADITIONAL' RURAL POWER STRUCTURE

In India, the 'traditional' rural power structure is often presented as one where a rich, ritually superior, 'dominant' caste wielded power over local affairs. The standard interpretation of the 'traditional' power structure of Sinhalese villages manages to avoid such a caste bias, but its depiction of leadership, power and influence as necessary adjuncts of certain occupations is no more successful.

Occupation and Power

The traditional village leaders came generally from those in the upper strata of village society like the school teacher, the ayurvedic physician, the monk of the Raja Maha Vihāraya, the village mudalali, and from the official world of the village headman. Recent changes in village society have resulted in the erosion of the power and influence of these personalities and new leaders are rising.[1]

Bradman Weerakoon's characterization of the rural power structure in Sri Lanka is typical of a tendency found in much of the writing on the subject: to view 'traditional' power holders as belonging to a discrete set of occupations.[2] Yet even if we allow the assumption that these occupations always bestowed power, this model of power fails to distinguish between the degrees of power that such persons may have held. For instance in the Rangama/Devideniya community successful landowners and mudalalis (loosely, 'rich people') had power over their economic dependants but could not be said to have constituted the power elite in the baseline period. Later, as will be seen, a schoolteacher and the largest landowner in the community did enter the highest strata of the power hierarchy – but the significance of this change is lost by lumping them together with bureaucrats (the only people who consistently occupied the highest strata of the power hierarchy prior to independence) as 'traditional' village leaders.

Not only does the model of the 'traditional' rural power structure neglect the fact that power holders have different degrees of power; its assumption that power is a necessary concomitant of certain occupations is itself erroneous. In Rangama/Devideniya, for instance, no Buddhist monk was a power holder in the first half of the century. Yet the Buddhist monk is invariably given a position of prominence in descriptions of the 'traditional' Sinhalese power structure. Since the notion of the power and influence of the village monk is so pervasive in both academic and popular literature on village life, it is worth examining in greater detail some of the reasons behind this misconception.

It is true that monks at the top of the Buddhist ecclesiastical hierarchy have for centuries been powerful and influential figures in national politics.[3] Certain monks also wield power in rural areas because they are incumbents of *vihāra* which control vast extents of village land. It does not follow from this, however, that the majority of ordinary village monks exercised power and leadership in their local communities.

The relationship between the laity and the ordinary village monk was (and is) essentially a reciprocal one. Villagers need monks to carry out religious rituals and act as a focus of merit-making activities. But it is important to realize that, equally, ordinary village monks depend on the laity for their food and material well-being.

The 'ideal' monk is respected and admired for his piety and 'other worldly' orientation. In practice, however, villagers have long been aware of corruption in the sangha, of the 'this worldly' orientation of many monks,[4] and of the fact that some monks flout even the basic rules of monkhood such as celibacy and abstinence from food after noon. Contemporary inhabitants of Rangama/Devideniya still prostrate themselves in the presence of monks but many, including older informants, claimed that they did so not because they respected the individual but in order to honour the saffron robe which symbolizes the Buddha. It is quite wrong therefore to construe such deference as an indication of the power of Buddhist monks.

From the beginning of the baseline period in 1885 until 1977, no monk in the Rangama/Devideniya community has been either a power holder or a leader.[5] Indeed in the 1940s the people of Rangama dispensed with the services of their monk altogether because he was openly flouting the rule of celibacy.[6] There is a certain irony in the fact that of all the incumbents of the Rangama *vihāraya* over the past century it is the present incumbent who occupies a central position in the power elite of this community. For, as will be shown, he is powerful for reasons which have nothing to do with the attributes of his vocation – his piety and the reverence of his congregation.

The Changing Pre-Independence Power Structure

The weakness of the model of 'traditional' power in Sinhalese villages lies not only in the imprecise and misleading identification of occupation and power, but also in its neglect of the changes that have taken place in local-level power hierarchies in pre-independence years. The power structure of the Rangama/Devideniya community, for instance, did not remain static between the baseline period and the ending of colonial rule, but underwent two significant changes – firstly the breakdown of the relationship between high-caste status and power; secondly the rise of new brokers into the ranks of the power elite.

The erosion of caste as a basis of power

During the baseline period high-caste status was a necessary condition for entrance into the highest stratum of the power hierarchy. The superordinate power holders were village bureaucrats who were, under the 'native headmen' system, drawn from the high castes. In the Kegalle district low-caste persons could only aspire to become subordinate headmen of low-caste villages within larger *vasama* units. At the turn of the century even this was beyond the aspirations of low castes in Rangama/Devideniya because neither village was officially recognized as being low caste. Thus although the neighbouring village of Galewala had its own low-caste headman (Vidāna Dēvaya – Vahumpura), bureaucratic office in this community was a high-caste monopoly.

Shortly after the baseline period the high caste monopoly of bureaucratic office in this community began to disintegrate. This was not the result of a deliberate dismantling of the caste based 'native headmen' system, but of low-caste prosperity and the self-interested manipulation of the headmen system by the Ratemahatmaya (chief native headman) of Paranakuru Korale.

In theory minor headmen were appointed by British administrators but in practice the latter relied heavily on the advice and recommendations of their chief headmen. To judge by their diaries, British officials seemed unaware of the fact that the Ratemahatmaya's decisions were not always based on administrative efficiency but often on pecuniary gain. The opportunity to gain such benefit derived from the continuation of certain ancient Kandyan customs. In the Kandyan kingdom all holders of bureaucratic office paid a fee to the King or Dissava (provincial governor) on appointment, as well as an annual tribute (däkuma) which served as a renewal of the appointment. Under the British, the payment of such fees for office continued, but in place of paying the King or Dissava, each applicant for minor headmanship offered to pay a fee to the Ratemahatmaya, and if appointed brought annual tributes to the Ratemahatmaya's *walawwe*. Thus the Ratemahatmaya stood to gain not only by appointing rich applicants but also by increasing the number of minor headmen under his authority.

In 1912 the Assistant Government Agent of Kegalle received a petition from the Batgam people of Devideniya to have a separate headman for their own community. Although the village was small and there was no administrative need for a separate headman, the Ratemahatmaya recommended to the Assistant Government Agent that their request be, granted. No doubt the Ratemahatmaya's enthusiasm for the idea was inspired by the knowledge that the Batgam had among their ranks a rich family (Ukkuwa Kankaniya's) willing to hold office. In 1912 Ukkuwa Kankaniya's second son was duly appointed Vidāna Duraya (Batgam village headman) of Devideniya.

This appointment was significant not only because it was the first time a low-caste person from Rangama/Devideniya had gained bureaucratic office, but also because the time-honoured method of administering low-caste villages was in fact being applied to a village which had, until recently, been considered an aristocratic one (see Chapter 3). The appointment of a Vidāna Duraya marked the official recognition of Devideniya as a Batgam village.

Low-caste achievement of bureaucratic office in the early decades of this century was not limited to headmanship of low-caste villages. In a radical departure from previous custom, a low-caste person was appointed Aracci of the Rangama *vasama* in 1926. This appointment was particularly unusual since in the Kegalle district unlike in the neighbouring Ratnapura and Kandy districts, low castes were not usually made headmen even over exclusively low-caste *vasamas*,[7] let alone one in which the inhabitants of the principal village were predominantly high caste.

The appointment of N.A. Ukkuwa, a Salagama[8] from Galewala, demonstrates the influence the Ratemahatmaya had within his administrative division. Prior to 1926 the Rangama *vasama* had had two unsatisfactory Goigama Araccis. J.R. Mudianse was suspended on account of 'highway robbery'[9] and his successor was barely literate. When the latter was dismissed because of involvement in a court case over cattle fraud, his son and N.A. Ukkuwa, who was the Vidāna Dēvaya of Galewala at the time, applied for the Rangam Aracciship. Older villagers claim that the Assistant Government Agent preferred the son of the former Goigama Aracci but that the Ratemahatmaya wished to appoint N.A. Ukkuwa because the latter outbid his competitor with a very high appointment fee. Thus despite the resentment of the Rangama Goigama and the Assistant Government Agent's preference, the Ratemahatmaya's choice prevailed and for the first time in its history the Rangama *vasama* was administered by a low-caste Aracci. According to H.R. Tikiri Banda, the former Vel Vidane, a further payment to the Ratemahatmaya secured for Ukkuwa the right to wear the dress of high-caste Kandyan Araccis.

The appointment of a low-caste person as Aracci of the Rangama *vasama* completely severed the link between caste and power in this community, a link which four decades later was to be officially severed by the abolition of the headmen system.

The rise of new brokers

The second change that occurred in the power hierarchy of this community in pre-independence years was the rise of certain non-bureaucrats into the ranks of the power elite. The superordinate power of the village bureaucrats at the turn of the century derived, as was seen in Chapter 6, from their role as brokers between the local community and the British administration. With the establishment of a police station (1917) and a hospital (1918) in Naranhena, and the introduction of universal franchise (1931), the range of important outsiders widened to include policemen, doctors, nurses and politicians. These changes, together with developments in the local area, enabled two individuals successfully to challenge the bureaucrats' monopoly control of the role of brokerage.

The changes that have taken place in the sphere of local–regional integration in post-independence Sri Lanka make it useful at this point to look more closely at the notion of brokerage. Originally developed within the Latin American context,[10] this concept is now generally used to refer to persons who control vital channels of communication between the local and regional/national levels. Brokers wield power through their role as intermediaries between local communities and the wider society. However, it is important to bear in mind that the notion of control is also integral to the concept of brokerage.[11] The role of broker thus implies possession of a degree of independence and control at the local level.

The Vel Vidane and the Aracci (the brokers during the baseline period), as well as the Vidāna Duraya, were all wealthy bureaucrats. Likewise the two new brokers who rose to prominence in the Rangama/Devideniya community in the 1930s and 1940s also possessed independent bases of control – landed wealth in the one case, and the less conventional resource of a superior education on the other.

In 1920 a school was started in the local area by the Buddhist Theological Society and for the first time a schoolteacher was resident in the vicinity of the community. The schoolteacher was more educated than the village bureaucrats and was better equipped than the latter to understand government circulars and publications. His education made him a useful mediator in interaction with regional-level figures such as policemen, government officials and Buddhist Theological Society officials. The latter were particularly useful in helping students gain admittance to advanced schools in towns and cities.

Another important development at the local level was the decreasing physical isolation of the community. In 1925 a wire bridge was constructed over the Maha Oya and in 1934–5 Nuwarapakse Mudalali, a rich Batgam, received a contract from the British government to construct a road to Devideniya. Nuwarapakse Mudalali constructed the road up to his house. Before such thoroughfares were in existence the 'rich' had power over their economic dependants, but could not be considered amongst the ranks of the local power elite because they could not compete as brokers with the village bureaucrats who had official connections to the outside. The Devideniya road changed the old patterns of communication with the outside. Regional personages began to visit the community because they no longer had to undergo discomfort to reach it. When they did, Nuwarapakse Mudalali's house was the most accessible. Policemen, politicians and government officials would travel up to Nuwarapakse Mudalali's house, stop for a cup of tea, and quite often transact their business through him. Nuwarapakse Mudalali used his wealth to reinforce his contacts with important outsiders. He contributed funds to the United National Party (UNP) and helped fund the electrification project of the police station at Doragala. He established such good relations with the police that he could intercede on behalf of villagers who got on the wrong side of the law,

In the 1930s and 1940s, therefore, the power elite in this community consisted of five people – the Rangama Aracci, the Vel Vidane, the Vidāna Duraya, the schoolteacher and Nuwarapakse Mudalali. Despite the significant change in the composition of the power elite, a certain continuity with the past was nevertheless maintained. This continuity lay in the fact that all members of the power elite in this period were, like their predecessors in the baseline period, local-level leaders, That is to say they were respected and admired members of the highest stratum of power who were able to command a following and to direct collective activity.

The leadership characteristics of the pre-independence power elite are emphasized by contemporary inhabitants of the Rangama/ Devideniya community. Contrasting it with the situation that prevails today, they recall the manner in which these power holders were able to rally people to engage in communal projects. They also exercised a prominent role in the settlement of disputes. Two of these men still remained in the Rangama/Devideniya community during the time of my fieldwork. One, H.R. Tikiri Banda, the former Vel Vidane, 80 years old, related how in the 33 years he held office he was able to mediate the settlement of all but five paddy land disputes. The other, Nuwarapakse Mudalali, also 80 years old, is a Batgam who became the largest landowner in the community. Nuwarapakse Mudalali's ability to exercise a leadership role in

Rangama was limited by his low-caste status, but his leadership in Devideniya was undisputed. In his heyday he was instrumental in mobilizing the collective activity of his fellow villagers and building the Devideniya *vihāraya* and the Devideniya school. Like the village bureaucrats and the schoolteacher, he seems to have been widely regarded as a father figure to whom people naturally turned as an arbiter in times of conflict. As a symbol of their position as leaders, each of these men was honoured with a tribute of betal leaves by their fellow villagers at the time of the Sinhalese New Year.

Members of this power elite had a virtual monopoly of office in statutory local organizations of that period – in the 1930s the Vel Vidane was elected president of the credit society; Nuwarapakse Mudalali and the schoolteacher were prominent members of the Co-operative Society; and Nuwarapakse Mudalali and the Rangama Aracci were members of the village council. These local bodies did not (and do not) bestow much power on their office-bearers – Village councils have had very limited powers and the co-operatives in Sri Lanka have not been involved in planning and development activities but have had as their main function the provision of consumer goods.[12] Today, office in such statutory organizations reflects the results of political party competition. In a period before political party competition had penetrated rural communities, election to such offices reflected the respect and admiration of the voters.

THE POWER HOLDERS IN CONTEMPORARY RANGAMA/DEVIDENIYA

The second half of this century witnessed a decline in the pre-independence power elite largely because the kind of brokerage which had constituted their power became increasingly redundant. Post-independence legislation introduced into the village setting a number of institutions which brought the community into closer contact with the outside world and obviated the need for the kind of mediation the pre-independence brokers had provided. Contemporary Rangama/Devideniya has three schools, altogether employing more than fifteen teachers, a resident midwife, a dispensary with a resident apothecary, two co-operative stores and a sub-post office. Divisional-level officials frequently visit the community. These include the Rural Development Officer and the Co-operative Inspector based at the divisional headquarters in Doragala, and the Agricultural Instructor who operates from the Agrarian Services Centre. The presence of specialist government officials within, or in close proximity to, the community has meant that contact with these officials is not problematic for the average villager. The intervention of higher-level and more distant bureaucrats in the resolution of problems is decreasing because of the political control of the administration (pp. 177–8 – this chapter), but, should it be necessary, the spread of education has meant that many families in Rangama/Devideniya have a relative in a white-collar job who can be prevailed upon to help in such a situation.

These legislative changes have also undermined the importance of wealth, education and bureaucratic office as bases of entry into the power elite, the break between education and power being the most decisive. In contrast to the situation in the early twentieth century, the introduction of universal free education has resulted in widespread literacy in Rangama/Devideniya. Many young people from the community have received secondary schooling in towns and cities, and are often more educated than the village schoolteachers themselves.

Although the erosion of wealth as a basis of power has not been as complete as that of education, post-independence legislation has significantly attenuated the functional relationship that prevailed between wealth and power in the baseline period. As was seen in the last chapter, redistributive and welfare schemes have made landed wealth an increasingly inefficient basis through which to secure power over the rural poor. Moreover, the longstanding link between wealth and power via bureaucratic office was severed with the abolition in 1958 of the post of Vel Vidane, and in 1963 of the 'native headmen' system. The 1963 legislation abolished low-caste headmanships (e.g. Vidāna Duraya) and replaced Araccis by Grama Sevakas selected on the basis of education and merit.

Bureaucratic office itself has not, however, become completely irrelevant as a basis of local-level power. Like the rest of the pre-independence power elite, local bureaucrats were adversely affected by the decline in the role of brokerage. They are not today holders of superordinate power. Nevertheless some of them at least continue to occupy an important, if lower, position in local power hierarchies.

The Contemporary Village Bureaucrats

The old posts of Vel Vidane and Aracci no longer exist in Sinhalese villages but, interestingly enough, despite a series of legislative changes affecting the administration of rural areas, the two principal bureaucratic posts at the local level today, Cultivation Officer (CO)[13] and Grama Sevaka (GS), are in many ways the counterparts of the administrative posts which were present under colonial rule. This does not mean, however, that the contemporary relationship between bureaucrats and villagers is similar to that which prevailed in pre-independence years. Bureaucratic office is no longer a sufficient condition for entrance into the ranks of the power elite, and neither of the contemporary village bureaucrats has taken over the mantle of leadership borne by the Vel Vidane and the Aracci.

Although the principal functions of the old post of Vel Vidane were the same as that of the contemporary Cultivation Officer – the supervision and improvement of agriculture – the CO is neither a power holder nor a leader. The Vel Vidane was invariably an experienced farmer. He was in charge of mediating paddy-land disputes and appearing as a witness when these disputes were taken to court. In contrast the Rangama CO has virtually no power. He is a political appointee and villagers are well aware that he has little knowledge of the land under his authority. Land disputes are today mediated by the Divisional Officer of the Agrarian Services Centre, and although the CO is present, he plays little part in the settlement.

The Rangama CO's lack of leadership qualities are clearly evidenced in his failure to organize any type of co-operative agricultural activity. Most farmers in Rangama/Devideniya do not even know the names of the office bearers of the Farmers' Society and the Young Farmers' Society which the CO has dutifully founded. During the period of my fieldwork his most important activity appeared to be that of compiling land registers, but even these were inaccurate.[14] The Rangama CO is an insignificant figure in the community and were he to disappear few farmers would be aware or concerned about it.

The Grama Sevaka's role in the Rangama/Devideniya community is more complex than that of the CO. Unlike the latter he is not devoid of power, but he resembles the CO in his inability to assume a role of leadership in the community.

The GS's power bears no comparison with that enjoyed by the Rangama Aracci of pre-independence years. The latter's duties were wide-ranging because he was the focal point of government authority in the community. The presence in contemporary rural Sri Lanka of a variety of specialized officials from many government departments has circumscribed the range of the GS's official duties. One of the most significant examples of the latter has occurred in the sphere of police work. As long as the 'native headmen' system remained, the police were required to work in collaboration with headmen and could not, for instance, enter, search and make an arrest in a *vasama* without the latter's presence. Contemporary police have no such restrictions on their actions and may choose whether or not they wish to enlist the help of a Grama Sevaka. Within the community the GS is not a mediator in the settlement of disputes as was the Rangama Aracci. Inter-village Conciliation Boards were established in the 1960s, and many rural people are now sophisticated enough to take their complaints directly to the rural court.

Despite considerable attenuation in his official duties, the GS cannot be dismissed in the same way as the CO. In their dealings with the outside, villagers are often required to produce a letter from their GS which serves as an identity-cum-recommendation – i.e. the GS certifies that the individual resides in his *vasama* and is of good character. Prospective employers (both private and government) often insist that an applicant for a job furnish such a letter. The GS's stamp of legitimacy is also required for numerous other activities such as transporting timber across district boundaries, felling jak or breadfruit trees, and even requesting a change of collection point for the rice ration. The receipt of welfare provisions is also (up to a point) at the discretion of the GS, since it is he who fills out, checks and examines eligibility claims – for example he collects information on income and land ownership for the purpose of determining eligibility for food stamps; and he estimates the extent of damage in a claim for government relief after a natural disaster.

The GS's official role in the community thus allows him to exert considerable influence over the inhabitants of his *vasama*. It also leaves ample room for self-enrichment. In 1979 when GSs were responsible for compiling lists of those eligible for food stamps, it was well known that the Rangama GS had upon payment of money, included certain individuals whose personal income would otherwise have warranted exclusion. Even without resorting to illegal means, the GS wields sufficient power to gain considerable extra emoluments. The Rangama GS frequently asks people for loans, timber, fruit etc, which they find difficult to refuse.

Since it is judicious to keep in the GS's good books, even the most snobbish Goigama, whatever their private reservations about his low-caste status, are circumspect in their personal interactions with him. Like others in the community, for example, they do not address him by his title, which means 'village servant', but by the more respectful term Aracci Mahatmaya, which harks back to the headmen system.

Despite the fact that villagers are dependent upon his co-operation, however, the GS is unable to act as a leader in this community. He is given official recognition in Devideniya village affairs, but even amongst the Batgam he is not a figure of respect and admiration. As for the Rangama Goigama, whilst careful not to antagonize him in personal interaction, where collective responsibility for an action may be assumed, as in Rangama festivals etc, they blatantly ignore him.

Several reasons account for the GS's inability to act as a leader in his *vasama*. Firstly, it is clear to everyone that the GS does not have complete discretion in the way he performs his official duties. He cannot act capriciously for he is accountable to his superior, the Assistant Government Agent, and increasingly to the MP as well. For instance, at the time I left the community, the Assistant Government Agent had received a large number of petitions from villagers complaining about irregularities in the way the Rangama GS was carrying out his duties. As a result the GS was suspended from work pending an inquiry.

Secondly, unlike the Araccis, contemporary GSs are selected on the basis of qualifications and are often 'outsiders' in the *vasama* to which they are posted. Moreover, on account of frequent transfers, they are also temporary residents in the area of their jurisdiction. The fact of being an outsider, and a transient one at that, makes villagers less inclined to look upon the GS as a figure worthy of fear, respect or admiration. And in the case of the present Rangama GS, these factors are exacerbated by his low-caste status.

Thirdly, and perhaps most importantly, the GS cannot act as a leader because he is no longer a member of the local-level power elite. For in recent years a new power elite has risen to prominence in the local-level power hierarchy which, for the first time in the history of Sinhalese rural communities, has displaced the village headman from the highest stratum of power.

The Power Elite in Contemporary Rangama/Devideniya

In contemporary rural Sinhalese communities, political support has replaced wealth, education and bureaucratic office as the basis of superordinate power. Two men constitute the power elite of the contemporary Rangama/Devideniya community – the monk of the Rangama *vihāraya* and Nuwarapaksage Siyathu, an overseer on Natha Kande estate. In most respects these two men are very dissimilar. The Rangama monk is a Goigama from an old established kin group; Siyathu is a Batgam. Siyathu is a die-hard UNP supporter whereas the monk's long-term political sympathies have been ambiguous and fluctuating. The monk prefers to operate covertly; Siyathu is openly aggressive. What they do have in common is the backing and support of the Naranhena MP.

It is these two men, rather than the GS, who have wide ranging and generalized influence over community decision making. The extent of their influence is a direct result of the degree of support accorded to each by the MP.

The MP's backing has, since 1977, enabled Siyathu to play an important part in determining the nature and even existence of local organizations. For example, because he was not elected president of the Devideniya Village Development Society (VDS), Siyathu successfully petitioned the MP to refuse to register the society on the grounds that there was an SLFP conspiracy to dominate it. The Rural Development Officer, who is responsible for the promotion of such societies, tried on two further occasions to establish a VDS in Devideniya but in the face of Siyathu's intransigence finally gave up the attempt. In this case, however, Siyathu's victory was not complete, since his desire to become president of the society was never realized. But in the case of the Natha Kande Workers' Welfare Society, Siyathu was able to put his aggressive stand to good use. He managed to undermine his main rival for the presidency, an SLFP supporter, by stressing that the society would be impotent if it had a known SLFP sympathizer as president. As a result of this pressure, Siyathu was duly elected president.

Of the two members of the power elite in this community, the monk of the Rangama *vihāraya* is in greater favour with the MP and this is reflected in the greater influence he has over local affairs. He does not encounter the semblance of opposition to which Siyathu is occasionally liable. For instance when a VDS was to be set up in Rangama, the monk did not have to manoeuvre for support but decided in advance who the office-bearers would be and assigned various people to propose and second his nominees. When the Rural Development Officer arrived to supervise the elections these nominees, M. Alwis (a Batgam whom some Goigama claim was chosen by the monk in order to curry favour with the MP) and the monk himself, were elected president and secretary unopposed.

An interesting example of the unbridled nature of the monk's power and influence in local affairs, which he is able to exercise under the protective aegis of the MP's favour, is the way in which he secured domination over the local Sarvodaya movement.[15] This 'self-help' movement is one cherished by planners and urban intellectuals for its potential to stimulate community-based rural development; but the 'power plays' engineered by the monk to wrest control of the local organization from a lesser power-holder in the community suggest that its success may be contingent on factors rather different to the spirit of 'community' on which its more optimistic supporters suppose it to rely.

It was the Rangama Grama Sevaka who started the first Sarvodaya organization in the Naranhena area. As with most activities in which he took the initiative, he embarked on this project with his caste fellows from Devideniya, and the first meeting was held at the Devideniya school in February 1979. Although this particular branch was set up to serve five villages (Rangama,

Devideniya, Galewala, Naranhena and Moragammana), the meeting was dominated by the Rangama GS and the people from
Devideniya. Dayananda from Devideniya was elected president of
the local organization's 'youth circle'. The Rangama monk was not
invited to attend either this meeting or the second meeting held
in March, but was belatedly invited to the third meeting by the
Sarvodaya 'youth circle' secretary, a young man from Naranhena.
At this meeting the monk spoke enthusiastically about the aims of
Sarvodaya, but was privately cynical about the whole enterprise.
He told me that despite Sarvodaya's grandiose ideal the local
organization had been set up by the Grama Sevaka and certain
Devideniya people for their own benefit.

Despite the proposal of innumerable schemes of rural development, Sarvodaya achieved nothing concrete in the Naranhena
area in its first five months. It was agreed that the initial project
would be a pre-school, for the under fives and the GS's mistress
was 'selected' to be the teacher. But no one was prepared to
donate a plot of land or a building to house the pre-school, and
neither the higher-level Kegalle Sarvodaya officials nor the local
office-bearers appeared to know how to proceed with the project.
Attendances at Sarvodaya meetings in the Devideniya school were
dwindling and the organization gradually ground to a halt.

Meanwhile the monk got in contact with the Sarvodaya officials
in Kegalle through the secretary of the local 'youth circle'. From
subsequent events the following bargain would appear to have
been struck. The monk would donate a plot of *vihāraya* land for
the pre-school and would make available the *vihāraya* preaching
hall until the building was constructed. In exchange Rangama
village would be made the central point of Sarvodaya activity in
the area.

In August 1979 a well-attended meeting of Sarvodaya took place
in the Rangama *vihāraya*. Dayananda and the GS were present
but the monk had now become the central figure. The monk was
instrumental in organizing a 'mothers' circle' which soon became a
puppet group through which he could run Sarvodaya in the way he
wished. A successful pre-school was established in the preaching
hall, but the GS's mistress was not the teacher. Claiming that
an 'outsider' (from Devideniya) was not suitable to teach in a
Rangama pre-school, the monk selected a Rangama girl instead.

Since their role in Sarvodaya had been usurped by the monk, Dayananda and the GS stopped attending Sarvodaya meetings. By the time I left the community the local Sarvodaya organization, from the selection of office-bearers to the distribution of benefits, was completely under the monk's control. His decisions were never opposed and he ran Sarvodaya as if it were his private company. Accusing the 'youth circle' of inactivity, he planned to cancel it and establish a new 'youth circle' – a move which will complete the exclusion of the GS and his Devideniya 'contingent' from the organization they initiated.

During my period of fieldwork the most striking example of the monk's power and influence over local affairs was evidenced in the way he manipulated and controlled what was perhaps the principal development benefit this community has received in many years – the supply of electricity.

Under the village electrification scheme funded by the Asian Development Bank, fifteen villages in the Naranhena area, including Rangama, were to receive electricity. Long before work started on the project the inhabitants of this community knew that the monk was actively involved in it. He had visited all the houses situated on or near the Rangama road and made a list of those who wished to have electricity. For this reason and also because the dispensary, a co-operative store and the largest school in the community were all situated towards the end of the main Rangama road (see Map 3, Chapter 2) most people reasonably assumed that the electricity line would continue along the road for approximately half a mile past the turn-off to the Rangama *vihāraya*.

As the months passed no definite information about the project reached the community and many people started getting anxious about the precise path the line was going to take. When the construction crews began to arrive in September 1979, several individuals (my landlady amongst them) went to ask the monk whether or not the electricity line was going to be constructed along the Rangama road as expected. The monk told them they had no cause for concern the project was proceeding smoothly.

One month later word leaked out from the construction crew that the line was only to be taken as far as the Rangama *vihāraya*, via the newly motorized road named after the MP.

Not unnaturally, people with houses on the main Rangama road past the *vihāraya* turn-off were annoyed and upset, but the monk was pleased to inform me that he was getting electricity to his doorstep at government expense. The disappointed people began to besiege the resident linesman from the Ceylon Electricity Board, demanding an explanation and requesting an extension of the line. The linesman advised them to petition the relevant authorities.

There was little else the linesman could do. From all accounts he and all the other employees of the Ceylon Electricity Board working in the area were under instructions from the MP to complete the project in a way that would please the monk. It soon became clear to everyone that no step could be taken without the monk's approval. The linesman confided in me that the monk determined the exact positioning of the connections and thus which particular house got electricity and which did not. Even the rich people who attempted to 'influence' the linesman were not acting independently but with the sanction of the monk. Indeed there is evidence to suggest that some of the negotiations between these rich people and the linesman were carried out at the Rangama *vihāraya*.

Perhaps the most striking indication of the monk's control was the fact that each time the Superintendant Engineer from Kandy visited the area he proceeded directly to the Rangama *vihāraya* to discuss the progress of the project. The monk had effectively become the local director of the Rangama electricity project.

PARTY COMPETITION AND THE POLITICIZATION OF THE LOCAL COMMUNITY

The power wielded by the Rangama monk and Siyathu over local affairs signifies the rise of a new power elite in rural Sinhalese communities. The emergence of this power elite, whose source of power derives from the support of an elected representative can only be understood through reference to the way in which democratic politics have developed in Sri Lanka.

Certain aspects of this development would, by most standards, be recognized as positive. This section will examine such 'positive' aspects as the growth of vigorous party competition in electoral politics and the transformation of the politically-alienated rural masses into a highly politically-conscious electorate.

However, the requirements of party building in 'developing democracies' have the effect of enormously extending the scope and intensity of patronage politics – a side effect of the democratic process no doubt unanticipated by its more idealistic proponents. As the subsequent section will demonstrate, the changes in Sri Lanka's rural power structures may be seen as a direct result of the operation of patronage politics in a developing democracy.

Electoral Politics in the 1930s and 1940s

Although Sri Lanka has enjoyed adult universal suffrage since 1931, the early decades of electoral politics were not characterized by competition between political parties. The structure of the State Council (1931–47) whose powers under the Donoughmore constitution of 1931 were severely limited, inhibited the growth and operation of national political parties. The 51-member State Council operated on a system of executive committees headed by a board of ministers who had no collective responsibility except for the annual budget.

With independence and the institution of a parliamentary system in 1947 under the Soulbury constitution, the political elite in Sri Lanka became aware of the organizational requirements of parliamentary government – particularly the need for permanent alignments in the legislature. To achieve this end the United National Party was formed through the merger of the Ceylon National Congress (CNC) – the prime mover in the struggle for independence – and a number of smaller ethnic political groupings such as the Sinhala Maha Sabha of S.W.R.D. Bandaranaike, the Ceylon Muslim League and a section of Ceylon and Indian Tamils.

The general election to the first parliament of independent Sri Lanka in 1947 was not seriously contested on the basis of party competition. In the Sinhalese areas of the island the UNP's only opposition came from the Marxist movement which had originated in the 1930s. But the left was seriously split in 1947 and the Marxist parties sought not so much to win parliamentary power but rather to use the election campaign to explain their revolutionary programme to the voters.[16]

The marginal role of party politics in the first two decades of universal franchise may be gauged from the number of independent candidates who stood for and were elected to the governing representative bodies. In the State Council elections of 1936 all candidates contested the election as independents. In 1947 half of the candidates who contested ran as independents and 21 (22.1 per cent) of the elected seats in parliament were won by independents.[17]

The pattern of electoral politics in these decades was elitist and personal. The parties were not broad based and the electors were ignorant of the issues of national politics. The political alienation of the masses was largely a result of the manner in which the independence movement took place in Sri Lanka. The leadership of the CNC was conservative and always opted for constitutional reform through negotiation. It did not, for example resort to the techniques of boycott and non-co-operation adopted by the Indian National Congress, which involved the participation of the masses and brought about a degree of political consciousness among the Indian people. The independence movement in Sri Lanka involved by and large only a small political elite.

It was this political elite that came to dominate the political parties.[18] The individuals who constituted the political elite were national and regional notables. These political notables did not need party backing to win elections. They were self-sufficient as electoral units. Their election campaigns were run by friends and relatives, and their success hinged by and large on their regional prominence. The UNP political notables, for instance, gained the vote of the rural masses by using local personages such as dominant landowners and village headmen as 'vote banks'. In return local personages received, or hoped to receive, roads, culverts, bridges, schools and dispensaries, as well as the not inconsiderable reward of the prestige of associating with the regional notable. The UNP did not find it difficult to obtain the support of these local personages.

For one thing there was little competition (in many electorates regional notables won their seats uncontested) and where there was, the UNP's standing as the most prominent national party gave them a competitive edge in capturing the support of the local 'vote banks'.

During the 1930s and 1940s the political notables who contested the seat in which Rangama/Devideniya was included used Nuwarapakse Mudalali and the Rangama Aracci as 'vote banks'. In the absence of serious competition, candidates avoided the hardships of the campaign trail, of door-to-door visits and 'pressing the flesh'. Election campaigning did not even involve much speech-making. Candidates simply visited the houses of Nuwarapakse Mudalali and the Rangama Aracci and enlisted their support to obtain the votes of their fellow villagers. Once the political notable had left the village the local 'vote banks' held one or more meetings, usually in the *vihāraya*, where they would tell the villagers that the regional notable had visited and requested their vote, and that they should vote for him. The majority of villagers complied with the wishes of these local personages.

Post-1950 Electoral Politics – The Rise of Party Competition

In 1947 the UNP was the only party that had established its presence in rural Sinhalese areas. This situation of one-party dominance ended with the formation of the Sri Lanka Freedom Party (SLFP) by S.W.R.D. Bandaranaike in 1951. Although a political notable himself, Bandaranaike championed the rights of the Sinhalese Buddhist masses in opposition to the westernized, English-speaking UNP political elite.

The SLFP contested and lost the 1952 general election. Like the UNP it had at the time little formal organizational linkage to the electorate. Candidates relied on their personal networks and campaigning was carried out much as it had been in the 1930s and 1940s.

The general election of 1956 was a watershed in Sri Lanka's electoral politics. Bandaranaike strove to undercut the electoral base of the UNP, which worked through village headmen and rich landowners, and adopted a new, populist style of election campaigning. Championing the causes of Sinhalese language and Buddhism, the SLFP won the support of many village school teachers and Buddhist monks. But it did not attempt to use these individuals as 'vote banks'. Rather the SLFP initiated a mass electioneering campaign with direct contact and appeal to the voter. In contrast to the aloof politician who worked through local personages, SLFP candidates began walking from house to house in rural villages, canvassing for votes. The first SLFP candidate who stood for this area in 1956, a rich, Radala-caste individual, is still remembered in Rangama/Devideniya for the way he mingled with villagers and accepted hospitality from even the poorest, low-caste houses. Indeed there was a deliberate attempt by the SLFP to woo the low-caste vote. SLFP politicians openly denounced the caste system and began publicly to eat and drink with low-caste persons and address them using familiar kinship terms.

The SLFP election strategy was successful; with the help of a few smaller parties, it swept the polls in 1956. The significance of this victory was twofold. Firstly, it established the presence of a democratic alternative to the UNP and thereby the importance of party competition in electoral politics. Since 1956 there has been a virtual two-party system in Sinhalese areas and independent candidates have almost completely disappeared from the political scene. Faced with the mass electioneering and populist strategies of the SLFP, the UNP has had to jettison the local notable technique of securing votes. Rallies, party meetings, speeches and house-to-house visits have now become the standard pattern of election campaigning for both parties. As a result parties have become identifiable entities to the voter and contemporary rural people constitute a highly politically-conscious and informed public.

Secondly, the SLFP victory, based as it was on appeals to Sinhalese and Buddhist values, encouraged the UNP as well as the SLFP to view Sinhalese chauvinism as a key means of gaining political support. In office both parties have promoted the Sinhalese language and the Buddhist religion, and pursued policies favouring the Sinhalese and discriminating against the Tamils.

Party Politics in Contemporary Rangama/Devideniya

In Rangama/Devideniya it is considered almost unnatural today to be neutral as far as party loyalty is concerned. Although people do change their allegiances, at any one time virtually everyone claims to be a supporter of either the UNP or the SLFP. The few who claim neutrality are simply disbelieved.

In contemporary Rangama/Devideniya party antagonism is deep-seated and reaches alarming heights in election years. After the 1977 UNP victory, rival party supporters refused to work together on *attam* teams and their children shunned one another in school. SLFP supporters were publicly insulted: as they collected their rice rations UNP supporters would jeer, 'you voted for the SLFP but now you are eating from our government.' Jubilant UNP members went to SLFP houses and forced the residents to worship pictures of president Jayawardena and the new MP for Naranhena. A few SLFP houses were stoned and burnt. Fearing harassment and physical injury, the Goigama president of the Rangama SLFP organization left the village, and SLFP-appointed labourers on Natha Kande Co-operative, who had received jobs under SLFP patronage, fled from their workplaces.

Although the intensity of political party antagonism diminishes after each election, UNP/SLFP rivalry is a constant feature of life in Rangama/Devideniya. In Devideniya, for instance, the SLFP-leaning monk has ensured that the lay organization of *vihāra* activities is dominated by SLFP supporters, and allows *vihāra* festivals to be used as an arena for demonstrating loyalty to the SLFP (e.g. using blue – the SLFP colour – decorations; thanking the former SLFP government for improving the village, etc). UNP members are therefore reluctant to involve themselves in *vihāra* activities apart from the customary, and in many ways inescapable, duty of providing meals for the monk. Party rivalry in this community has the potential of erupting into violence over even minor provocations. In March 1980, almost three years after the general election, a government announcement of a price increase in bread led to a violent confrontation between rival party supporters. An SLFP supporter had the temerity to remark in a Rangama shop that even if the government raised the price of a pound of bread to Rs 10, he would still be able to afford it. A

UNP sympathizer who heard this remark correctly detected in it an insult to the UNP and a hint that the party was failing to help the people. The brawl that ensued was so serious that people were hospitalized and a court case was initiated.

THE MP'S RAJ

The intensity of party affiliation in rural Sri Lanka does not simply signify the fact that contemporary rural people possess political consciousness and an awareness of national issues. It is equally a reflection of the high degree to which virtually every aspect of rural life is politicized. Since independence there has been considerable expansion of state activity in rural areas in spheres such as the supply of agricultural inputs, the marketing of crops, education, health, land distribution etc. The MP's control over these activities has increased in recent decades to such an extent that the rural electorate has been aptly termed the 'MP's Raj' by political commentators. Using the MP as the principal distributor of state benefits, political parties increasingly employ these extensive state powers as levers of political patronage.

Political Control in Rural Sri Lanka

The extension of patronage politics in Sri Lanka may, as in other developing democracies, be seen as an inevitable consequence of the growth of party politics. Competitive electoral politics in Sri Lanka operates in the absence of autonomous provincial institutions capable of constraining the activities of the elected representative. In such a context there is little check on the rural MP's propensity to distribute state benefits, not according to recognized policy criteria, but as a device for building party support.

The lack of any effective institutional constraints on the activities of the rural MP in Sri Lanka is most clearly evidenced in the functioning of local government. Local government in rural Sri Lanka has, until recently,[19] been carried out by village councils (VCs). However, VCs have had very modest powers and their principal function appears to have been that of providing a springboard into national politics. VCs lacked power principally because they have never been autonomous bodies. Under

British rule Ratemahatmayas (chief native headmen of the provincial administration appointed by the Governor) were ex-officio chairmen of the VCs. And both before and after independence the functioning of VCs as locally-representative bodies has been severely hampered by the lack of an independent revenue base, as well as by the high degree of control over their activities and budgets exercised by central government authorities. The central government retained the right to dissolve VCs and place them under the direct control of the officials of the Department of Local Government. In recent years, 'the punitive dissolution of VCs has become increasingly common and the grounds for dissolution increasingly diffuse'.[20] Far from the VC acting as a check on the MP's activities, the MP had the power to dissolve an 'unco-operative' VC. The UNP government that came into power in 1977 dissolved all VCs. New elections to reconstitute VCs, although mooted in 1979–80, were never held.

The MP's control over every aspect of state affairs in the electorate has been further strengthened by the politicization of the administration which has taken place in recent decades. After independence the highly-centralized administrative system of the British was gradually dismantled and all the major government departments established branches at the district level; some even at the divisional level. (The Kegalle district has ten divisions, one of which is Naranhena.) In order to co-ordinate the activities of the various government departments at these levels, District Co-ordinating Committees and Divisional Co-ordinating Committees were set up in the mid-1950s. MPs whose constituencies lay in these administrative areas were included in the committees, but the key figures in these early years were the principal administrators – the Government Agent at the district level and the Divisional Revenue Officer (now called the Assistant Government Agent) at the divisional level. Politicians were, however, critical of the administrative service, which was accused of being backward looking and insensitive to the needs of the people. Indeed the idea 'gained currency that the bureaucracy should be brought under "political control" at all levels, in order to link the aspirations and needs of the public more effectively with the working of the administration'.[21] Thus in the 1960s MPs became more involved in decision making and plan implementation in their electorates, to the irritation of regional administrators. In 1973 the SLFP government increased the influence of politicians in the running of the district administration by creating District Political Authorities (DPAs). Each Political Authority was an MP from the district appointed by the Prime Minister to give political direction and control to the work of the district administrators. In 1977, under the UNP government, DPAs became District Ministers but the latter's relationship to district administrators remained unchanged.

Political control of the administration has meant that bureaucrats' careers (appointment, promotion, transfer) are largely determined by political representatives. MPs are consulted prior to the appointment of minor bureaucrats, such as Grama Sevakas, and at all levels of the provincial bureaucracy MPs 'act as a local check on the work of administrators and constitute in a sense the first level of accountability which the district administrator faces. . . . The centre's evaluation of one's performance depends on, or is guided by, the acceptance which one obtains at the local political level.'[22] As in the case of VCs, far from the administration functioning as a check on the MP's activity, the latter can remove 'unco-operative' bureaucrats. An 'unco-operative' bureaucrat includes any bureaucrat (including the Government Agent) who opts for initiative and direct action rather than toeing the MP's line, because such action is seen as a threat to the MP's power and influence.[23]

It has been the SLFP which has been primarily responsible for most of the radical changes in rural society. The abolition of the post of Vel Vidane and the 'native headmen' system; the experiment in agrarian democracy through cultivation committees; the Paddy Lands Act and the Land Reforms: all these were changes introduced by Bankaranaike's party. But the logic of party competition has meant that the UNP has become equally involved in the process of extending the scope of patronage politics. Nothing that the UNP government has done since its election in 1977 suggests that it is in any hurry to dismantle the patronage structure that has been created over the past few decades.

The urge of both parties to underwrite the MP's powers over his local electorate meant that the MP became unequivocally the most important regional power holder.

The Regional Power Structure in Naranhena

The concentration of power in the hands of the Naranhena MP is not hard to detect. As the 'commandant' of all bureaucrats in Naranhena, he has transferred many Grama Sevakas suspected of being sympathetic to the SLFP and refers patronisingly to the chief bureaucrat of the region as 'my AGA'. He makes no secret of the fact that it is within his power to have the Government Agent of the Kegalle district removed should he prove 'unco-operative'. The MP's influence also extends over bureaucrats from outside his electorate who are involved with projects located in Naranhena. For instance, a high official of NADSA (National Agricultural Diversification and Settlement Authority), operating from headquarters in Kandy, felt it judicious to consult the MP and accept his decisions on all matters pertaining to the NADSA project, even though it clearly hampered the project's efficiency.[24]

In Naranhena not even the forces of law and order are above the influence of the MP. The principal police station in the constituency is situated in Doragala and is in the charge of an Inspector of Police (IP). The IP's relationship with the MP is not dissimilar to that of a bureaucrat. It is well known that he frequently receives, and accedes to, requests from the MP to drop charges against caste fellows or political supporters. The MP's influence over the police has led to a situation where certain individuals commit crimes against property with impunity. The superintendant of a state-owned plantation near this community, for example, is widely known to steal crops from the estate. Yet no one reports the thefts to the police because the estate superintendant and his father are very close to the MP, and it was the MP himself who gave the former his job.

Control over employment opportunities constitutes perhaps the best evidence of the MP's prominent position in the regional power structure. Despite the fact that the demand for jobs far outstrips the supply there nevertheless remains a sizable pool of jobs available for disposal by the MP. The extension of state activity in rural areas has increased the number of employment opportunities over which the MP has control, not only through the process of introducing new enterprises to the area (e.g. the pencil factory in Naranhena) but also through the opportunity for employing a far larger number of labourers on existing government enterprises (e.g. estates) than is economically necessary. Moreover after each general election certain government jobs become available again for distribution because of the sacking of many of the post-holders appointed by the losing party. This occurs most frequently in unskilled manual jobs but is not uncommon even in clerical and secretarial jobs.[25]

In Naranhena all state jobs are distributed via the MP's office. It is well known in this community that in order to get a job as a labourer in a government department or estate, an applicant needs to possess a letter from his local UNP organization and usually must then obtain clearance from the MP's office. The application is then submitted to the relevant bureaucracy which sends a list of 'suitable' employees to the MP's office for final approval. The MP adds or deletes names as he sees fit and sends the list back.

The procedure for the distribution of white-collar jobs, such as the very popular teaching posts or bank clerk posts, is somewhat different, but the MP's discretion in the final choice is still critical. Applications for teaching vacancies, for example, are sent to the Education Ministry; but it is common knowledge that prior to appointing anyone the Ministry draws up a list of candidates with the appropriate educational qualifications and forwards it to the MP's office for approval. A well-placed source within the government told me that there is tacit acceptance in the Ministry that MPs may (and often do) insert the names of other persons onto the list, some of whom do not have the necessary qualifications for the job.

Whilst the financial resources of certain SLFP supporters have enabled them to override the disqualification of their party affiliation, the MP's control over state employment in the electorate has led to a situation where most SLFP sympizers have resigned themselves to the futility of applying for government posts. They are biding their time until the next general election, in the hope that the SLFP will be returned to power and it will be their turn to receive employment.

The Naranhena MP's power within his 'raj' is rarely contested. On the single occasion when it was during my stay in the Rangama/Devideniya community, the challenge did not come from the administration, the police force or independent interest groups. It came rather from a more senior political representative of the same party – the Minister of Power and Highways – who was briefly drawn into the internal affairs of the Naranhena electorate because of the petty rivalry that existed between two village monks. The monk of the Nugapitiya *vihāraya*, who had a long history of enmity with the Rangama monk, was angry that his *vihāraya* was not going to receive electricity under the Village Electrification Scheme, whilst his rival's would. The Nugapitiya monk had three important extra-local connections: an official in the Kegalle Kachchery (district administrative headquarters), a bureaucrat in the President's office, and a high-ranking monk of the Malwatte chapter.[26] It was probably through these contacts that the Nugapitiya monk was able to get the Ministry of Power and Highways to allocate funds for the 'Nugapitiya electricity project'. Whilst the Rangama project had come to a standstill because of charges of bribery and corruption, the Nugapitiya electricity line was completed by June 1980 with the backing of the Minister of Power and Highways. But the Naranhena MP had promised the Rangama monk that the latter would not have to suffer the loss of face of seeing the Nugapitiya monk switch on his lights first. Thus instructions were passed to the Superintendant Engineer of the Ceylon Electricity Board to delay actual transmission of electricity on the Nugapitiya line until the Rangama line was completed. The Superintendant Engineer probably estimated correctly that the Minister had lost interest in what was for him a minor case, and that he had more to lose in defying the MP in whose constituency he was working. He complied with the MP's request. The Nugapitiya monk had to wait over a year to get electricity to his *vihāraya*. In July 1981 the Rangama line was completed and both monks held elaborate celebrations to mark the inauguration of electricity to their *vihāra*.

The Integration of Local and Regional-level Power Structures

The extensiveness of the MP's power in the electorate and the degree to which he can directly or indirectly influence the lives of those living within it has made the regional power structure an increasingly important determinant of the local-level power structure. The patronage that today's MP distributes is not only vastly greater in extent than that distributed by his predecessor, the political notable, but is also much more individualized. It is not restricted to the provision of collective goods like wells, roads and electricity but extends to matters involving control over individually attributable benefits such as who gets a one-acre government allotment and who gets a job as a casual labourer on a state building project. Indeed the system of political patronage is so highly developed that it has resulted in a change in the role of the rural MP. Before 1956 the MP was a regional notable primarily concerned with national legislative affairs and had little direct contact with the voters in the constituency. In recent decades, however, MPs 'have been content to leave the manipulation of parliamentary affairs to the party managers, and to accept the determination of policy by the party leaders'.[27] Their principal role has become the distribution of patronage to individuals in the electorate.

The development of the MP's raj and the MP-centred regional power structure has meant that those individuals who are able, through the MP's support, to manipulate the distribution of specific resources, have risen to prominence as the power elite of local communities. Of the three groups of people – personal contacts, party officials and henchmen[28] – with access to the MP, it is the latter who have the greatest degree of backing and have emerged as the new power elite in their local areas.

Personal contacts
───────────────
Unlike their urban, westernized, English-speaking predecessors, most contemporary MPs have their roots in the rural areas. They have usually lived and worked in their constituency and have extensive grass-roots kinship and friendship networks. The extent to which relatives and friends benefit from their links to the MP depends not only upon whether they campaigned for him

but also on the nature of their relationship in the non-political sphere. In the Rangama/Devideniya community the individual with the closest personal contact to the Naranhena MP is B. Jayasena, a prominent SLFP supporter. Jayasena's mother and the MP's paternal grandfather were siblings and despite opposing political sympathies their relationship has been characterized by goodwill. After the 1977 election B. Jayasena escaped political victimization. Unlike many others he retained his job on a government estate to which he had been appointed by the previous SLFP regime. When he was dismissed subsequently on account of drunkenness and negligence, the MP gave him a white-collar job at the newly-built pencil factory. His relationship to the MP has also enabled B. Jayasena to receive occasional favours for others. It is alleged for instance that caste appeals to the MP from this community are usually directed via B. Jayasena.

Party officials

With the establishment of party competition in Sri Lanka's electoral politics, both the UNP and the SLFP made a concerted effort to establish local-level party organizations. In theory, each party may have up to three village organizations: the branch organization, the youth organization and the young women's organization. In practice, party activity tends to be dominated by either the branch or the youth organization.

In both parties the most dedicated workers are the educated youth who hope to obtain employment after the elections. The structure of the UNP and SLFP local organizations in this community are, however, rather different. The SLFP youth in both villages has not been able to challenge the leadership of older persons who, in the late 1950s, took the radical step of throwing their lot in with the SLFP. UNP organizations in both Rangama and Devideniya on the other hand are dominated by young people. In principle they secure their position through election; but in practice they do so by arranging to meet the candidate's campaign staff prior to an election and getting themselves registered as the local party organization.

Party organizations become extremely active prior to general elections. Officials organize meetings in the village, gather supporters to attend party rallies in various parts of the electorate, and issue membership cards. After the election the activities of the losing party organization come to an abrupt halt. The local organization of the victorious party on the other hand tends to remain active for some months after the change in government, because they have a stake in determining the distribution of manual jobs which become available after the election. During these early months there is considerable uncertainty as to who will receive these jobs. In Rangama/Devideniya, for instance, many people found themselves on and off the employment register of Natha Kande estate as interested parties competed to have their favourites included. Once the distribution of most of the manual jobs has been settled, however, whether or not the local organizations of the victorious party continue active in party affairs (e.g. become involved in local elections) depends to a large extent on the officials' post-election relationship to the MP.

A crucial component of this relationship is the extent to which the MP is prepared to reward the organizations' officials. In return for their campaign work the party officials expect to gain prestigious white-collar jobs (e.g. as a teacher or a bank clerk). But there is no binding obligation on the part of the MP so to reward local party officials, especially since the balance of reciprocity shifts in his favour after he wins the election. The Naranhena MP neglected the claims of many party officials and chose to distribute scarce white-collar jobs according to a criterion which was materially advantageous to himself. The majority of UNP officials were unwilling to abide by this criterion to secure jobs which they felt they had earned as of right.

A look at the post-election careers of the four principal UNP party officials in Rangama/Devideniya shows that whilst not neglected by the MP they nonetheless failed to secure the kinds of job they wanted:

W.R. SISIL BANDARA (President – Rangama):
Got a job as a security guard.
M.W. ABEYRATNE (Secretary – Rangama):
Appointed Cultivation Officer. Upon receipt of petitions against the appointment, however, the MP saw fit to cancel it and

gave Abeyratne a minor job as an overseer on a small extent
of NADSA land.

S. JAYARATNE (President – Devideniya):
Received a job as an English teacher. He lost this job soon after-
wards when it was discovered that he had used forged certificates.
The MP has not bothered to give him another job.

S. PIYASENA (Secretary – Devideniya):
Offered a licence to manufacture *bīdi* (local cigarettes), which he
declined.

All four men feel they have been inadequately rewarded and
have lost interest in their organizations. During the period of
fieldwork both UNP organizations were just as inactive as the
local organizations of the losing SLFP party. Indeed Jayaratne
and Piyasena, the Devideniya UNP officials, have left the village
in order to avoid the scorn levelled at them by their fellow
villagers for having failed to receive the prestigious white-collar
jobs they expected. Jayaratne's departure was also motivated by
the fact that his attempts to obtain manual jobs for some of his
relatives were successfully frustrated by an MP's henchman in the
community. After Jayaratne's departure this henchman took over
the Devideniya UNP organization.

The MP's henchmen

Henchmen may or may not be relatives, friends or party officials.
What differentiates henchmen from others with access to the MP
is that the extent of support they have has enabled them to rise to
prominence as the power elite in their local communities. One or
more of the MP's henchmen are invariably in attendance on him,
both at his residence and at the functions which he graces.

In the Rangama/Devideniya community the monk of the
Rangama *vihāraya* and N. Siyathu are henchmen of the Naranhena
MP. The most direct way in which the MP's support enables these
two men to wield power is through manipulating the distribution
of particular resources of high value to people in the community.

In theory every person in the electorate has access to the MP.
Yet most people realise that making a personal request to the MP
is one thing and having it fulfilled another. The effectiveness of
working through a person who is known to be favoured by

the MP is therefore readily understood by individuals in the Naranhena electorate. Acting as an intermediary, Siyathu has secured a variety of favours for people in this community. On one occasion he obtained a job as conductor on Natha Kande estate for S. Dayananda, a political activist who until just before the 1977 election had been a stalwart SLFP supporter. It is likely that the MP and Siyathu felt it advisable to give Dayananda this post over the claims of more educated persons who had had a long-standing association with the UNP, in order to cement Dayananda's new allegiance to the UNP.

The henchmen's role may also be used in a negative way. For henchmen can remove people's names from employment lists which are routinely sent to the MP's office for approval. Siyathu frequently indulges in this activity, because his loyalty to the UNP is so obsessive that he cannot countenance anyone with SLFP sympathies getting a job under a UNP government.

It is not essential in all cases, however, to be a committed UNP supporter when seeking the help of henchmen to secure a job. Not all henchmen, nor indeed all MPs, favour applicants on the basis of party criteria alone. With regard to white-collar jobs in particular, which are highly valued and therefore marketable commodities for those who have control over their distribution, the opportunity for financial gain can be an important motive for MPs, particularly when they are not seeking re-election. When this applies, however, the 'purchase' of such jobs cannot be seen to happen in a visible way and MPs therefore rely on selected henchmen to organize such transactions.[29] The recipients are selected not on the basis of party loyalty but rather on the price they are prepared to pay, and the degree to which the henchman feels they can be relied upon not to make public the transaction.

The power that the monk and Siyathu wield in Rangama/ Devideniya is not, however, limited to the supply or withholding of individualized state benefits. They also, as we have seen, exert wide-ranging influence over community decision making. In part at least their ability to dominate local affairs derives from the control they have over state patronage – there is general recognition on the part of their fellow villagers that it is in their self-interest to acquiesce to henchmen's wishes. Equally important, however, is the fact that villagers know that henchmen operate under the aegis of the MP: villagers are aware that the actions and decisions of these henchmen will be sanctioned and upheld by the MP. In this context opposition to their wishes is largely futile. Moreover, when certain individuals are under the MP's aegis there is a tendency for lesser regional personages to lend their support as well. These personages include the Inspector of Police, the Assistant Government Agent, and certain other officials all of whom, though ultimately under the control of the MP himself, nevertheless enjoy limited discretion within their own spheres of action. From the point of view of the villager, therefore, the henchmen enjoy the protection not only of the ultimate regional power-holder – the MP – but also of other important personages who are often in more direct contact with the local level than the MP himself.

It is the protective aegis of the MP (and other personages), and the MP's largesse in allowing them to control the distribution of state patronage in their communities, that has enabled henchmen to occupy the highest stratum of local-level power hierarchies. The integration of local-level power structures with those of the regional level therefore takes place through the MP–henchman relationship.

The increased political integration of the local community with the regional level, which has taken place through changes in rural Sinhalese power structures, bears similarities not only with post-independence developments in neighbouring India (below) but also with recent changes in parts of rural Europe. For instance, Silverman's account of post World War II changes in the relationship between a central-Italian community and the larger society contains remarkable parallels with the Sinhalese situation.[30] Concomitant with free elections, universal suffrage, the penetration of the state into local areas and the spread of welfare provisions, the padrone's role as broker had been eliminated and rural communities were increasingly drawn into contact with the wider society through political intermediaries. Likewise, in western Sicily, Blok finds that villages are increasingly integrated with the regional and national levels through the sphere of politics.[31] Until very recently the mafiosi operated as power brokers in rural Sicily, controlling the links that tied the peasant to the larger society and the state. That situation no longer prevails. As one of Blok's informants described the change in Sicily: 'before it was mafia; today it is politics.'[32]

Thus the decline of the pre-independence brokers in Sri Lanka in the context of democracy and party building has close parallels in the decline of the padrone and mafioso in central Italy and Sicily respectively. All these power elites have been replaced by political intermediaries – people who are powerful because their extra-local political contacts allow them to manipulate state resources and distribute benefits and favours.

Whether in India, Italy or Sicily, in situations where local–regional integration takes place through political intermediaries the interactions involved at each level are depicted in the literature in terms of the exchange of favours for votes.[33] The political intermediary is in some sense perceived as obtaining blocks of votes, either for himself or for higher-level party members, through the distribution of benefits. In the early decades of electoral politics in Sri Lanka also, local personages, as we have seen, acted as 'vote banks', delivering blocks of votes to parliamentary candidates in exchange for development benefits.

It is therefore interesting to note that the contemporary MP–henchman relationship in Sri Lanka is not one of exchange of favours for votes. The level of political consciousness of rural Sinhalese people today is such that it is difficult to conceive of anyone 'delivering' the vote of another. Certainly in Rangama/Devideniya the monk and Siyathu cannot influence people's voting patterns and can in no way therefore be considered 'vote banks'. They are better considered as information banks, providing the MP with inside information about the constituency which he needs in order to maximize returns (i.e. further his own and his party's interests) from the extensive power and highly individualized patronage at his disposal. Although most contemporary MPs are rural-based, the size of their electorates (well over 25,000 voters from more than ninety villages in Naranhena) makes it difficult for an individual to gather the necessary detailed knowledge of local affairs for himself. He therefore relies on his henchmen to supply him with up-to-date information about which party member's support is worth reinforcing and which opposition activist could be converted by patronage, about whether local-level bureaucrats are supporting his development plans or sabotaging them, and so on.

Although the MP–henchman relationship contains elements of reciprocity, the balance of reciprocity is always, unambiguously, in the MP's favour. The MP chooses his henchmen, not vice versa. Thus although certain aspects of the henchmen's role in local communities resembles that of a broker, he lacks the independence of position usually associated with the term 'broker'. If the relationship between the MP and a particular henchman were to break down, the latter ceases to have power. The MP simply selects another henchman.

Given the considerable advantages attached to being a henchman there is no dearth of candidates for the position. The nature of the MP–henchman relationship is such that the vital prerequisite for assuming the role of henchman is not control over some resource, or possession of a particular skill, nor evidence of long-standing and devoted party allegiance. Rather the emphasis is on trust and personal loyalty to the MP. This means that officials of local party organizations are by no means automatic candidates for henchmanship. Neither is the extent of support extended to a henchman necessarily related to intensity of party support.

In the Rangama/Devideniya community the henchman most favoured by the MP is not the die-hard UNP supporter Siyathu but the far less 'committed' monk. The evidence of the goodwill that exists between the MP and the monk is reflected in many of the prominent improvements that have recently taken place in Rangama. For example, it was due to the MP that the footpath to the Rangama *vihāraya* was converted to a motorable road, and that the school founded by the monk was nominated one of only two model schools in the constituency, thereby being earmarked for special facilities. The MP has also promised to construct a bridge over the Maha Oya behind the Rangama *vihāraya*. The special regard which the MP has for the monk was demonstrated when the MP left for London as a member of a parliamentary delegation. On that occasion the monk was one of a select group of people who accompanied him to the Colombo airport for the 'departure ceremony'.

The close relationship the monk has with the MP has impressed important regional figures no less than villagers. It is therefore not surprising that the Inspector of Police and the Assistant Government Agent see it as judicious to make themselves available to attend and speak at Rangama *vihāraya* festivals. The AGA often accompanies the monk on social visits outside the community and the IP even went to Kandy with the monk to help him buy electrical equipment for the Rangama *vihāraya*.

The relative unimportance of long-standing party support on the henchman's part is further underlined when one examines the monk's tarnished record of UNP support. The monk is not simply less committed than Siyathu to the UNP. He was in fact, until recently, an SLFP supporter. His relationship with the previous SLFP government was sufficiently close for him to secure a permanent building for the Rangama school he had started in 1958. Moreover, during the 1977 election campaign the monk had initially supported the SLFP candidate and had even allowed the latter to use the Rangama *vihāraya* for a campaign meeting. The SLFP candidate's reluctance to promise certain improvements to the Rangama *vihāraya* alienated the monk who thereafter supported the UNP candidate.

Even today in his role as a member of the Rangama/Devideniya power elite the monk is not averse to rewarding SLFP supporters with state patronage, though he may have to disguise such activities from the MP. On one occasion, for example, he secretly secured a highly-valued application form for the Job Bank (a government scheme to distribute jobs) for a youth who was a prominent member of the Rangama SLFP organization. Because the MP might well have resisted this selection on party grounds the monk allowed the MP to believe that the youth was his nephew.

It is ironical therefore that in a system of power which has evolved through competitive party politics, the intensity of party support is not of crucial importance either in the MP's choice of henchmen or in the degree of support and backing that he gives them. Local-level power hierarchies in Sri Lanka have undergone radical change because national political parties rely on patronage politics to secure party support. Yet a long-standing and proven record of party support is not a sufficient nor even a necessary condition for entering the ranks of the local-level power elite.

POWER WITHOUT LEADERSHIP

The growth of democratic politics and its effect on local-level power in Sri Lanka may, as has been seen, share common features with rural societies in Europe. But perhaps the society which bears the most interesting parallels with post-colonial developments in Sri Lanka is India, the only other South Asian country with an unbroken tradition of democracy since independence.

One feature common to electoral politics in both countries has been the growth of party competition. In recent decades new parties have emerged challenging the dominance of the political party that took over the reigns of government from the British. The electoral competition that the SLFP presents to the UNP in Sri Lanka is paralleled in India by the challenge to the Congress Party from a small number of national parties and a large number of regional parties.

A second feature common to both countries has been the rapid extension of state activity in rural areas. This in turn has given rise to a wide-ranging system of patronage politics which has served to integrate local-level power structures with those at the regional level. In India this integration has been facilitated by Panchayati Raj – the three-tier structure of local government which controls the Community Development Programme. Panchayati Raj links the local level to the block and district level not only through a system of indirect elections but, more importantly, through the elaborate network of political patronage that Panchayat members operate. In rural India obtaining jobs, loans, licenses or even a place in college entails securing state patronage through a political broker.[34]

Finally, in both these South Asian democracies, the expansion of state activity and the increase in the elected representatives' control over the distribution of state resources have resulted in the politicization of the local-level power structure. The pre-independence power elite has been displaced by a new elite whose source of power is based essentially on political party connection. The counterparts of the Sri Lankan MP's henchmen in rural India are those individuals who control the allocation and distribution of government resources – village panchayat presidents and chairmen of local co-operatives.[35] These are elective offices, and because local elections in India are usually extensions of village factionalism, wealth and caste retain more relevance in local power hierarchies in India than they do in Sri Lanka. Nevertheless, given the penetration of party politics into Indian village life and the tendency for each faction to ally itself with a political party, it would be misleading to ignore 'party connection' as an important basis of power within the Indian context.

Whilst the impact of democracy on local-level power structures in South Asia has been the subject of extensive scholarship, one of the most important implications of these changes has been improperly understood, because scholars have failed to distinguish between the terms 'power' and 'leadership'.[36]

The Absence of Leaders in Rangama/Devideniya

The emergence of a new power elite in Sinhalese communities does not mean that 'new leaders are rising'.[37] The way in which the members of the new power elite in this community exercise influence may in many respects be dissimilar (the monk is secretive, Siyathu aggressive), but their style of wielding power shares one important characteristic: they are neither of them leaders. They do not command a following and the authoritative nature of their actions and opinions does not derive from the respect and admiration that villagers hold for them.

Both men are unpopular. Although villagers praise Siyathu to his face and although they continue to give the monk the respect accorded to the sangha, in private they frequently express resentment at the activities of both men. Overt opposition is uncommon. During my stay in the community the only act of overt opposition to a member of the power elite occurred during a Devideniya temple festival. Siyathu's daughter was performing a dance, and during the performance the brother of the secretary of the local SLFP organization, apparently under the influence of alcohol, shouted that the dance was going on too long and others should get their chance to perform. Such incidents are rare. But as long as anonymity can be preserved many residents of the community are quick to express their covert antagonism. For example, numerous petitions have been sent to the MP and NADSA to have Siyathu dismissed from his post as overseer on Natha Kande estate. Other forms of covert protest have been employed against the Rangama monk. The *vihāraya* police book, signed by the police each night, has twice been stolen, and in January 1980 two of the monk's dogs were poisoned. Shortly afterwards, in a symbolic show of antagonism to the monk's relationship with the MP, the signboard bearing the MP's name which marked the road to the *vihāraya* was stolen. I also learned from a reliable source that the monk is so suspicious of the ill intentions of certain families that when it is their turn to provide the daily meals for the *vihāraya* he accepts the food but does not eat it for fear of being poisoned.

Another important aspect of the absence of leadership is the fact that the power of the monk and Siyathu is temporary. Between 1970 and 1977, for instance, neither man was a power holder of any description, let alone a member of the power elite. During that time it was B. Jayasena, a henchman of the previous SLFP MP, who was the principal power holder in this community.[38] The monk and Siyathu became power holders in 1977, and their power will last only as long as the UNP and the present MP for Naranhena remain in office.

The lack of leadership in the Rangama/Devideniya community is perhaps best evidenced in the failure of local institutions and organizations to foster local participation, despite the best efforts of government and administrators. It has been suggested by some scholars that the political awareness of Sinhalese villagers has resulted in a high level of popular participation in local-level institutions,[39] but the empirical evidence from this community flatly contradicts this observation. True, a large number of rural people hold elective or appointed office. But this is a result of the multiplicity of local-level institutions[40] and says nothing about the actual level of participation in, or effectiveness of, these institutions. Usually after an initial meeting in which office bearers are elected, the organization exists in name alone. Thus there are several people in Rangama/Devideniya who are addressed as *lēkam mahatmaya* (Mr Secretary) and *sabhāpati mahatmaya* (Mr Chairman), but in virtually every case they are office bearers of moribund societies.

Villagers cite two reasons for the failure of these institutions.

On the one hand they point to the fact that local-level institutions, government and non-government, often become sources of corruption, and that the only organizations in which people show an interest in holding office are those which have the potential of receiving outside funds (e.g. Village Development Society, Sarvodaya). Villagers insist that officials of these organizations (including the monk and Siyathu) are not motivated by enthusiasm to develop the community but rather by the hope of material gain. The inhabitants of this community also (correctly) identify disunity as a cause of the ineffectiveness of local organizations. This disunity is manifested not only in caste and class antagonism but also, in recent years, through the conflict engendered through rival party affiliation.[41]

The dismal performance of local organizations is, however, equally the consequence of the absence of leaders in contemporary rural communities. Sinhalese villages today do not have men of the stature of the Vel Vidane or the Aracci, men who are respected and admired and who inspire sufficient confidence to enable their followers to overcome disunity and work together to improve the community. The relationship between the new power elite and the villagers is not one which makes it possible for the former to mobilize communal effort for the collective benefit.

The new rural power elites in India appear from the literature to share many of the characteristics of their Sri Lankan counterparts. The new village power holders are unpopular and disliked. Villagers are cynical about their activities and regard their route to power as built upon deceit and self-interest.[42] The new power elite is also constantly depicted as being incapable of mobilizing local initiative and carrying out programmes of rural development.[43] For example, Sharma, writing of Arunpur, says that villagers claim 'today no one obeys anyone, all think themselves big.'[44] And this inability of the new power holders to direct collective activity is hardly surprising in view of the fact that 'the tendency to discriminate on political grounds in the distribution of benefits has not encouraged broad-based, generalized support for village *leaders*'[45] (my emphasis).

Many observers of rural India have, however, failed to reach the conclusions which their own empirical evidence indicates, because of the lack of definitional clarity in their frameworks. The relationship between power and leadership in local communities cannot be properly understood if, for instance, the panchayat president regardless of his role in the community is consistently described as a village 'leader'. The changes in the rural Indian power structure are thus variously described in terms of a change in the type of leader (from 'real', 'traditional', 'natural' leaders to elected, official leaders); a change in leadership style (from expressing the community consensus to recruiting a ruling coalition); or a change in leadership function (from maintenance of social order and reinforcement of village values to brokerage and patronage).

The evidence from the Rangama/Devideniya community, and indeed the Indian literature itself, suggests that it is misleading to talk of the changes that have taken place in rural South Asian power structures in terms of changes in type, style or functions of leadership. Whatever else they may or may not be, members of the new rural power elite do not appear to be leaders. To describe as leaders people who do not lead, and by all accounts have no followers,[46] results in confusion and tends to overlook perhaps the most significant aspect of local-level change in these South Asian democracies – the demise of the village leader. Local communities today are characterized not by 'the inability of rural leadership to mobilize power',[47] but rather by the inability of the new power holders to act as leaders.

It is the party political basis of their power which denies the new local power elite the ability to acquire the qualities of leadership. The regional and national power structures from which their power derives is liable to change at each general election, rendering their tenure of power essentially temporary. More importantly the local power hierarchies over which they preside are integrated to these larger power structures through a system of political patronage which involves victimization and favouritism.

A future resurgence of leadership in rural South Asian communities seems unlikely. Patronage politics is, after all, the operation of the 'politics of scarcity', where the demand for government benefits far outruns the supply. And in the stagnant or declining economic environment of South Asia it seems unlikely that the 'politics of scarcity' will disappear in the near future. Even were it to do so however, in Sri Lanka at least, the indications are that the demise of leadership is not a temporary phenomenon. For the impact of democracy has not only denied the new power elite the qualifications of leadership; as will be seen in the next chapter, it has also fostered egalitarian ideologies which have ensured the demise of followers.

12   The Contemporary Ideology of Stratification

This chapter analyses cultural conceptions in the contemporary Rangama/Devideniya community by building upon the distinction that has been made between the descriptive and evaluative components of an ideology of stratification. This basic model was adequate for the examination of conceptions of inequality in the baseline period, because of the ideological consensus that prevailed at that time. That ideological consensus no longer applies, however, and the conceptions of inequality now displayed present a far more complex picture; a picture of attitudes shared at some points by some groups, and divergent on others.

To capture the ideological diversity that now prevails in the Rangama/Devideniya community, the basic model is developed to incorporate a further level of categories (see Figure 7). It should be stressed that these are analytical categories; there is no suggestion that people's views of stratification are consciously compartmentalized in this way.

Within the descriptive component of the ideology of stratification, 'subjective definition' refers to the way in which people define a particular dimension of inequality – their own definitions of caste, class or power. The 'perception of hierarchy' on the other hand, refers to the way in which these definitions apply to their society: the way they see their society divided into strata according to the different types of inequality.

Within the evaluative component of the ideology of stratification, 'evaluation of the hierarchical system' refers to the evaluation of the presence of ranked strata with reference to a particular type of inequality. The 'evaluation of the system's operation', on the other hand, evaluates the patterns of interactions that prevail between strata – the way in which different groups act towards each other.

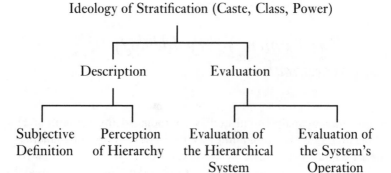

Figure 7   Model of the ideology of stratification

Having first looked briefly at the influences which disrupted the ideological consensus of the baseline period, and their effects on the religious theory which held that consensus together, I shall go on to analyse the contemporary ideology of stratification in light of the categories outlined above.

THE DECLINE OF CONSENSUS AND THE INCREASE IN IDEOLOGICAL DIVERSITY

As was seen in Chapter 7, the ideology of stratification which prevailed in the baseline period was characterized by consensus. The vast majority of people subscribed to, and believed in, ideologies which benefited the higher strata. Such uniformity of cultural conceptions is far less evident amongst contemporary inhabitants. The upper strata of the hierarchies of caste, class and power cannot be said to exercise 'hegemony'.

In recent decades the ideology of stratification in Rangama/Devideniya has been heavily influenced by the democratic and socialist ideals espoused by post-independence national governments. The impact at the local level of these national-level ideologies has been to lay stress on the theory of local-level participation and on the notion that all rural people should have an equal say in the development of their community. Local receptivity to this national ideology has been facilitated by the widespread extension of education, which has not only made it easier for villagers to understand national-level issues, but is also in itself a practical illustration of the ideal of equality of opportunity.

The underlying basis of the ideological consensus of the baseline period rested on adherence to the Buddhist karmic theory of causation. This theory served as a powerful justification of social inequality. The confrontation of the karmic theory with the populist doctrines of secular idealism has served to undermine the primacy of the religious theory. Nominal allegiance remains, but its usefulness to 'believers' as an explanation of social inequality is highly attenuated.

For a small minority of the inhabitants of contemporary Rangama/Devideniya, karma still provides a satisfactory explanation of social inequality. They are not for example discomfited by the fact that some individuals rank high on one dimension of inequality (e.g. class) but low on another (e.g. caste). They will say that men like Nuwarapakse Mudalali and B. Jayasena were born rich because they were generous in their past lives, but were born low caste because they did not give with the good intention of gaining merit, but with arrogance and pride (*mānna sahitava pin karā*); or because they flouted caste etiquette in their previous existences.

Such wholehearted belief in the karmic theory of causation is, however, largely restricted to the old, as well as to some middle-aged inhabitants. For many others, belief in karma no longer implies acceptance of the doctrine as the explanation of all types of social inequality. Many, for example, see it as a correct explanation of material inequalities in society, but not of birth status ones. Such a position avoids the logical inconsistency present in an acceptance of caste as karmically determined. For if caste status was dependent upon accumulated merit and demerit, one's ancestors and one's children could belong to a different caste from one's own.

More significantly, however, there are a considerable number of people who reject an explanation of inequality founded on karma altogether, even though continuing to profess allegiance to Buddhism. This is particularly noticeable amongst the young, but there are many middle-aged farmers also who, for instance, insist that the degree of wealth a person possesses is directly related to his striving and effort (*utsāhaya*) rather than accumulated merit and demerit in past lives.

For a few of the more educated persons in the community, such rejection of karmic theory is often given a logical or 'scientific' basis. The Grama Sevaka, for example, felt karmic theory to be 'logically' unconvincing because it did not take into account the relativity of suffering. A worm does not suffer by being in a cess pit, so how can it be said that a human being who sins receives punishment by being reborn as a worm? More surprisingly, perhaps, the scepticism towards karmic theory is even shared by some Buddhist monks. One monk told me that it is his duty to maintain the truth of karma to the villagers. Yet his own personal belief is that certain Buddhist doctrines propounded over two thousand years ago are rendered questionable in the light of advances in science and man's increased understanding. Science, for instance, has gone a long way in explaining the origins of the world, whereas Buddhist doctrine enjoins people not to bother with this problem because it is beyond their comprehension. With the advance of knowledge and scientific thought it is equally difficult to accept the Buddhist karmic theory of causation as an explanation of social inequality.

Exposure to the democratic, socialist ideologies of the national level and the attenuation of adherence to the karmic theory of causation, have not, however, resulted in the simple replacement of notions of hierarchy by those of equality. Since the baseline period, the Rangama/Devideniya people's perceptions and evaluations of caste, class and power have not changed in a uniform manner. Rather the contemporary ideology of stratification is characterized by a high degree of diversity in which notions of hierarchy coexist with those of equality.

THE CONTEMPORARY IDEOLOGY OF CASTE

Low-caste resentment of high-caste privilege and repudiation of caste etiquette are the most striking changes in caste ideology that have taken place in this community since the baseline period. It is tempting to conclude, therefore, that in democratic societies such as Sri Lanka, the caste hierarchy is rejected by those who are ranked unfavourably within it. The importance of examining the ideology of caste by reference to the analytical framework outlined above is that it affords a quite different and more complex picture of the perception and evaluation of birth status inequalities among rural Sinhalese.

Subjective Definition

Contemporary inhabitants of Rangama/Devideniya most commonly express the meaning of caste in terms of an historical division of labour organized under one of the early Sinhalese kings. In this understanding, therefore, the caste system is a derivative of a royal decree (*rāja nītiya*). But differences which are in some sense 'natural' are also seen to distinguish one caste from another. The view that people of different castes are inherently different is widespread, with people from both low and high castes agreeing that all people are not the same – all people are not equal. Few see the contradiction between the view of caste as based on a royal decree on the one hand, and some 'natural' difference on the other. Those that do, resolve the dilemma by saying that the way in which the king assigned noble and demeaning tasks to his subjects was based on pre-existing differences between groups.

Beyond a conviction that caste groups were inherently different from each other, most low-caste persons found it difficult to explain what constituted the basis of this 'natural' differentiation. Indeed, many seemed to find the question too obvious to require explanation. Some referred to *vansa* (pedigree), others to character (*carita*, *gatiguna*). Many when pressed resorted to the circular argument that the difference between themselves and the high castes lay in the fact that the latter were 'good people' (*honda minissu*), descended for generations from good people.

Not surprisingly, the Goigama proffer a more explicit account of why some groups of people are inherently superior to others. Many Goigama identify such personal characteristics as dress, speech, manners, etc, as the difference marking off a high-caste person from a low-caste person. A few of the more educated Goigama go further and point to an explicitly physiological difference between castes – a difference described by the former Vel Vidane as one of 'blood heritage' (*lē urumayen ätivena venasvīmak*).

According to this view the character, morality, appearance, dialect and even cleanliness and smell of the various castes are 'naturally' determined attributes. Moreover, because these distinguishing attributes are 'natural' ones, it follows that low castes can never erase inferior and unrefined forms of behaviour and speech. For example low-caste women would never be able to drape their saris in the modest and decorous manner of the high castes, and even if low-caste men rose to be MPs and Ministers of State they could never eradicate inferior speech patterns (e.g. the consonant 't' at the end of verb forms rather than the 'n' or 'd' of high-caste speech). The Vel Vidane claimed that although Buddhism does not support the caste system, the very fact of the Buddha's birth into a high-caste family proves the existence of caste among men. The Buddha was such a great man that he had to be born into a superior caste.

In a broad and general way, therefore, the Goigama view of the meaning of caste resembles Marriott and Inden's theory of 'the cognitive non-duality of action and actor or code and substance.'[1] But the fact is that this view is by and large restricted to the Goigama, and even then is fully expressed only by the more educated among them. The evidence from Rangama/Devideniya thus throws doubt upon the general applicability of this theory as an account of the underlying ideology of caste in the South Asian region.

Goigama not only have the most explicit view of the meaning of 'natural' difference but also go furthest in the degree of significance they attach to birth status inequalities. The Goigama subjective definition of caste contains certain ideational features which were widespread in the baseline period but are today not present among the lower castes. During the baseline period an ideational equivalence between the different dimensions of inequality such that each implied the other, was common to all inhabitants of this community. Today the Goigama alone persist in a view that caste and class imply each other. To be high caste is to be wealthy and vice versa. Goigama also continue in the view that caste-status differences necessarily imply certain patterns of inter-caste interaction which must be maintained by the rules of caste etiquette and which entail deference by the low castes to the high castes. Non-Goigama in this community, whilst identifying caste as based on 'natural' birth status differences, no longer see high caste status necessarily implying wealth and privilege.

There are some middle-aged and young Batgam in the community, who, in sharp contrast to the Goigama, claim to disbelieve entirely the theory of natural difference between human beings of the same race. They assert that it was only ignorance and foolishness that allowed earlier generations to suppose that Sinhalese people are divided into superior/inferior groupings. But this rejection of birth-status differences is purely verbal and superficial, for in other contexts most of them are just as eager to claim caste distinction as any Goigama. Hence these same people will often proclaim their superiority over the Vahumpura and Hēna castes because the latter are service castes; will be at pains to point out the superiority of their names in contrast certain other castes;[2] and will frequently denounce inter-caste marriages with those below them in the caste hierarchy.

There are only a few cases where verbal denial of the meaning of 'natural difference' matches a genuine lack of belief in birth status differences. These are to be found amongst certain Batgam youths who, unlike their parents, show no desire to assert their superiority in the caste hierarchy.

Perception of Hierarchy

It is quite possible to recognize the presence of a hierarchy of birth status even though rejecting the notion of natural differences existing between people of the same race. And indeed young Batgam do have a clear perception of the way their society is hierarchically structured in relation to caste differences. This is a perception shared by all other members of the community.

There are a number of ways in which this shared perception of the caste hierarchy diverges from the contemporary structural reality examined in Chapter 9. To begin with, although Muslims are regarded, and regard themselves, as of relatively good-birth status, they are excluded from a formal ranking within the caste hierarchy. Conversely, the ideology of villagers continues to categorize the Walawwe people as the highest caste, despite their absorption into the Goigama caste. Villagers speak disparagingly of the economic decline of the Walawwe people but are, by and large, convinced of their superior caste status. But this perception may be undergoing change. Increasingly, remarks are made on the extent of intermarriage with the Goigama. And the Rangama monk observed that quite apart from poverty, such intermarriages themselves had 'finished off' the Walawwe caste (*ēkenma valavva ivarayi*).

The most marked discrepancy between the perception of the caste hierarchy and the structural reality is the widespread conviction among the Goigama that caste differences have little bearing on village life today. Although they share with members of other castes recognition of hierarchically ranked caste groups, Goigama, unlike members of other castes and contrary to the behavioural reality, feel that these groupings are becoming increasingly insignificant in their society. They see the contemporary caste system as a shadow of its former self, and some poor Goigama, among whom this attitude is particularly intense, even go so far as to say that there will be nothing called caste in five to ten years time.

Evaluation of the Hierarchical System

Whereas the general themes of the descriptive components of the ideology of caste are relatively similar across different groups, the evaluation of the system differs markedly across the castes.

The Goigama, as one would expect, solidly support the caste hierarchy. Since for them the division of society into castes is the proper and natural order, the legitimacy of the caste system is not in doubt. It appears self-evident to them that a system which ranks those who *are* superior higher than those who are inferior must be a correct one.

Many Goigama look upon colonial rule as a time when the caste hierarchy was strong and society functioned well, and see the passage to democracy as the harbinger of subsequent decline. In particular they blame Bandaranaike who, according to them, was the architect of the decline of caste. Bandaranaike ruined things (*vade kava*) by introducing and popularizing an ideology of equality in which all citizens obtained equal rights.

In contrast to the Goigama, the majority of Batgam disapprove of the caste system. Apart from the old, there is universal agreement among them that a society free of caste would be better than one in which caste distinctions prevailed.

The attitude towards the caste system of people of intermediate caste status is marked not by approval or disapproval but rather by a sense of inevitability and acceptance. Many feel it is futile to talk of the merits or demerits of a system which is unlikely to disintegrate.

Evaluation of the System's Operation

Evaluation of the way the caste system operates varies across a high-caste/low-caste axis. Non-Goigama are united in their denunciation of the way the system operates and feel that the rules of caste etiquette entail unjustified discrimination against some and equally unjustified privilege for others. Whilst each low-caste group resents acts of discrimination perpetrated by all castes higher than itself in the caste hierarchy, negative evaluation is principally directed against the exclusivity and discrimination of the Goigama.

The only exception to the otherwise generalized low-caste denunciation of the caste system's operation is to be found among the older people. Age, in fact, is an important variable amongst the low castes in determining the intensity of their opposition to the rules of caste etiquette. Older people, for example, consider it morally wrong to serve food to the high castes (p. 84), whilst many middle-aged low castes, though wishing commensal restrictions were abolished, are not prepared to take the initiative to do away with them. Low-caste youth, however, are incensed by the commensal exclusivity of the Goigama and some have been known to contrive situations in which Goigama are forced to eat food prepared in low-caste houses.[3]

But negative evaluation of the caste system's operation is not a low-caste preserve. Goigama for their part feel the liberties assumed by the low castes in dress, naming conventions etc, are highly improper. Goigama deplore the way the caste system operates today, where superior people who deserve respect and deference no longer receive it. They recall with fondness the occasion when B. Jayasena (one of the richest men in the community and a member of the Batgam caste) attended the funeral of the mother of one of his Goigama tenants. Owing to his position as a landlord, B. Jayasena was offered a chair rather than a bench to sit on, but had nevertheless chosen the bench saying 'If I was found fit to be born a Padu [derogatory term for Batgam], then what does it matter if I sit on a bench?' Goigama may wish that all low-caste persons would be as humble as B. Jayasena, but they neglect the probability that the latter's behaviour is motivated not by his belief in the morality of caste etiquette but (ironically) by his political ambitions within a party (the SLFP) which in theory, if not in practice, denounces the caste system.

In the absence of a framework which makes an analytical distinction between the various components of an ideology of stratification, the near universal rejection of caste etiquette and negative evaluation of caste discrimination by low castes may have led to an assumption that low castes reject the caste hierarchy and do not subscribe to a belief in birth status inequalities. The analysis of caste ideology presented here shows, on the contrary, that rejection of the way a particular caste system and the groups within it operate is not mutually exclusive with widespread belief in the presence of 'natural' differences, nor even with an acceptance of the hierarchical ordering of unequal groups. Many low castes in Rangama/Devideniya do not repudiate the superior birth status of the high castes. What they take issue with is the translation of that superiority into patterns of behaviour which entail discrimination and privilege.

THE CONTEMPORARY IDEOLOGY OF CLASS

Just as with caste, the most striking changes in class ideology have taken place in the cultural perception of the lower strata. Even a short visit to the Rangama/Devideniya community will confirm the widespread antagonism harboured by the poorer classes against the rich.

Understanding of the ideology of class assumes particular significance in the light of the implications that such resentment is held to carry for revolutionary change on the one hand, or democratic stability on the other. Those who feel that the resentment of the contemporary rural poor against the landed classes is a prelude to the organization of peasant resistance do not just have to look to communist China as their example. In recent decades, what has been seen as the emergence of class consciousness amongst the landless and land-poor agricultural labourers in parts of South India, is held to have occasioned the organization of unions, political activity and violent disputes with the upper classes.[4]

Outside of careful analysis of the nature of local ideology, it would be easy to extrapolate from the South Indian evidence and succumb to the idea that Sinhalese peasants would readily participate in insurrectionary activity. The analysis presented here, however, reveals a complexity of attitude that makes it quite mistaken to interpret the antagonism of the Sinhalese peasantry as a desire for a classless society. Not only, as stressed in Chapter 7, is the distinction between the ideology of class and 'class consciousness' quite fundamental, but within the former the diverse nature of belief systems in Rangama/Devideniya makes the notion of an undifferentiated and 'radical' attitude towards class cleavages nothing less than fanciful.

Subjective Definition

Even at the turn of the century the inhabitants of Rangama/Devideniya had a well-defined awareness of the nature of material inequality. Wealth (*dhanaya*) was unambiguously associated with paddy-land ownership. Today, however, the cultural preference for paddy land is not as strong nor as exclusive as it was in the baseline period, although it is still considered highly prestigious to own sufficient paddy land to meet household requirements. Contemporary inhabitants of Rangama/Devideniya set great store by the commercial value of high land, and recognize possession of money (as long as it is accompanied by land ownership) as an important constituent of wealth. Though considerably different in content, this contemporary definition is just as clear cut and as uniform throughout the community as was the definition of material inequality in terms of paddy land in the baseline period.

Perception of Hierarchy

The change in the nature of the subjective definition has also brought about a change in the way people perceive the ranking of classes within the community. No longer is the landlord–tenant relationship seen to encompass the relationship between classes. And no longer is the class hierarchy seen in terms of the land tenure and productive processes of paddy cultivation.

Contemporary perception of class hierarchy defines itself against a clear cut notion of a highest stratum of rich people/land-owners/moneyed men (*dhanapatiyo/idam himiyo/salli kārayo*). The position of everyone else in the hierarchy of material inequality is seen in relation to this upper stratum. If one does not belong to the select group of 'rich' people then one is first and foremost 'non-rich', only secondarily comfortably off, poor or destitute as the case may be.

This perception of the critical dividing line of the class hierarchy is shared throughout the community, but the degree to which it is seen as significant in the operation of village life is not. As in the perception of caste hierarchy, in the perception of class hierarchy also it is the Goigama view that diverges most markedly from the behavioural reality. Goigama conviction of the decline of caste is matched by a conviction of the pre-eminence of class inequalities in their society. The following statements reflect the widespread belief among the Goigama that material inequalities are increasingly overriding those of caste as the basis of respect and prestige:

Young woman (middle farmer class):
People who deserve respect don't receive it any more;
with wealth one inherits the highest position in society.

Rangama monk:
There is no meaning to aristocratic birth if one is poor.
Those who have wealth don't need caste. Today Nuwarapakse Mudalali has become a Walawwe man.

Middle-aged man (poor class):
Low-caste status can be erased by money.

Scion of a Walawwe (very-poor class):
Today's birth status is wealth.

There is thus a certain irony in the fact that the group of people most obsessed by material inequality, and who perceive their relative deprivation most keenly, could in many ways be described as the most conservative group in the community.

Evaluation of the Hierarchical System

Contrary to what the antagonism and resentment which characterizes inter-class relations might suggest, the hierarchical system in which certain groups are economically better off than others is considered legitimate by the vast majority of people in contemporary Rangama/Devideniya.

Villagers do not expect everyone to be equally well off and do not wish for a classless society in which the scarce land is distributed equally among all the inhabitants. The 'non-rich' may be envious of the 'rich' but do not question the legitimacy of 'rich' people possessing more than they do. Land is highly valued by all and the inalienability of private property is a notion strongly held by the majority of people, rich and poor alike. For example, except for those tenants who gained security of tenure over substantial extents of paddy land, the Paddy Lands Act is looked upon with disfavour primarily because it contradicts the proprietarian view that the owner of a plot of land should have control over it. People refer to the process of the Act taking effect on fields as 'fields being captured' (*kumburu ahuvunā*). Most tenants feel that the landlord's right to half the crop is fair as long as he does not try to evict them. For instance, M.R. Podiappuhami, who belongs to the 'poor' class, took his legal ¾ share for a few years after his landlord tried unsuccessfully to evict him. Once he was confident that the landlord would not attempt to evict him again, however, he reverted to the traditional half share.

The class system *per se*, as opposed to its operation, is considered unjust by only a very small number of people in this community. Included among this number are a few destitute people who are of the opinion that the present class structure does not allow for class mobility, and that they are therefore condemned to a life of poverty. These people, however, cannot be said to possess 'class consciousness'. Their attitude is more akin to the philosophy of liberal democracy – the stress is on the need for greater equality of opportunity – than to that of the socialist ideal of equality of material possession. 'Class consciousness' does exist but is restricted to a tiny minority of educated youth who espouse radical land reform and claim they would like to transform their society to one more akin to Russia or China: countries where, they believe, everyone is equal.

Marxist parties in Sri Lanka have, over the years, had to face the fact that such radical ideologies hold little fascination for the majority of rural Sinhalese. In the 1977 general election the Marxist parties suffered a resounding defeat all over the island, and in the Naranhena electorate the Trotskyist Lanka Sama Samaja Party candidate obtained only just over 1 per cent of the vote.

It is not just acceptance of the legitimacy of material inequality which has contributed to the failure of Marxist parties to capture the Rangama/Devideniya people's vote. Equally significant is the widespread conviction among the non-Goigama that material inequalities have become far less pervasive in recent decades, and the near universal belief (Goigama included) that class mobility is a very real possibility. Villagers attribute the increasing prosperity of the indigent to estate employment and free education, and are quick to point out the humble beginnings of many of today's 'rich' people.

Evaluation of the System's Operation

The widespread inter-class resentment and antagonism in contemporary Rangama/Devideniya has therefore little to do with a negative evaluation of material inequality itself. Rather it derives from a dissatisfaction with the actions of particular groups within the contemporary class hierarchy.

The principal criticisms levelled against the 'rich' are that they are selfish, miserly and indifferent to the welfare of the indigent. The perceived 'stinginess' of the 'rich' (held to be so extreme that they do not even spend on themselves) prompts the 'non-rich' to compare the former's wealth to a moon shining in a forest – there is no illumination and no one benefits from it.

The 'rich' are also disliked for what is seen to be their arrogance and lack of sympathy towards those less well off than themselves. Poor people are reluctant to ask for help because of the belief that the 'rich' would publicize their own largesse and call attention to the dependence of their supplicants.

The fact that the antagonism towards the 'rich' is ubiquitous and strident does not mean that negative evaluation of the way the class system operates is a prerogative of the 'non-rich'. The antagonism of the 'rich' is not so evident (they are usually more careful in their pronouncements on the subject) but is felt with equal conviction.

The resentment of the 'rich' is directed not at 'middle farmers' but at the two lowest classes. At first it may appear that the 'rich' resent the indigent because they feel pressured (against their will) to 'sacrifice' some of their wealth for the benefit of the poorer classes. Indeed 'rich' people often complain that poor people expect too much of them, and that it is unreasonable for the few 'rich' people in the community to be vilified for their failure to make lavish contributions to every local enterprise and festival.

On closer examination, however, it becomes evident that a more basic reason for the antagonism of the 'rich' lies in the fact that they can no longer count on the subservience of the indigent as a prerogative of economic superiority. Large landlords regret the way that customary forms of honouring the landlord are falling into disuse; they look with nostalgia on the time when poor people would carry sacks of grain for them as a gesture of 'friendship', not in expectation of payment. What is seen to be missing is that aspect of inter-class relations regarded as fundamental to the proper operation of the class system – the idea of 'good will'. This implies a willingness on the part of the indigent to be at the beck and call of the 'rich', just as it implies a readiness on the part of the 'rich' to offer help in times of crisis or emergency. So, in many ways, the 'rich' would probably like to see more, not less, supplication by way of confirmation of the 'good will' system. What they find now, and what they most resent, is that independent attitude of mind on the part of poor people which expects the 'rich' to contribute more to community affairs (there are increasingly few occasions when purely personal requests are made), without a corresponding willingness to pay the price for such largesse. 'Their [poor people's] arrogance prevents them from working for us or asking for anything – they'd rather do without than ask for help'.

Examination of class ideology as a monolithic entity is likely to lead, as in the case of caste ideology, to an erroneous interpretation of the place of hierarchy in the Rangama/Devideniya people's cultural system. The analysis carried out in this section makes clear that the pervasiveness of class antagonism in this community is the result of the mutual dissatisfaction on the part of the 'rich' and the indigent with regard to the other's behaviour. It is the result of a rejection of the system's 'operation', not of the class hierarchy itself. It does not therefore signify the rise of class consciousness among the rural poor. Indeed, as comparison with the villagers' evaluation of the caste and power (see below) hierarchies makes evident, material inequalities are felt to be illegitimate by fewer people than either those of birth status or power. Marxist parties may have been unsuccessful in rural areas in the past because the rural poor believed karma to be the cause of their poverty. But attenuated adherence to karma has not increased the appeal of the Marxist doctrine. Expropriation of land and communal ownership are ideas that hold little attraction to people who value private ownership of land, and who feel that education, enterprise and effort can be rewarded with wealth.

THE CONTEMPORARY IDEOLOGY OF POWER

Studies examining the changing perceptions of hierarchy in rural South Asia have emphasized the rejection of the caste hierarchy by the lower castes[5] and the rise of a new class consciousness among the lower classes.[6] Analysis of the contemporary ideology of stratification in the Rangama/Devideniya community affords a rather different picture of people's attitudes towards social inequality. As has been seen in this chapter, the hierarchies of caste and class are accepted or even approved of by the majority of people in this community. Widespread rejection of hierarchy does occur, but it is not with regard to material inequality or birth status. Rather it is in reference to a dimension of inequality which people no longer perceive to be operative in their society – power.

Subjective Definition

Unlike that of caste and class, the subjective definition of power has remained virtually unchanged since the baseline period. Although there is less emphasis on office as a basis of power, the majority of people still believe that if power is to be found it must be a derivative of high-caste status and wealth. Moreover, just as it did to their predecessors at the turn of the century, for contemporary villagers also power implies the ability to command and have one's commands obeyed. Power holders are thought of as leaders who are respected and admired by the powerless, and who have the ability to rally a group of followers to get something done.

Perception of Hierarchy

A commonly held opinion in the Rangama/Devideniya community is that of the three types of social inequality the most drastic change has taken place in the sphere of power. In this the villagers' perceptions correspond with the realm of social action where, as has been shown in preceding chapters, the power hierarchy has undergone more fundamental change than either that of caste or class. The correspondence between idea and action, however, ends there. For the villagers' perception of the contemporary power hierarchy bears little resemblance to, and indeed flatly contradicts, the social structure of power in this community.

Only the Rangama monk and Siyathu recognize the presence of power in the contemporary community. But although they are not unaware of their ability to influence local affairs, even they do not describe themselves as power holders. Nor do either of them attribute their influence in the community directly to the MP's backing and support. Characteristically, Siyathu attributes the source of his influence to his reputation as a staunch UNP supporter, and the monk makes reference to his eloquence, his service to the community and his religious authority.

Despite the fact that the monk and Siyathu (and to a lesser extent the Grama Sevaka) are able to influence the actions of others and bring about an intended state of affairs, the majority of villagers are convinced that they live in a society that is egalitarian with regard to power. They insist that the ability of one person to impose his will on another is a phenomenon of the past and that no individual in the contemporary community could be described as power holder. Their own explanation of the demise of power holders invariably makes reference to the fact that wealth no longer entails the ability to influence others:

People are developed enough these days not to accept being dominated by a wealthy man.

Today people are not frightened of another's wealth – a rich man cannot order around even the poorest man today.

Today the country has improved. Even the poor have money. If you have enough to eat and drink you need not be subordinate to anyone else, however much he has.

Even the Goigama who attach a high degree of significance to wealth, and see it as being increasingly more effective than birth status in gaining respect and prestige, share the view that wealth is no longer a basis of power. Thus though villagers think of wealth as a necessary condition for power, they do not see this functional relationship operative within their own community.

The complex interaction between idea and action which accounts for the near universal conviction that power is absent in the contemporary community will be analysed in the next chapter. It will be seen that this perception of power, which diverges radically from the behavioural reality is largely the product of the continuation and stability of the subjective definition of power.

Evaluation of the Hierarchical System

Given that the people of Rangama/Devideniya do not perceive their society to be hierarchically structured with respect to power, the evaluative component of the ideology of power revolves around attitudes towards the presence or absence of a power hierarchy, not towards its operation.

With the exception of the 'rich', who regret their declining ability to dictate to, and receive the subservience of, the indigent, there is universal approbation of the perceived absence of a power hierarchy in this community. The majority of people claim that the society in which they live is superior to that of their forebears because no individual has to bow and scrape before another and no one is subservient (*yaṭat*) to anyone else.

It is interesting to note that the widespread negative evaluation of a hierarchical system in which some people are subordinated to others, has resulted in the increased prominence of a belief in the indignity of hired labour.

Labour in and of itself is not devalued. Many people, for instance, gain pleasure in working on their own land, particularly in their paddy fields. The same applies to *attam* labour, which implies control over some land. Labouring on another's land is devalued not on account of toiling but because it implies a degree of subservience. Because of the increased control that tenants have acquired as a result of the Paddy Lands Act, working on another person's paddy land as a tenant is considered to be qualitatively different from labouring on another person's high land. It is the latter and not the former which is degrading.

The concept that labouring on another's land is demeaning is not new in the system of meaning of the Sinhalese. What is new is that an attitude previously restricted to the ideational system of the upper strata is now internalized by everyone in the community. The attitude of the rural poor today is 'Why should we demean ourselves by labouring? We'll manage with what we have'.

The comprehensiveness of the negative evaluation of the power hierarchy contrasts with the Rangama/Devideniya people's evaluation of the other hierarchies of social inequality. Only a small minority of radical youth and destitute people feel the class hierarchy is unjust. And although many of the Batgam feel the same way about the caste hierarchy, they are well outnumbered by those who accept as legitimate the presence in their society of a hierarchy of birth status.

There are two main reasons for the widespread rejection of the idea of a power hierarchy – one internal to the community, the other external. The internal factor is related to the differential flexibility of the various hierarchical systems. For instance, the near universal acceptance of the class hierarchy is largely a consequence of a belief in the possibility of class mobility.

People are unlikely to perceive as illegitimate the possession of a resource which they themselves value and feel is attainable. In contrast, however much people may value the possession of power, achievement of it is far more remote than the possibility of 'getting rich'. Change of caste status is of course even more unattainable than power. But unlike the power hierarchy, a considerable number of people, including many low castes (e.g. Paṭṭi, Gallat, Vahumpura) are well placed enough within the hierarchy to contemplate its existence with approval or at least equanimity.

The external factor is related to the different emphasis that national ideology has placed on inequalities of power on the one hand, and caste and class on the other. Post-independence national governments have freely and frequently denounced domination and subservience, and in many ways applied this aspect of national ideology at the local level. For example, all national governments have tried to promote popular participation in local-level institutions and to encourage the democratic election of office bearers in such institutions.

In contrast, national attitudes and action towards the ideal of a caste-free or classless society have been, at best, ambiguous. It is true that compared to the pre-independence colonial government, national governments, both UNP and SLFP, have been more responsive to the disadvantaged groups in rural areas. Welfare policies and redistributive legislation have, as shown in Chapter 10, improved the economic position of the rural poor. Yet it is only the 'rich' and the Goigama in Rangama/Devideniya who would go so far as to claim that post-independence years have witnessed a 'social revolution' in the spheres of birth status and wealth. UNP governments have, in fact, been so temperate in their denunciation of class and caste, that the party was, and still is, perceived by large sections of the rural populace as the party of the aristocracy and the rich. And whilst Bandaranaike's 'sympathy' for the lower strata is recognized, most villagers do not consider SLFP achievements in the direction of establishing a caste-free and classless Sri Lanka to have been spectacular. They are not unaware, for instance, that the governing elite of the SLFP, no less than that of the UNP, has largely been dominated by a closely-related group of Goigama. Moreover, it is clear to everyone in Rangama/Devideniya that the SLFP land reforms, although beneficial to the poor, were hardly radical. They only resulted in the confiscation of land of a very small minority of large landowners and did not affect a redistribution of land *within* the local community. The basic conservatism of the SLFP is reflected in the fact that the half-hearted land reform was itself a response to an attempt to overthrow the SLFP government by an insurgent movement in large part motivated by the rising but unfulfilled expectation of certain low-caste and poor youths.

It is not difficult to see why national political parties have been less than whole-hearted in their attempts to eradicate caste and class inequalities. Quite apart from the desire of leading politicians to protect their own personal privileges, it is quite simply politically expedient to avoid alienating large and middle-sized landowners on the one hand, and high-caste individuals on the other. Goigama are, after all, numerically preponderant among the Sinhalese. By contrast, not only is the power elite in rural areas numerically smaller than either the landowners or the high castes, but power is a less easily identifiable attribute than either wealth or birth status. To assert that all citizens should have equal rights does not single out a readily identifiable group whose privileges will be withdrawn in order to achieve this end. Thus the more comprehensive rejection of the power hierarchy by the inhabitants of Rangama/Devideniya may be seen, in part at least, as a reflection of an egalitarian and democratic national ideology which has been, and is, more consistent and unambiguous about the merits of a society in which no individual is subservient to another than about the merits of a caste-free or classless society.

13 Conclusion

In order to understand the phenomenon of stratification, this study has developed and employed a theoretical framework which makes analytical distinctions between various aspects of social reality – between the social and cultural realms; the hierarchies of class, status and power; and the descriptive and evaluative components of ideology.

During the period under investigation interaction between the social and cultural realms of stratification in the Rangama/Devideniya community has taken place in two principal ways. Examination of these patterns of interaction shows that there is no justification for treating behaviour or ideology as a fundamental, causally prior, form of social reality

The first and most straightforward pattern of interaction is that of direct influence of one realm upon the other – idea upon action or action upon idea. One example would be the way in which changes have taken place in people's 'subjective definition' of class since the baseline period. This can be seen as the direct result of changes in the agrarian social structure.

Social Action		Ideology
Paddy Lands Act reduces Landlord's power over tenant		Reduced cultural value of paddy land; material inequality is no longer only perceived in terms of differential ownership of paddy land
+	$\longrightarrow$	
Rise in value of, and better marketing outlets for, high-land crops		

In the same way changes in ideology have had their influence upon social action. In contemporary Rangama/Devideniya, for example, the reluctance of even the poorest villagers to work on a 'rich' man's land, despite the possibility of material gain, can be traced directly to the influence of ideology. Certain men who have no choice but to work as casual labourers themselves, encourage those of their sons with secondary-school education to be idle at home. These sons will wait indefinitely for the chance of prestigious employment, rather than accept work as labourers. This contemporary reluctance to work on 'rich' men's land stems from cultural influences – the negative evaluation of subservience and the ideology of the indignity of hired labour. As a result of these cultural influences certain kinds of labour are more stigmatized than others. For example, one common agricultural activity – the climbing of trees to harvest fruit – is now regarded as the ultimate symbol of subservience. Until recently poorer people were quite ready to perform this type of work for payment in kind (e.g. one coconut for every tree climbed). Today the wealthy in Rangama/Devideniya are increasingly hard put to find anyone willing to harvest their fruit trees. Many poor people would feel insulted even by the request to do so.

The direct influence of idea upon action and vice versa is not the only way in which the social and cultural realms interact. The interdependence of idea and action also occurs in a more complex manner – namely where a component of ideology and an aspect of behaviour act in combination to influence another type of action or idea. This second more complex pattern of interaction between action and idea, makes comprehensible the behaviour of tenants in response to the Paddy Lands Act, a response which at first glance appears to be contradictory. Tenants are eager to obtain security of tenure and resist eviction. Those who have achieved security have ceased performing a myriad of customary extra-cultivation duties. Moreover, symbolic acts of deference to landlords are gradually falling into disuse. Yet these same tenants continue to give the landlord half the crop although the Act legally entitles them to a larger share. The tenants' responses to the Act become comprehensible when attention is paid to the degree to which different provisions of the Act are compatible with local ideology.

The Paddy Lands Act of 1958 thus provides an interesting example of the way in which external legislation interacts with local ideology to influence local social action. Seen in reference to

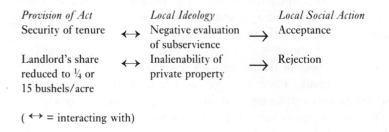

Provision of Act		Local Ideology		Local Social Action
Security of tenure	↔	Negative evaluation of subservience	→	Acceptance
Landlord's share reduced to ¼ or 15 bushels/acre	↔	Inalienability of private property	→	Rejection

(↔ = interacting with)

the disapprobation of power and near universal perception of the legitimacy of material inequality, the differential responses of the Rangama/Devideniya tenants are easily understandable.

Aspects of social action and ideology interacting with one another influence not only the sphere of behaviour (as above) but also that of cultural perception. Examination of the way in which this type of interaction influences ideology explains some of the striking instances where lack of correspondence prevails between behavioural reality and cultural perceptions in contemporary Rangama/Devideniya.

The close correspondence or 'fit' that existed in the baseline period between the power structure and people's perception of it, has been replaced in the contemporary period by a comprehensive divergence between idea and action. The widespread belief in the reality of a society egalitarian with respect to power, contrasts with the presence of a small, but forceful, power elite. Here the lack of 'fit' between idea and action is common to almost all members of the community. By contrast, in the dimensions of caste and class, the divergence between perception and behaviour is primarily restricted to a single group – the Goigama. Remarkably, the Goigama of Rangama, the most snobbish and exclusive people in the manner of their behaviour, are at the same time convinced at the ideational level that birth-status inequalities are being superseded by those of wealth.

The lack of correspondence between these contemporary 'perceptions of hierarchy' and the behavioural reality may be seen as the result of a stability of 'subjective definitions' interacting with changing aspects of social structure.

It is interesting to note that Goigama perceptions of the way

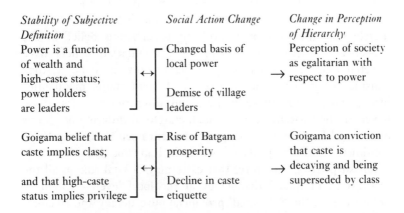

Stability of Subjective Definition	Social Action Change	Change in Perception of Hierarchy
Power is a function of wealth and high-caste status; power holders are leaders	Changed basis of local power / Demise of village leaders	Perception of society as egalitarian with respect to power
Goigama belief that caste implies class; and that high-caste status implies privilege	Rise of Batgam prosperity / Decline in caste etiquette	Goigama conviction that caste is decaying and being superseded by class

their society is changing bear striking similarity to the 'class replacing caste' interpretation of social change put forward by many South Asianists.[1] Indeed the above analysis of Goigama perceptions helps reveal some of the biases present in these interpretations. In this regard one might point not only to the assumption that 'traditional' South Asian society was a primarily caste-based society in which wealth was a manifestation of caste status, but also to the presupposition that inter-caste interaction necessarily involves discrimination/privilege. When such assumptions are present it is easy to interpret such facts as the breakdown in hereditary relations between castes, the refusal of low castes to carry out certain tasks, the divergence of caste and class inequalities, and rising low-caste wealth, as evidence of the attenuation of caste and the corresponding pre-eminence of class. Thus, perhaps ironically, the preoccupation with caste often leads to interpretations of change which see the caste hierarchy undergoing decay in modern South Asia.

The framework employed in this study enables us to discern a quite different and more complex picture of socio-cultural change. That picture shows that in contemporary Rangama/Devideniya caste still constitutes a significant means for structuring relations between people. What has changed since the turn of the century is not the salience of caste but its expression in non-conventional behaviour patterns – most notably caste segregation. The increasing land control by low castes in this community, far from leading to a decline of caste, has in fact promoted caste segregation and exacerbated hostility between the Batgam and Goigama.

The continuing salience of caste at the behavioural level is matched at the ideational level by a persisting belief in the existence of birth status inequalities. Egalitarian beliefs have affected most people's ideology of caste only in so far as they consider illegitimate the translation of birth status inequalities into privileges for those higher, and discrimination for those lower, in the caste hierarchy. The hierarchical ordering of groups of unequal birth status – the caste system itself – is accepted as legitimate by the majority of people in Rangama/Devideniya. It is not surprising, therefore, that caste plays a vital role in all the institutions of liberal democracy at the local level – voluntary organizations, the 'reformed' provincial bureaucracy and electoral politics.

If the resilience of caste in the Kandyan highlands in the democratic environment of the late twentieth century is depressing to the liberal, the failure of the Sinhalese peasantry to engage in insurrectionary activity must be equally frustrating for the Marxist. The sharp disparities in land control which result in widespread poverty, the callous self-interest of the landed elite and the antagonism of the rural poor towards the former should, in simple theory, make contemporary rural Sri Lanka a fertile ground for peasant insurrection.

But Sinhalese peasants do not revolt. In 1971 the Kegalle district was the scene of fierce fighting between rebels and government forces. But the insurgency was hardly a peasant revolt.[2] It was mounted by a minority of educated youths, and had little popular support in the villages. In Rangama/Devideniya only eleven youths were associated with the movement and even they could hardly be described as 'committed'. Their involvement was limited to attendance at a few preliminary 'lectures' and ceased well before the actual fighting. These youths found unacceptable the codes of conduct imposed upon participants, especially that enjoining abstinence from alcohol and tobacco. In addition the fact that ten of the eleven were members of the Batgam caste suggests that their interest in the movement stemmed more from low-caste resentment than poverty.

The failure of the Sinhalese peasantry to organize, let alone revolt has been regarded by certain scholars as a result of the nature of the agrarian social structure: the close relationship between landlord and tenant, and the gradualism of the agrarian spectrum which acts to limit polarization.[3] But the analysis of class in this study has shown that the relationship between the landed elite and the rural poor is distant and strained, and that there *is* a sharp distinction in cultural perceptions between the 'rich' and the 'non-rich'.

The Marxist use of the concept of mystification to explain why 'exploited' peasants do not revolt is equally unhelpful in understanding the behaviour of peasants in the Rangama/Devideniya community. As this study's analysis of class ideology has shown, it is simply inaccurate to describe the lower classes in Rangama/Devideniya as victims of mystification: that they are in some sense unaware of the real conditions of their existence. Though the indigent in this community do accept as legitimate the 'hierarchy' of material inequality, their ideas about the 'operation' of the system are in direct opposition to those of the 'rich'. The poor feel the meanness of the 'rich' is unjust, and reject the notion which the 'rich' uphold that economic inferiority should be accompanied by subservience.

Several scholars who accept that peasants *do* have a clear awareness of economic injustice claim that they are nevertheless unwilling to challenge the system because of fear of repression and their economic dependence on the landed elite.[4] But again this does not explain why the rural poor in Sri Lanka have consistently failed to support Marxist parties in parliamentary elections – an action which has no short-term or long-term adverse consequences for the voters, and is all but costless. Like the Marxists such scholars make the mistake of assuming that peasant awareness of deprivation automatically occasions the impulse to change the system of material inequality. When peasant insurrection does not occur, only one of two explanations is then possible: either peasants are not in fact aware of their deprivation or they refrain from challenging the system because the costs of political participation are too high.[5]

As we have seen these factors do not apply in the case of Rangama/Devideniya, even if they may obtain to a greater or lesser degree in various other societies. The important point that is seldom recognized is that acceptance on the part of peasants that the hierarchy of material inequality in their society is legitimate tends to act as a powerful disincentive to challenging the established social order. The examination of class ideology in this study shows that resentment and antagonism of the rural poor towards the landed elite should not be interpreted as class consciousness. In Rangama/Devideniya it reflects a rejection of the way groups within the class hierarchy act – not the class hierarchy itself. The response of the tenants to the Paddy Lands Act shows that in situations where the presence of material inequality is accepted as legitimate, even the prospect of immediate material gain is not sufficient to secure the support of rural people. Thus whilst a Migdal-type analysis might suggest that the electoral failure of Marxist parties in Sri Lanka lies in the fact that they do not offer the rural poor tangible material incentives,[6] I argue that the Marxists' lack of success lies precisely in what they do offer. Marxist parties have consistently failed to capture the vote of the rural poor in Sri Lanka because they offer to change a system which the poorer classes among the peasantry do not want changed.

My examination of stratification in the Rangama/Devideniya community from 1885 to the present day thus shows that the democratic, socialist ideologies of the national level have not affected the local level in a simple or uniform manner. Democratic ideologies have indisputably undermined the karmic theory of causation which explained and justified inequality in the past. But although hierarchical values have been challenged in Rangama/Devideniya, there have been no fundamental changes in the way the people evaluate the hierarchical systems of caste and class. My analysis shows that the rejection of discrimination by lower castes, and the expectation by lower classes that they should receive more material help from the landed elite – a phenomenon often observed in contemporary rural South Asia – is not mutually exclusive with a belief in, and acceptance of, birth status and material inequalities. In other words, egalitarian ideologies may affect people's evaluation of the way in which different groups within a hierarchy act towards each other, whilst leaving intact their evaluation of the hierarchical system itself.

Radical change in this South Asian community has occurred not in the caste and class hierarchies but in the hierarchy of power.

The transition from British colonial rule to independence, and the development of democracy and political party competition, have fundamentally altered the structure of local-level power. Community power structures are now integrally related to the 'MP's raj' at the regional level; wealth and caste – the pre-independence bases of power – have been superseded by political backing; a new power elite has risen to prominence which, for the first time in the history of rural communities, has displaced the village headman as a superordinate power holder. Radical changes in local-level power are not limited, however, to the realm of social structure. In contrast to the continuities that exist in local caste and class ideologies, there has been a comprehensive rejection of hierarchy in the dimension of power. With the exception of the 'rich', there is universal condemnation of domination and subservience.

The socio-cultural changes analysed in this book do not auger well for the development of the rural community. The presence of egalitarian values in the cultural conceptions of the Rangama/Devideniya people has had an adverse effect on the social harmony that existed in the past – co-operation and goodwill have been replaced by caste segregation and class antagonism. Contemporary Sinhalese communities would benefit from the presence of leaders capable of overcoming disunity and mobilizing local activity. But the development of democracy in Sri Lanka has ensured that leadership is, and will continue to be, an unavailable commodity in Sinhalese villages. On the one hand the political source of their power disqualifies the rural power elite from assuming the role of leaders. On the other hand democratic ideologies and the widespread disapprobation of subservience have created an inhospitable environment for followers. Sinhalese villages disunited by caste, class and political party allegiances, now, more than ever before, require leaders. But leaders and their followers have disappeared entirely from rural Sri Lanka.

Epilogue

During the past decade Sri Lanka has been torn by violent conflict. Tamil separatists fighting for an independent state in the north and east, the anti-UNP Sinhala Janatha Vimukthi Peramuna and many other armed groups have contributed to the violence and terror in the island.

Despite the political violence, intimidation and confusion the past four years have witnessed a spate of elections in Sri Lanka. As a military solution began to look increasingly unlikely, the ruling UNP turned to political initiatives to end the ethnic conflict. Provincial council elections were held throughout the island in 1988 as a means of achieving devolution of power. The SLFP boycotted these elections on the grounds that the provincial council system would weaken the unitary state and lead ultimately to the division of the country. The UNP success in the provincial council elections in the Sinhala-speaking areas of the island was repeated in the Pradeshiya Sabha (divisional Council) elections held in 1991. More importantly, UNP victories in the presidential election (1988) and the general election (1989) have resulted in almost 15 years of unbroken UNP rule.

The establishment of provincial councils has been promoted as a radical restructuring of planning, administration and representation in rural areas. Provincial councils are to obtain wide-ranging powers, among them the responsibility for housing, social services, agriculture, health, education and the formulation and implementation of development projects. The sweeping changes envisaged under the new system represent a clear challenge to the control the rural MP has hitherto exercised over his constituency, a challenge exacerbated by the introduction of proportional representation in elections. Under proportional representation the MP's traditional link with his constituency would in principle no longer obtain, since the MP's 'seat' is no longer the relevant electoral unit. Voting at general elections is now carried out on a district basis, transforming each district into an electorate. Instead of an MP representing a single constituency, under the new electoral system, districts have become multi-member electorates.

To date, however, provincial councils and proportional representation have not led to any real devolution of power or a fundamental change in the legislator-constituent relationship.[1] As far as rural people are concerned changes legislated at the national level have made virtually no impact. On a recent visit to Rangama, a young man summed up the feeling expressed by many others when he told me – 'the only things that have changed are the names of government institutions and the titles of government officials'.

Two reasons can be adduced for the continuity evident in rural politics. The first lies in the fact that despite proportional representation the concept of the MP's 'seat' remains significant for political parties, MPs and voters. Political parties have not adapted their structure or organization to coincide with the logic of proportional representation. Although the district rather than the single member constituency is now the relevant electoral unit, neither the UNP nor the SLFP has developed the district-level party organization as a significant unit of party structure. Instead, the constituency-level party organization continues to be the pivot of party structure. Prior to an election it constitutes the locus of a potential MP's campaign organization, since his principal party workers are all members of it. Although MPs did canvass for votes outside their constituency in the 1989 general election, the greatest number of votes an MP received was naturally from his local area. This explains the post-election predilection for an MP to nurture this block of votes and give priority to the needs of people from his 'seat'.

It is hardly surprising therefore that although people within any given district are now represented by several MPs, the concept 'our MP' has not lost its salience. Indeed in 'seats' where the local candidate failed to get elected as a district MP in 1989, almost everyone agrees that not having 'their own' MP is a serious disadvantage. Naranhena is one such area, and people here complain that since an MP is primarily concerned with is own 'seat', their requests to MPs from other seats have little chance of success. They also point out that Naranhena has not received any benefits from the decentralized budget allocated to district MPs;

and they are concerned that without a local MP there is now no one with an interest in obtaining central government benefits such as school laboratories, factories and so on for their area.[2]

The second reason for the continuity evident in rural politics lies in the inability of provincial councils to function as alternative sources of power. The ineffectiveness of provincial councils has invited hostile public comment from the time of their inception. Provincial councils are charged with being white elephants, a drain on scarce national finances and with achieving little apart from the generation of 'Pajero culture.'[3] Although some politicians attribute the present ineffectiveness of provincial councils to teething problems, this is unduly optimistic. There are much stronger indications that they will remain the victims of lack of commitment on the part of central government, which continues to constrain their independence. One can point to the small proportion of their budgets over which provincial councils have any real discretionary control, the centre's continuing hold over district and divisional level bureaucrats, and the central appointment of provincial council ministers.

Perhaps of equal concern with regard to the effectiveness of provincial councils is that such central government influence has not been challenged or opposed in any serious way by provincial councillors in the Sinhala-speaking areas of the island. Here, where there was never any demand for provincial councils, the attitude towards the devolution of power is at best lukewarm. Many provincial councillors receiving salaries and pajeros see no reason to rock the boat and insist on more power. In 1991, the much publicized disagreements between MPs and provincial councillors focused not on problems of representation or responsibility but rather on what privileges and emoluments were being received from the government. It is therefore unlikely that provincial councils in Sinhala-speaking areas will assume and act upon the powers that have formally been accorded to them.

Rural Sri Lanka has been bequeathed a system where the issues of local government and administration are the common concern of district MPs, provincial councillors, Pradeshiya Sabha members and bureaucrats. But the way in which these different political actors will share responsibility for making local policy remains unresolved. Judging by the present performance of the new local bodies there is every reason to suppose that the historically established patronage structure focused on the MP and his constituency will, with some modifications, survive the creation of provincial councils and continue into the foreseeable future.

Tamara Gunasekera
London 1992

Appendix I: Kandyan Names

Kandyan Sinhalese in the Rangama/Devideniya community use two types of names – formal and informal. The formal or official name consists of a *vāsagama* followed by a personal name. *Vāsagama* literally means village of residence, and in certain parts of the island is associated with a village or hamlet.[1] Often, however, the *vāsagama* name carries associations beyond this restricted meaning. In this community, as in the time of the Kandyan kingdom,[2] it refers not only to village of residence but also to ancestry, house, field, occupation, official status or title. Tambiah and Robinson are therefore mistaken in their claim that when taken beyond its literal meaning a *vāsagama* name refers exclusively to an illustrious ancestor.[3] The claim is probably the result of a Goigama bias in their work. For the majority of low-caste *vāsagama* names in the Rangama/Devideniya community do not refer to ancestry, and when they do the ancestors are not regarded as illustrious in any sense. In the case of Robinson's discussion of *vāsagama* names a further distortion arises because she confuses the *vāsagama* name with a specific form of it – the titled *patabändi* name.

In certain parts of the Kandyan highlands individuals possess another type of formal name – the *gedera* (house) name which establishes connection to an ancestral home. In the Rangama/Devideniya community there is no separate class of *gedera* name. Some *vāsagama* names, however, have a *gedera* referent. These are not associated with an estate and are therefore more akin to the *gedera* names described by Robinson[4] than those described by Tambiah[5]. *Vāsagama* names with a *gedera* reference always include the term *gedera* and are quite distinct from the numerous *vāsagama* names that end in 'lage', despite the fact that *gē* as well as *gedera* means house in Sinhalese. The 'lage' ending (e.g. Mudianselage, Heneyalage, Rallage, etc.) refers not to a house but rather signifies belonging to a particular group and/or descent from a specific ancestor.

The second type of name used in the Rangama/Devideniya community is an informal house-site name. The informal name is a practical necessity since within each caste many individuals have identical formal names. It consists of the name of the land on which an individual's house stands followed by his personal name. The name of the land itself is determined by a salient natural feature, a type of vegetation, a building etc., which characterizes it. For example:

Kande Kade Dingiri Banda (Dingiri Banda of the shop on the hill)
Pera Kotuwe Rankira (Rankira of the guava patch)

In the baseline period household heads who shared a house-site name were close kinsmen and these names were thus probably equivalent to the 'compound group' name described by Robinson.[6] It is also probable that in the past, possession of a common house-site name implied common rights to a specific plot of land. But property and kinship connections among those who share a house-site name are much attenuated today. With the advent of government sponsored village expansion schemes, some contemporary house-site names refer to the name of the land carved up for settlement or even to the extent of land granted for settlement. For example:

Rangama Watte Liyanna (Liyanna of Rangama Estate)
Akkara Thun Kale Vincent (Vincent of three quarter acre)

When villages were newly established house-site names may also have been indicative of caste status. But even in the baseline period house-site names had lost their caste association on account of mobility within the community coupled with in and out migration. Today Bodhipaksage Ariyadasa, a Batgam man, is known informally as Walawwe Watte Ariyadasa (Ariyadasa of the manor garden) because he happens to live on the site on which the famous Devideniya *walawwe* stood.

Appendix II: Some Forms of Inter-Caste Address in the Baseline Period[a]

SPEAKER	ADDRESSEE							
	Walawwe	Goigama	Muslim	Patti	Gallat	Vahumpura	Hēna	Batgam
Walawwe			nāna (M) ācci (F)		galladda (M) nāccirē (F)		hēna māma (M) ridī nända (F)	personal name + ajja (M) (e.g. mutuva – mutuajja)
Goigama	bandāra mahatmaya (M) menike (F) appe (young)		tambi (M) ācci (F)				,,	,,
Muslim	,,	rālahāmi/ nilame (M) menike (F)		appuhāmi (M) etanahāmi (F)			,,	,,
Patti	,,	,,	mudalali (M) ācci (F)				,,	,,
Gallat	,,	,,	,,	bande (M) tikiri unnähē (F)			,,	,,
Vahumpura	,,	,,	,,	,,	bās unnähē/ gurunānse (M) upāsikava (F)		,,	,,
Hēna	,,	,,	,,	,,	,,			,,
Batgam	,,	,,	,,	,,	,,			

a Where the speaker is of superior status (right side of diagonal) and no specific term is present, the personal name was used irrespective of age.

Appendix III: Income/Cost Analysis for 1 Acre of Rubber 1979/80

GROSS INCOME/ACRE/YEAR
Number of days trees are tapped/year	= 230
Average yield/day	= 7 lbs dry sheet rubber
Average price of dry sheet rubber	= Rs 3.40/lb
Gross Income/Year	= *Rs 5474.00*

(i) NET INCOME IF TAPPING TREES ONESELF
Costs/Acre/Year: (landowner taps trees)
(a) Chemicals used on trees	= Rs 53
(b) Weeding land and cleaning trees	= 200
(c) 8 lbs Sodium @ Rs 6/lb	= 48
(d) 6 pints acid @ Rs 7/pint	= 42
(e) Sheet rolling charges	= 84
(f) Drying Charges	= 168
Total Cost	= Rs 595

Net Income (i)	= *Rs 4879.00*

(ii) NET INCOME EMPLOYING RUBBER TAPPER AT FIXED RATE/LB
Costs/Acre/Year: (employing rubber tapper at the rate of .75 cents/lb.)
a, b, c, d, e, f as above	= Rs 595
Wages for rubber tapper	= 1207
Total cost	= 1802

Net Income (ii)	= *Rs 3672.00*

(iii) NET INCOME EMPLOYING RUBBER TAPPER ON A HALF SHARE BASIS
Costs/Acre/Year (employing rubber tapper on a half share basis)
a and b as above	= Rs 253
Half the cost of c, d, e, and f	= 171
Rubber tappers share (i.e. half Gross Income)	= 2737
Total Cost	= 3161

Net Income (iii)	= *Rs 2313.00*

Appendix IV: Income/Cost Analysis for 1 Acre of Paddy 1979/80

Average yield/Acre/Year (i.e. two seasons)	= 120 Bushels
Price/Bushel	= Rs 40
Gross Income/Year	= Rs 4800.00

Cultivation costs/Acre/Year (owner cultivator)	
Buffalo hire	= Rs 500
Food for attam teams	= 300 [1]
Fertilizer	= 480
Seed Paddy	= 120
Pesticide	= 64
Transport	= 56
Winnowing	= 20
Total cost	= 1540
NET INCOME/YEAR FOR AN OWNER CULTIVATOR	= Rs 3260.00

On land cultivated by a tenant costs and benefits are shared in such a way that the landlord receives two thirds of the net income (see Appendix VI).

NET INCOME/YEAR FOR A LANDLORD   = Rs 2173.00

Appendix V: The Kannamāru Tenurial System and its Combination with Taṭṭumāru

By *kannamāru* I here refer to a tenurial system which occurs when there is differential fertility (due to distance from water source, availability of sunlight, etc) in an undivided field owned by share owners. Under the simplest *kannamāru* arrangement co-owners have equal shares of the total field which is informally divided into as many equal parcels as there are share owners. All share owners cultivate simultaneously but change or rotate the parcels each year. Thus, if a field has four co-owners, each cultivates a different parcel for four years before returning to the original parcel.

The complexity of these tenurial systems is exacerbated by the frequent combination of *taṭṭumāru* and *kannamāru* in the same field. For example if two brothers, A and B, inherit equal shares in an undivided field, and the shares are of unequal fertility they will cultivate the field on the *kannamāru* basis changing plots each year. If A has three sons and B has two sons, A's sons will inherit ⅙ share of the field, and B's sons will inherit ¼ share (See Figure 8). After the death of A and B, if each group of sons decides it is not economical to cultivate simultaneously, they will agree to cultivate the two plots on a *taṭṭumāru* arrangement among themselves. Thus each year half the field is cultivated by one of B's sons, while the other half is cultivated by one of A's sons. The next year the plots are rotated in *kannamāru* but another of A's sons and the other of B's sons get usufructory rights. Thus under the two separate *taṭṭumāru* arrangements agreed upon by the two sets of brothers, B's sons get rights to ½ the field every other year, whereas each of A's sons gets rights to ½ the field every three years.

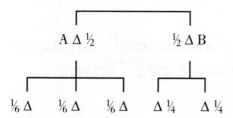

Figure 8 Combination of *taṭṭumāru* and *kannamāru*

Appendix VI: Cost and Income Sharing between Landlord and Tenant: Anda System

(Half an Acre of Paddy for One Season)

Average yield/season/ ½ acre	= 30 Bushels
Price/Bushel	= Rs 40
Gross Income/Season	= Rs 1200

Tenant				*Landlord*
Gross Income		*Costs*		*Gross Income*
Rs 600	125	Buffalo Hire	–	Rs 600
	135	Food for attam teams	–	
	60	Fertilizer	60	
	8	Pesticide	8	
	15	Seed paddy	15	
	10	Winnowing	–	
	7	Transport	7	
	360		90	

NET INCOME [TENANT] = Rs 240
NET INCOME [LANDLORD] = Rs 510

Total Net Income	= Rs 750
Landlord's share of Net Income	= ⅔
Tenant's share of Net Income	= ⅓

Notes

1: Introduction

1 See Chapter 11, pp.187–8; S. Silverman 'Patronage and community – Nation Relationships in Central Italy', *Ethnology*, 1965, vol 4(2), 172–89; A. Blok, *The Mafia of a Sicilian Village, 1860–1960.*

2 The widely-used 'dominant caste' concept was originally developed from within the anthropological literature. M.N. Srinivas, 'The Dominant Caste in Rampura', *American Anthropologist*, 1959, (61), 1–16; A. Mayer, 'The Dominant Caste in a Region of Central India', *Southwestern Journal of Anthropology*, 1958, vol 14, 407–27.

3 As Ishwaran points out, power holders in a community are not necessarily confined to a single caste. Nor is it the case, as the concept implies, that in those situations where power holders do belong to a single caste, all members of that 'dominant' caste are powerful ('Introduction' in K. Ishwaran (ed.), *Change and Continuities in India's Villages*, 9–10).

4 M. Weber, 'Class, Status, Party' in H.H. Gerth and C. Wright Mills (eds), *From Max Weber.*

5 W.G. Runciman, 'Class, Status and Power?' in W.G. Runciman, *Sociology in its Place*, 102–40.

6 D. Schneider, *American Kinship: A Cultural Account.*

7 By ideologies I refer to cultural perceptions with regard to a particular type of inequality. An ideology as used in this study does not imply a sharing of cultural perceptions and ideational features across the whole community. It allows that the ideology of stratification in a particular society contains diversity both with regard to different types of inequality as well as between different groups of people.

8 W.G. Runciman, 'Class, Status and Power?' in W.G. Runciman, *Sociology in its Place*, 111.

9 W.G. Runciman, 'Class, Status and Power?' in W.G. Runciman, *Sociology in its Place*, 108.

10 L. Dumont, *Homo Hierarchicus.*

11 E.R. Leach, 'Introduction: What Should We Mean by Caste?' in E.R. Leach (ed.), *Aspects of Caste in South India, Ceylon and North-West Pakistan*, 1–10; B. Ryan, *Caste in Modern Ceylon*; N. Yalman, *Under the Bo Tree.*

12 F. Barth, 'The System of Social Stratification in Swat, North Pakistan' in E.R. Leach (ed.) *Aspects of Caste in South India, Ceylon and North-West Pakistan*, 113–46; G Berreman, 'Caste in India and the United States', *American Journal of Sociology*, vol 66, 1960, 120–7.

13 A. Beteille, *Studies in Agrarian Social Structure*, 71; J. Mencher, 'A Tamil village; changing socio-economic structure in Madras State', in K. Ishwaran (ed.), *Change and Continuities in India's Villages*, 206.

2: *Research Setting*

1 *Ethnic Distribution of Sri Lankans, 1971*

Ethnic Group	Number (in thousands)	Percentage of population
Sinhalese		
Low Country	5,426	42.8
Kandyan	3,705	29.2
Sub-total	9,131	72.0
Ceylon Tamils (a)	1,424	11.2
Indian Tamils (b)	1,175	9.3
Muslims (c)	899	7.1
Burghers (d)	45	0.4
Others	16	0.1
TOTAL (e)	12,690	100.1

Source: Census of Population, 1971, vol II, Part I, 25.

(a) Descendants of South Indian peoples who migrated to Sri Lanka between the second century B.C. and the ninth century A.D.

(b) Descendants of South Indian labourers brought by the British to work on plantations in the nineteenth century.

(c) Descendants of Arab traders, Indian Muslims and Malays.

(d) Eurasians. The majority are the descendants of Dutch and Portuguese colonial officials.

(e) Discrepancies in totals are due to rounding.

Religious Groups in Sri Lanka, 1971

Religion	Number (in thousands)	Percentage of population
Buddhists	8,537	67.3
Hindus	2,239	17.6
Christians	1,004	7.9
Muslims	902	7.1
Others	8	0.1
TOTAL	12,690	100.0

Source: Census of Population, 1971, vol II, Part I, 27.

2 Portuguese 1505–1658; Dutch 1658–1796; British 1796–1948.

3 Unless otherwise stated, the sources consulted for this section are: C.R. de Silva, *Ceylon Under British Occupation 1795–1833*; L.S. Dewaraja, *The Kandyan Kingdom 1707–1760*; R. Knox, *An Historical Relation of Ceylon.*

4 B. Ryan, *Caste in Modern Ceylon*; R.L. Stirrat, 'Caste conundrums: views of caste in a Sinhalese Catholic fishing village' in D.B. McGilvray (ed.), *Caste Ideology and Interaction*, 8–33.

5 Evers estimates that quite apart from the forests and high lands owned by these religious institutions, as much as 10 per cent of all paddy land in the

region belongs to monasteries, and an even higher percentage to temples. (H.D. Evers, 'Monastic landlordism in Ceylon', *Journal of Asian Studies*, 28(4) August 1969, 688.

6 The concept 'monastic landlordism' was developed by Max Weber (*The Religion of India*, 257). It refers in the Sinhalese situation to the ownership of land by Buddhist monasteries and temples, and to their role as landlords in renting out land in lieu of services.

7 Monastic and temple lands were exempted from the scope of the British ordinance of 1832 which abolished *rajakāriya*. They were, however, included in the provisions of the Paddy Lands Act of 1958, in the hope that this would lead to the abolition of service tenure on such lands. Although successive national government were able to withstand sangha demands that monastic and temple lands be exempted from the Act, this hope has not been realized. Most caste services continue as in the past because of pressure from monks and considerations of religious merit on the part of tenants.

The Land Reform Acts of 1972 did not bring about any significant change in the institution of 'monastic landlordism'. The United Front government of 1972 specifically exempted monastic and temple lands from the purview of the Acts for fear of antagonizing the powerful sangha.

8 Chief monks and temple lords who control and administer the lands owned by monasteries and temples, respectively, belong to the Radala caste.

9 The Kandyan highland region includes the whole of the Kandy and Nuwara Eliya administrative districts and parts of the Kegalle, Matale, Badulla, Moneragala and Ratnapura administrative districts.

10 The word 'Walawwe' will not be italicized when used as a caste name. It is interesting to note that village aristocrats in this community are not known as Radala, but by reference to a term denoting a 'manor house' (Sinhalese: *valavva*). Since the English rendition for the word *valavva* is used in the text – i.e. *walawwe* – I have retained the form of the English rendition in referring to this caste.

11 The boundaries of the community are not co-extensive with the administrative or geographical boundaries of these two villages. Four families who reside in the neighbouring villages of Moragammana and West Galewala are included in what I have called the Rangama/Devideniya community, because their principal source of income is derived from tenancy of paddy land in the Rangama paddy tract. These four households therefore constitute part of the Rangama/Devideniya class hierarchy.

3: *The Baseline Period*

1 As in the time of the Kandyan kingdom, Muslims had a monopoly over trade in these interior highland villages.

2 In the Kegalle district the population of Hatara Korale was three times that of the plantation region of Thun Korale. Yet the amount spent on public works in the latter in 1888 was three times as much as that spent on Hatara Korale. (Diary of the Assistant Government Agent, Kegalle District, June 1899).

3 In the Rangama/Devideniya community a handful of people including the Buddhist monk were literate in Sinhalese. No one was literate in English

and older informants well remember the time when telecommunications were conducted only in English and telegrams had to be taken all the way to Naranhena (two-and-a-half miles away) to be read.

4 Prior to the baseline period Berawila and Natha Kande were principally coffee estates. The coffee industry in Sri Lanka suffered a severe setback with the appearance of a fungal leaf disease in the early 1870s. Over the next fifteen years coffee production declined rapidly and tea replaced coffee as the major plantation crop. Indeed by the turn of the century tea had become so widespread that in the Kegalle district as a whole there were more acres of tea under cultivation than there were of paddy.

5 According to the *sannasa*, Rangama *vihāraya* owned 100 *amunu* (approximately 250 acres) in a number of villages in the vicinity. Certain lands were donated in order to enable the *vihāraya* to receive the services of various caste groups in lieu of land rent. Thus, for example, the *vihāraya* owned land in the nearby village of Telleke (*tel* means oil) and recieived oil from those who cultivated the *viharāya* fields.

6 High Land Register Rangma Vasama, Thumpalata Pattuwa West, Paranakuru Korale, 1897.

7 All the colonial registers cited use the Sinhalese measures – *amunu*, *päl*, *kuruni* or *lās* (10 *kuruni/lās* = 1 *päla*; 4 *päl* = 1 *amuna*). I have therefore converted all land extents into contemporary measures on the basis used in the Kegalle district which is 16 *kuruni/lās* = 1 acre of paddy land; 8 *kuruni/lās* = 1 acre of high land.

8 The term *walawwe* will be in italics when it is used in reference to a manor house.

9 Grain Tax Assessment Register, Kegalle District 1869–1875.

10 It is alleged however that B. Ariyadasa, a very old Batgam man who today lives on the *walawwe* site, is an illegitimate child of Devideniya Nilame and a Batgam woman. B. Ariyadasa himself claims (usually when drunk) that he is an aristocrat by birth and tries to manifest this in his interaction with members of other castes. He addresses the Goigama by terms of equality, and although not welcome to eat inside Goigama houses, prefers, when he visits Rangama, to eat in the courtyard of a Goigama house rather than in a Batgam one.

A single family in the community today can claim kinship to the aristocrats of the Devideniya *walawwe*. H.M. Lokubanda, an old, indigent tenant cultivator, is related to the *walawwe* through his mother, who had the same *vāsagama* name (Chandrasekera Mudianselage) as the owners of the Devideniya *walawwe*.

4: *The Caste Hierarchy in the Baseline Period*

1 H.N.C. Stevenson, 'Status evaluation in the Hindu caste system', *Journal of the Royal Anthropological Institute*, 1954, vol 84, 45–65.

2 M. Marriott, 'Interactional and Attributional Theories of Caste Ranking', *Man in India*, 1959, vol 39, 92–107.

3 Levinson, for instance, uses honorific and dishonorific forms of address as the medium of social exchange through which to rank castes. ('Caste rank and verbal interaction in western Tamilnadu' in D.B. McGilvray (ed.), *Caste*

Ideology and Interaction, 98–203.)

4 High-land registers constitute a more accurate source for locating the resident household heads in a community than paddy-land registers for two reasons:

(1) Most people who invested in land outside their own villages bought paddy land because of the cultural preference for paddy land and the presence of an institutionalized method of tenant cultivation (the *anda* share-cropping system). Thus the number of 'outsiders' listed in paddy-land registers is much higher than in high-land registers.

(2) High-land ownership was much more widespread than paddy-land ownership since even the poorest people could lay claim to at least their house site. Thus high-land registers almost always included all resident household heads.

5 A statement such as, 'In some areas certain of the sub-castes stand practically as caste groups themselves' (B. Ryan, *Caste in Modern Ceylon*, 98) is unfortunately far from uncommon in the literature.

6 Pieris, for example, regards the Nilamakkārayo as a sub-caste division of the Goigama caste but describes the exceptional case of marriage between 'men of the Goigama *caste proper*' and 'women from the Nilamakkaraya sub-caste' as infringements of the 'taboo on *inter-caste* marriages' (emphasis mine; R. Pieris, *Sinhalese Social Organisation,* 177).

7 'All members of that caste (Goigama) are not equal; there are within it mutually exclusive groups, there are aristocratic ones that will not intermarry with the less aristocratic.' (A.M. Hocart, quoted in R. Pieris, *Sinhalese Social Organisation,* 171).

'The (Goigama) caste is today divided into a number of endogamous subgroups having distinctive status positions.' (B. Ryan, *Caste in Modern Ceylon*, 97).

8 For a detailed discussion of Kandyan names with special reference to the forms employed in the Rangama/Devideniya community, see Appendix I.

9 In the seventeenth century the title Mudianse was bestowed by the Kandyan king for conspicuous military exploits. The title was conferred in a ceremony akin to knighting when the king tied (*bända*) a silken strap (*pata*) round the head of the recipient. Hence *patabändi* names.

10 B. Ryan, *Caste in Modern Ceylon*, 147.

11 The Patti are a group of people usually described in the literature as a sub-caste of the Goigama caste. John Davy is an exception and lists them as a separate caste beneath the Goigama (*An Account of the Interior of Ceylon and of its Inhabitants,* 12). Some authors claim that Nilamakkārayo is an alternative caste name for the Patti (J. Davy, *An Account of the Interior of Ceylon,* and R. Pieris, *Sinhalese Social Organisation*) but Ryan asserts that the former are a separate sub-caste of temple servants (B. Ryan, *Caste in Modern Ceylon*, 101, footnote 5).

12 R. Knox, *An Historical Relation of Ceylon*; J. Davy, *An Account of the Interior of Ceylon.*

13 B. Ryan, *Caste in Modern Ceylon*, 94 and 201.

14 For as long as people in this community can remember, a small number of Oli families have lived in the neighbouring village of Galewala.

15 Dura is a suffix attached to several of the lower Kandyan castes – e.g. Panna Dura, Batgam Dura, Valli Dura, etc. No definite statements, however, can be made with regard to which castes bear this suffix, or what they have in common. For instance, whilst A.A. Perera (*Sinhalese Folk Lore Notes*) lists the Vahumpura as a Dura caste (Kande Duraya), few other observers include it in this category. Disagreement is also present regarding what the term Dura means. Gilbert (*Ceylon Historical Journal*, 1952, vol 2, 328) claims that it is employed for castes that performed palanquin bearing duties. Ryan, on the other hand, states that 'durayi' was originally a term given to headmen of certain low castes and that it subsequently became an honorific applied ot all members of those castes (*Caste in Modern Ceylon*, 91). Whatever the original reason, in contemporary times the appellation Dura is not indicative of any shared characteristics.

16 R. Pieris, *Sinhalese Social Organisation*, 56; 105–6.

17 R. Pieris, *Sinhalese Social Organisation*, 190.

18 The vocative and the second person singular pronoun are not, however, mutually exclusive. The vocative was occasionally used in the baseline period in lieu of the second person singular pronoun.

19 In hierarchical order from the highest to lowest these included:
    i)   straight-backed chair
    ii) bench
    iii) small low chair akin to a child's chair
    v)   low stool (*kolomba*) usually used in the kitchen
    v)   mat

20 Poor people who could not afford such long-drawn-out celebrations telescoped the festivities into a couple of days by inviting each caste group at a separate time rather than on a separate day.

21 Although the term māma is a kinship term, in inter-caste interaction it clearly denotes the addressee as being of lower caste status than the speaker.

22 Even today, long after the basis of entrance to white-collar employment has been changed from birth status to educational qualifications, the results of British policy are in evidence in rural areas. A disproportionate number of senior white-collar positions are occupied by members of the higher castes. For example, the managers of all three co-operative stores in the vicinity of the community are Goigama, as are two of the three headmasters of the schools in the community.

23 Domestic religious rituals were usually *pinkam* (merit making occasions) to transfer merit to a dead relative. *Pinkam* take the form of all-night *pirit* (sacred texts) chants by a minimum of ten monks, who sit inside an ornate structure called a *pirit kotuva* (pirit cage). Refreshments are served to all who attend the ceremony and the monks are provided breakfast and an elaborate luncheon feast the following day.

24 The British enforced strict licensing laws on the sale of intoxicants. As a result the supply of legal arrack and toddy was far below the demand and many people (such as the Batgam in Devideniya) trafficked in the manufacture and sale of toddy.

5: *The Class Hierarchy in the Baseline Period*

1 R. Redfield, *Peasant Society and Culture*; M. Marriott, 'Little Communities in an Indigenous Civilisation' in M. Marriott (ed.), *Village India*, 171–222.
2 The information regarding the British tax structure at the turn of the century was gathered from the diaries of the Assistant Government Agents of the Kegalle district.
3 The population of this community has increased by 200 per cent since the baseline period. In contrast, the increase in the extent of cultivated land (especially paddy land) is relatively low.

| | Baseline | | | 1979–1980 | | | % |
	A	R	P	A	R	P	increase
Paddy land	103	1	15	116	1	30	12.6
High land	188	2	10	336	3	25	78.6

Two reasons underly the 78.6 per cent increase in high land. Firstly, former jungle land has gradually come under cash-crop cultivation. Secondly, under village expansion schemes, post-independence governments have acquired parts of plantations and redistributed this land among poor villagers.
4 The following official pamphlet, distributed in all the villages of Hatara Korale in 1896, deserves to be quoted in full because it demonstrates so well the paternalistic concern of certain British officials to preserve the prosperity of the region: 'in the Four Korales there are as many Kandyans as the fields will grow food for. Therefore there should be no strangers introduced. If you sell your chenas you will lose part of your food supply; and the rest of your food supply will be destroyed through the fields being silted up from the drains in the high lands. If you sell your chenas, you will lose your lands and will someday soon have to work as daily labourers for other people who have obtained possession of your lands. You are happy now because you have only to work for yourselves to provide yourselves with sufficient food. When you lose your lands you must work as daily labourers and must always work whether you wish to or not, or whether you are well or sick; for if you do not earn wages you will starve. You will be cheated by Kanganies who will keep back part of your wages, or who will get you into debt by giving you advances on high interest. When once you have got into debt, you will never escape; as if you go away you can be brought back on warrants. Furthermore your children will learn the vices of their masters. You will see your children learning to drink strong drink and to fight and to swear. They will copy the vices of the Europeans and not all their manly virtues. So do not be persuaded to sell your lands, but keep your ancestral lands to yourselves and let the Four Korales remain what it has always been, the most favoured garden of the Kandyan Provinces. There is plenty of room for tea plantations in the Three Korales, and up in the hills where there are no paddy fields, only a few villages.' (Diary of the Assistant Government Agent, Kegalle District, Oct 1896.) N.B. *hatara* means four; thus 'Four Korales' refers to Harara Korale. Kanganies were overseers on plantations.
5 Far from an excess of labour, even in 1920 there was a shortage of labour in rural areas. At this time the Assistant Government Agent of the Kegalle

district claimed that transplanting was not carried out on paddy fields because there was insufficient labour to undertake this labour-intensive task. (Diary of the Assistant Government Agent, Kegalle District, Oct 1920.)

6 Low-country Sinhalese responded to the economic opportunities arising from the British presence and migrated to the hill country to work in British enterprises. A considerable number worked as labourers in the plumbago mines and on plantations, whilst others worked in the capacity of overseer or *bās* (masons, carpenters, etc.). The British preferred Kandyan labour, however, because the Low Countrymen were not under the jurisdiction of the Kandyan headmen and therefore constituted a labour force that was more difficult to control. In 1894 the Assistant Government Agent of Kegalle requested each chief headman to supply confidential reports of the number of Kandyans in each village willing to work on estates. These reports showed that in an area which had 17,570 able-bodied men only 1,847 were prepared to work on tea estates, and that 'in many villages *none* of the inhabitants wish to earn their living in this way.' (Diary of the Assistant Government Agent, Kegalle District, July 1894.)

7 As low-caste persons, the Batgam had less to lose by working on British plantations than did high-caste persons. Moreover, the economic incentive would for them have been more compelling. In 1904 the Assistant Government Agent of the Kegalle district wrote: 'The lower caste villagers in this district are poor and sickly. Mr. Fairweather (a planter) tells me that they willingly work for him on the estates which he is now opening.' (Diary of the Assistant Government Agent, Kegalle District, February 1904.)

8 Unlike in the Maritime Provinces where all 'waste and unoccupied' land was considered crown property, in the Kandyan Provinces the British, in accordance with local usage, recognized and accepted the fact of private ownership of chena land. Even after the passage of the Waste Lands Ordinance of 1840, which sought to define crown and private rights in land, Kandyans were permitted to establish their title by prescription on lands that could only be cultivated periodically – i.e. chena. (M. Roberts, 'Land Problems and Policies c. 1832 to c. 1900' in K.M. de Silva (ed.), *History of Ceylon*, vol III, 121–2.)

9 By 'rice' I refer to the cereal grain obtained from varieties of paddy grown on 'mud land'. This is to be distinguished from the less appreciated hill paddy varieties grown on chena land which did not constitute the staple food but were used only as a supplement to rice.

10 It is not implausible that some coffee may have been grown for sale in garden plots in this region prior to the baseline period. Although certain authors have shown that the extent of indigenous coffee cultivation in the nineteenth century has been overestimated in the literature (M. Roberts and L.A. Wickremaratne, 'Export Agriculture in the Nineteenth Century' in K.M. de Siva (ed.), *History of Ceylon*, 97–8), coffee grows well in the Kegalle district and Muslim traders were bartering coffee berries at the ports long before the advent of large-scale coffee plantations (91). However, the coffee-leaf fungus severely affected small holdings in the 1870s and with the rapid decline of coffee cultivation that followed, coffee was virtually non-existent on garden land in this community during the baseline period.

Neither did cocoa, pepper, tea or rubber, all of which were to become important high-land crops in the future, have any appreciable impact on garden cultivation during this period. By the end of the nineteenth century cocoa and pepper were just being introduced by the British to be grown as village-garden cash crops, and tea and rubber cultivation on small holdings began much later in the 1920s and 1930s.

11 V. Samaraweera, 'Economic and Social Developments Under the British' in K.M. de Silva (ed.), *History of Ceylon*, 52.

12 L.S. Dewaraja, *The Kandyan Kingdom*, 184.

13 Paddy tracts are always designed to have a gradient (gentle in the valleys and steep on the hillsides) to facilitate drainage. The tract is not, however, a continuous sloping piece of land. It is divided by low ridges (*niyara*) into strictly-level plots of irregular shape and size (determined by the contours of the land), and thus visually resembles a patchwork quilt. The *niyara* serve a variety of purposes. Their chief function is to retain water in each separate field, since at particular stages of cultivation the fields need to be completely inundated. *Niyara* are also used as footpaths and as boundaries separating one person's plot from another's.

14 'I tried to persuade some villagers of Rangama, at work ploughing their fields, to bury green leaves and give this manure a trial. But I doubt if my arguments had much success. If I were to order them to use green manure, they would comply. But I doubt if they would not attribute any increase in fertility to good fortune or to the propitiousness of the day on which the ploughing was begun, or to some agricultural rite. These remote Kandyans have vague ideas of the laws of causation.' (Diary of the Assistant Government Agent, Kegalle District, Oct 1920).

15 Today women also carry out the recent cultivation technique of transplanting the young paddy plants from the nursery to the fields.

16 For an extended discussion of these latter tenurial arrangements see pp. 122–3.

17 Each arecanut tree yielded on average 300 nuts per annum, and at 1,200 trees per acre the crop was worth from Rs 87 gross to Rs 66 net per acre (*Ferguson's Ceylon Handbook and Directory*, 1895–6, 120). In contrast an acre of paddy during the same period yielded on average 25 bushels per annum, since only one season was cultivated in this community. Twenty-five bushels of paddy is approximately equal to 11 bushels of husked rice. (A bushel of paddy when husked yields slightly less than half its volume of rice.) For revenue purposes the British government valued rice at Rs 3.50 per bushel (*Ferguson's Ceylon Handbook and Directory*, 1909–1910, 512). Even in the unlikely event that the selling price of rice in rural areas was one-and-a-half times as much (i.e. Rs 5.25), the annual income from an acre of paddy would be Rs 57.75 and still below the income from an acre of arecanut.

18 'On the principle of buying in the cheapest and selling in the dearest market, it would certainly appear that the people of Ceylon (with but few exceptions in the Matara, Batticaloa and Jaffna districts), could more profitably turn their attention to plantation and garden products such as coconuts, areca or betal nuts, pepper ... then selling the product to advantage, they could buy rice from Southern and Northern India and Burmah more

cheaply than they can produce it' (J. Ferguson, *Ceylon in the Jubilee Year*, 44–5).

19 Tenancy rights were inherently insecure. A tenant's material well-being fluctuated from year to year and he lacked the security of food supplies possessed by those who had ownership rights in paddy land.

20 During the period 1869–1888, the Batgam increased their paddy-land holdings by nine acres. Five of these nine acres were land that had belonged to the Devideniya *walawwe* prior to its disintegration, and the four remaining acres were purchased. Even if Batgam purchase of land had doubled over a similar number of years, 1888–1910 (unlikely since apart from Ukkuwa Kankaniya no other Batgam during the baseline period obtained a well-paying job on the plantations), they would still have owned only eighteen acres of paddy land.

21 M. Roberts, 'Aspects of Ceylon's Agrarian Economy in the Nineteenth Century' in K.M. de Silva (ed.), *History of Ceylon*, 160.

22 Claim under ordinance No. 1 of 1897 and No. 1 of 1899 with respect to Upalagoda Tenna Hena at Rangama in Tunpalatapattu of Paranakuru Korale in the Kegalle District (Ceylon Government Archives).

6: *The Power Hierarchy in the Baseline Period*

1 Diary of the Assistant Government Agent, Kegalle District, Sep 1908.

2 The area of jurisdiction of low-caste headmen varied from district to district. Whilst it was limited to a village in the Kegalle district (H. White, *The Ceylon Manual, 1912–1913*, 388), in the Ratnapura district, which was also in the province of Sabaragamuva, low-caste headmen were appointed over *vasamas* and in some cases even over *patttuwas* (H. White, *The Ceylon Manual*, 387–8) of predominantly low-caste people.

3 This code specified the uniform of Ratemahatmayas and Koralas as 'the dress of Kandyan chiefs' and that of minor headmen as 'dress according to respective castes' (H. White, *The Ceylon Manual*, 388). Some British officials even fined native headmen for appearing before them without their hats, which was considered an 'essential' part of their uniform (Diary of the Assistant Government Agent, Kegalle District, 1903).

4 A candidate for an administrative post thus routinely cited the bureaucratic posts, honours and awards received by this father, grandfather, uncles, etc., as reasons why he considered himself to have a 'right' (*ayitivāsikama*) to the job.

5 Diary of the Assistant Government Agent, Kegalle District, Dec 1909; July 1888.

6 The Aracci's role in police work did not decline with the introduction of rural police in 1892. He remained the local policeman. Fourteen police stations in charge of a police sergeant were established in the Kegalle district in 1904, but the Naranhena area did not have a regular police station until 1917.

7 Diary of the Assistant Government Agent, Kegalle District, Apr 1915 and Jan 1887.

8 'Held inquiry regarding complaint by Mr. Mant that the Rangama Aracci had crimped some of his coolies ... I have reliable information that Mr.

Mant has a private grudge against this Aracci, and I think his complaint to me is attributable to this grudge.' Diary of the Assistant Government Agent, Kegalle District, Nov 1888.

7: *The Ideology of Stratification During the Baseline Period*

1 L. Dumont, *Homo Hierarchicus.*

2 'On the Purity of Women in the Castes of Malabar and Ceylon', *Journal of the Royal Anthropological Institute*, vol 93, 1963, 25–58; N. Yalman, *Under the Bo Tree.*

3 B. Ryan, *Caste in Modern Ceylon*; R.L. Stirrat, 'Caste Conundrums: Views of Caste in a Sinhalese Catholic Fishing Village' in D.B. McGilvray (ed.), *Caste Ideology and Interaction*, 8–33; D.B. McGilvray, 'Mukkuvar Vannimai: Tamil Caste and Matriclan Ideology in Batticaloa, Sri Lanka' in D.B. McGilvray (ed.), *Caste Ideology and Interaction*, 34–97.

4 Older informants repeat the story of the moneyed man in a situation of scarcity of paddy. When he approached a poor farmer to buy some paddy, the farmer climbed on the rich man's back in order to reach his storage bin. This story illustrates the superiority of the owner of paddy land, and the humiliation suffered by those who are forced to purchase paddy.

5 G. Obeyesekere, *Land Tenure in Village Ceylon.*

6 L. Dumont, *Homo Hierarchicus.*

7 J.V. Femia, *Gramsci's Political thought.*

8 G. Berreman, 'Self, Situation and Escape from Stigmatised Ethnic Identity', in 70th Meeting of the American Anthropological Association, New York, 1971.

9 Diary of the Assistant Government Agent, Kegalle District, Oct 1920.

10 J.V. Femia, *Gramsci's Political Thought*, 24.

11 A.T. Kirsch, 'The Thai Buddhist Quest for Merit', paper read at the American Anthropological Association meeting, Washington, Nov 1967.

12 The popular cults include the propitiation of deities, the placation of demons, the exorcism of evil spirits, astrology, etc.

13 The pantheon presented here is largely derived from the pantheon in the village of Rambadeniya described by Obeyesekere ('The Buddhist pantheon in Ceylon and its Extensions', in M. Nash (ed.), *Anthropological Studies in Theravada Beddhism*, 1–26). It is not a 'real' phenomenon specific to one or more areas, but a general construct, the lower levels of which are in reality variable from region to region.

As the propounder of the faith, and as a being who has achieved Nirvana, the Buddha heads the pantheon. The Buddha is also the ultimate repository of power. This power he delegates to the other super-natural beings according to the state of karma they have achieved.

14 The Buddha admitted into his order individuals of all castes, and claimed that the fourfold varna division in Indian society was functional rather than birth ascribed.

8: *The Contemporary Community*

1 Four village expansion schemes have enabled landless and land-poor households in this community to gain control of land:

Name of Scheme	Year of Settlement	Extent allotted per household
Appallagoda	1940	1 acre
Berawila	1950	¼ acre
Buthmallawa	1959	2 acres
Udayapura	1975	1 acre

2 In July 1982 Rangama village received electricity. Today one house and the Rangama *vihāraya* enjoy the benefit of electric lighting.

3 J. Jiggins, *Caste and Family in the Politics of the Sinhalese, 1947–1976*, 73.

4 Provincial Councils were established throughout the island in 1988 (see Epilogue).

5 A third village, West Galewala, also belongs to the Rangama *vasama*. The *vasama* has almost always been an essentially administrative unit. Inhabitants of the multi-village Rangama *vasama*, for example, have never felt a sense of '*vasama*-based' identity. In 1978 the people of West Galewala along with those of East Galewala (which belongs to the neighbouring *vasama*) petitioned the Member of Parliament to create a new *vasama* – Galewala – incorporating the two halves of their village. This action reflected the alienation of Galewala villagers from the inhabitants of their respective *vasamas*.

It is also not the case that inclusion in an administrative unit makes for intensive interaction within that unit. In this region, for example, *vasama*-based voluntary organizations are markedly more moribund than village-based ones.

It was only between the years 1958 and 1977 that the *vasama* achieved an importance outside its purely administrative role. During this period it became a significant unit in the local-level power structure because the *vasama* was usually co-extensive with the area of jurisdiction of cultivation committees. But the abolition of cultivation committees by the United National Party government in 1977 has rendered obsolete the extra-administrative importance of the *vasama* unit.

9: *The Contemporary Caste Hierarchy*

1 In 1935 my landlady's father, a wealthy Vahumpura from Rangama, wished to name his daughter Udumawathie – a clearly non-Vahumpura name. The registrar refused to register the name on the grounds that it was too grand for a Vahumpura child. The child's father filed action and took the case to court, before he was successful in registering the name of his choice.

2 The Paṭṭi alone among the low castes have presumed to register the Banda/Manike suffixes as part of the formal name of their children. Yet Banda and Manike have, along with the high-caste honorific 'Hamu', become in effect the name of many low-caste children because contemporary low-caste parents have a tendency to use these terms as nicknames for their children.

3 Only middle-aged and old people in the community today have caste-associated personal names, such as:

Siyathuhamy, Pinhamy	– Paṭṭi
Naide, Etana (suffixes)	– Gallat
Aungo, Mungo, Dewaya	– Vahumpura

| Kuda Henaya, Kuda Ridi | – Hēna |
| Kiri Duraya, Rana | – Batgam |

Some older lower-caste persons find themselves being re-named by their children who insist for example that their father's name is Ranasinghe (a Goigama name) and not Rana.

4 The Ralahamy/Manike honorifics are used most extensively by Muslim middlemen who visit the community to buy spices. The Goigama, however, derive no joy from this because contemporary Muslim traders freely use theses titles on anyone they trade with. According the Goigama they do so in the hope that such flattery will enable them to buy spices from low-caste villagers at a cheap rate.

5 In 1972 the parliament of Ceylon was renamed the National State Assembly. Representatives are therefore Members of the National State Assembly. They are, however, still popularly known as MPs and the term MP will be retained throughout this study.

6 In lesser degree this is true of every caste in its relationship to a caste lower than it in the caste hierarchy.

7 The Goigama–Gallat union that KDK exploited had been the cause of inter-caste hostility long before the April disturbances. A group of Goigama men had attacked a Gallat man believed to have encouraged the romance, and the Goigama landlord of the Gallat girl's father had threatened to evict the latter. Nor is opposition to inter-caste marriages confined to the Goigama. A Vahumpura girl from Rangama who eloped with a Batgam boy from Devideniya was kidnapped by her relatives and imprisoned in her parents' home until the police intervened. The girl has not seen her parents since then.

8 Village Development Societies are expected to initiate projects such as building wells, dams, footpaths etc., for the improvement of the village. Once a project is approved by the Department of Rural Development, sufficient funds are allocated for it and are handed over in instalments after each phase of the project is completed.

9 Funeral Aid Societies are non-governmental organizations. Members receive a fixed sum of money when a death occurs in their family which enables them to meet the funeral expenses. Many families join this organization because it is considered a sensible scheme. Their participation, however, rarely goes beyond the payment of subscriptions.

10 In the 1956 general election, most of the floating Goigama vote in Rangama went to a Goigama from a respectable family in a nearby town, even though he was an SLFP candidate.

11 During the baseline period Koralas and Araccis (high-caste headmen) were in charge of policing rural areas. In 1980, of a 25-strong police force stationed in Doragala, only the inspector and four constables were Goigama. The rest of the force belonged to the Batgam caste.

12 They are sometimes able to help the Goigama in cases which involve the district police headquarters in Kegalle. For instance, according to some villagers, when the Kegalle police requested the inspector's help to apprehend a Goigama youth from Rangama who had deserted from the Navy, the inspector is alleged to have reported that the youth was not in

the Naranhena area, although he was aware that the youth was hiding is his father's house.

13 Although these Vahumpura do reside in Rangama, I have included them in the Rangama/Devideniya community not simply on account of their residence, but because the majority of their land is in Rangama and they therefore constitute part of the Rangama/Devideniya class hierarchy.

14 The smaller caste groups cannot afford the luxury of caste-exclusive domestic rituals and are constrained to solicit the participation of non-caste fellows.

10: *The Contemporary Class Hierarchy*

1 B. Ryan, 'Socio-Cultural Regions of Ceylon', *Rural Sociology*, vol 15, no. 1 (March 1950), 14.

2 K. Gough, *Harijans in Thanjavur*, 223.

3 A household is defined as a group of people who have the same source of income or who pool their incomes and form a separate economic unit. A household thus defined is not coterminous with 'those living in a single house', or 'a group that shares a hearth' (i.e. cook and eat together), because of the presence in the highlands of what may be termed complex houses. Complex houses are those where groups of people (usually close relatives) who keep their incomes separate, nevertheless live in the same house and sometimes even share the same hearth. In the latter case the groups share the expenses for meals and cook together for convenience, but keep their incomes separate and constitute separate economic units.

The majority of households in contemporary Rangama/Devideniya are composed of nuclear families or nuclear families and one or two very close relatives. The 'household head' is taken to be the principal income earner in the household. With few exceptions the household head is the eldest male in the household.

4 Apart from bananas which are cultivated as a cash crop by a few people, all other fruit trees are grown principally for household consumption. Excess fruit is sold to itinerant traders who in turn sell the fruit to larger traders in bazaars or to retail shops in towns.

5 Although Berawila and Natha Kande are no longer thriving rubber planta-tions, rubber remains the most important plantation crop in the vicinity of the community. There are four rubber estates bordering the community, the largest being the hundred acres of Berawila which remained privately owned after the 1972 land reforms. The absentee owners of these estates live in towns and cities and visit their estates a few times each year. The estates are run by managers who, like the majority of the labourers on these estates, tend to come from outside the Rangama/Devideniya community.

6 See Appendix III for an income/cost analysis of rubber cultivation during 1979/80.

7 The employee taps the trees, coagulates the latex and rolls the rubber into sheets, and dries the sheets. He receives half of the sheets as wages. The landowner provides the implements and chemicals for the trees. Landowner and rubber tapper share the expenses for the acid used to coagulate the latex and for the rolling machines and ovens.

8 See Appendix IV for an income/cost analysis of paddy cultivation during 1979/80.

9 In 1948 the government introduced the Guaranteed Price Scheme (GPS) for paddy with the primary aim of increasing production by offering the cultivator a fair and stable price for his produce. Although the guaranteed price has on occasion been lower than the open market price, the GPS has ensured that the price is stable and that a minimum price for paddy is maintained which is higher than the cost of production.

10 In this community the terms *taṭṭumāru* and *kannamāru* are used interchangeably to describe both tenurial patterns. For convenience I shall use the term *taṭṭumāru* for the more common pattern in keeping with the usage in the rest of the island, and *kannamāru* for the other.

11 For an extended discussion of the second system and the way in which both systems are combined in the same field see Appendix V.

12 In order to minimize exhaustion for the bulls, threshing is not carried out during the heat of the day, but is begun in the late evening and is carried on through the night. Landlords visit the threshing floor in the evening but tend not to stay all night. They claim that by observing the stacked paddy they are able to obtain a fairly accurate estimate of the yield. They return the next morning for the crop division.

13 The contract system on paddy land in rural Sri Lanka incorporates the traditional *attam* labour arrangement. The contractor does not pay his labour team cash wages, but returns their labour by working on each of their fields.

14 Although the Land Reform Acts created employment for a considerable number of individuals, over 150 people (the majority below 35 years of age) in this community are unemployed. Between 15 and 30 young people migrate temporarily to the dry zone each year. Settlers in certain dry-zone colonization schemes have been allotted relatively large extents of paddy land which are difficult to cultivate with family labour alone. During the periods of peak labour requirements in the paddy cultivation cycle, labour recruiters visit their natal villages and collect labour teams. The lack of employment opportunities in the Naranhena region forces young men and women from this community to migrate for a few months each year to the dry zone to carry out harvesting and transplanting respectively.

15 In this region the landlord only contributes towards the cost of seed paddy, fertilizer and pesticide, and (since the PLA) the cost of transporting the paddy from the threshing floor to the granary. All other money costs are borne by the tenant. Certain tasks have to be carried out during a short space of time (e.g. second ploughing, transplanting, harvesting and threshing) and require outside assistance. These tasks are carried out on *attam*. The food costs for co-operative labour teams are considerable and they are borne solely by the tenant. They constitute the single largest item of cost for small farmers. For a detailed analysis of the cost and income sharing between landlord and tenant see Appendix VI.

16 Eight tenants who are not protected by the Act, but who stand in the relationship of son or son-in-law to the landlord, are also considered to have control over one-third of the land they cultivate. This overcomes the

distortion that would otherwise arise when young men who work on fields they will eventually inherit are seen as landless.

17 In compiling statistics of land control, I have discounted 20 perches (one-eighth of an acre) from the garden land of each household because the presence of the house and yard on garden land renders such an extent non-income yielding.

A considerable amount of rubber land in the Rangama/Devideniya community is low yielding. In order to make land extents comparable in terms of income yielding potential, I have for the purposes of the class analysis presented here, discounted the extent of these rubber holdings by two-thirds.

18 In theory control over all three types of agricultural land may be obtained in these three ways. In practice, however, only owner management bestows control on all types of agricultural land. Tenancy on high land is not unknown. In the past individuals who had large extents of high land sometimes appointed another person to look after the land in exchange for half the crops. This practice has now fallen into disuse because of the alleged thieving which took place when the owner was not in direct contact with the land. Usufructuary mortgages and leases are confined to paddy land for another reason. It is unwise from the borrower's point of view to allow the creditor temporary use of land on which perennial crops are grown (i.e. high land). Borrowers prefer to allow creditors to use paddy land because there is no risk of damage to, or misuse of, income-yielding perennial crops.

19 Fifty-seven young people (below 30 years) in this community are also engaged in non-agricultural occupations. These persons generally contribute part or all of their income to the household economy. Although a few young people from the lowest classes have 'higher-income' jobs, it would be mistaken to assume that they are capable thereby of enhancing the class position of their households. The majority had been working for only a short time – either because they had just entered the job market or because they had got these jobs through political connections (see Chapter 11) after the UNP victory in 1977. Moreover their contribution to household economy is a transient phenomenon not only because jobs gained through political connections are usually lost if an opposition party wins the next national election, but also because these people are of marriageable age and will, within the next few years, marry and start households of their own.

20 M. Robinson claims that in Morapitiya 'the norm is that attams must be returned for equal time and in kind', *Political Structure in a Changing Sinhalese Village*, 63.

21 The branch of the Bank of Ceylon at Doragala (six miles away) provides credit only if the borrower can leave an item of gold as security until the loan and interest is paid up. Many poor people, however, do not possess pieces of gold jewellery, and even for those who do, it is often of little use since the bank lends money at any one time only up to the value of one third of the item.

22 See, for example, J. Scott, *The Moral Economy of the Peasant*, and J. Migdal, *Peasants, Politics and Revolution*.

23 Direct state intervention in rural areas began in 1932 with the formation of

the State Council in which control over agriculture was, for the first time, placed in the hands of Sri Lankans. Since then the economic position of many poor families has been improved through village expansion schemes, resettlement schemes, the PLA and the Land Reform Acts, as well as through wide-ranging welfare legislation. The latter include the free or subsidized rice ration, the dole, old age supplements, food stamps and the spread of free education and health care.

24 L.A. Wickremaratne, 'Peasant Agriculture', in K.M. de Silva (ed.), *Sri Lanka*, 251.

25 The Land Reform Act of 1972 restricted *individual* ownership of land to 50 acres of high and 25 acres of paddy. No one in this community owned more than 25 acres of paddy and the one individual who owned land in excess of the high-land ceiling was not affected because he, like many others in the country, simply divided his landholdings legally among his children.

26 The Land Reform Commission acquired over 50 acres of jungle land which was part of Rangama Watte estate situated on the southern boundary of Rangama village. The SLFP government attempted to redistribute this land to the poor in one-acre blocks. The allottees were asked to pay Rs 60 to cover the cost of surveying the land, but few thought this investment worthwhile for a piece of rocky jungle land. In 1977 the UNP government cancelled the scheme. Those few allottees who had paid the survey fee have to date got neither the land nor their money back.

27 Sessional Paper XVIII, 1951 – The Report of the Kandyan Peasantry Commission, 249.

28 In the baseline period the landed elite also included two Gallat households. The Gallat, like the high castes, have suffered economic decline. All six Gallat households in the contemporary community belong to the poorest classes.

29 Sinhalese operate as wholesale traders in Dambawala but the larger spice traders in this region are still Muslims. Muslim traders are at a competitive advantage over their Sinhalese rivals because they work in conjunction with the large spice exporters in Colombo. The latter advance large sums of money to their provincial colleagues, who are thus, because of their larger capital base, able to 'out bid' the Sinhalese traders in the competition for 'leasing' spice crops.

30 Although the acreage under rubber in the island had almost doubled, from 100,000 to 188,000 acres between 1906 and 1910, tea remained the principal plantation crop in the vicinity of the Rangama/Devideniya community. The Naranhena region belonged to the Kegalle administrative district but the Dolosbage planting district. The latter was in 1909–10 still a predominantly tea planting area, as is shown by the following table.

	Dolosbage planting district (acres)	Kegalle planting district (acres)
Extent cultivated	14,795	16,967
Tea	11,687	2,009
Rubber	796	10,000

Ferguson's Ceylon Handbook 1909–1910, Planting review, xi.

31 Two smaller estates were also opened up during this period in the vicinity of the Rangama/Devideniya community:
   – Rangama Watte Estate, situated south of Rangama village: 100 acres
   – Buthmallawa Estate, situated east of Rangama village: 75 acres

32 Diary of the Assistant Government Agent, Kegalle District, Feb 1925.

33 Three households descended from this carpenter are the only Goigama households in Devideniya today. All three households are in the 'middle farmer' class.

34 Non-residents and the Rangama and Devideniya *vihāra* also control land in the community. A minority of non-residents who control paddy land in the community are people who have worked in Rangama or Devideniya (as schoolteachers, Grama Sevakas etc.) in the past. However, the majority of non-residents who control paddy land, and virtually all non-residents who control high land are people who were born in the community and now live in urban areas. Their land is taken care of by a close relative who in the case of paddy often works the land as a tenant. Like other outsiders who control land in this community, their principal economic interests lie elsewhere and most only visit the community once or twice a year to collect the crops.

35 The four Vahal households in the contemporary community are no longer in a position of economic servitude to the Watte Gedera Walawwe family. Lacking the means to support them, the *malawwe* allowed them to work as tenants for others. Today, owing to the PLA, the Vahal families control some paddy land. One individual was the recipient of a two-acre government allotment when the Buthmallawa rubber estate was divided up in 1959, and is therefore in the 'middle farmer' class.

36 In the past Megoda Devideniya referred to that part of Devideniya village that lay east of the Maya Oya. Megoda Devideniya does not exist today. It is unambiguously part of Rangama village, not only in the perceptions of villagers but also in official records.

37 Agricultural productivity committees were set up in 1972 under the Agricultural Productivity Law. They were regional bodies which supervised the activities of 10 to 12 cultivation committees.

38 Peace councils were set up with the aim of settling minor disputes in an amicable way without taking them to court.

11: *The Contemporary Power Hierarchy*

1 B. Weerakoon, 'Emergent leadership at the village level', *Economic Review*, Jan 1976, 12.

2 T. Fernando, another exponent of the 'traditional' rural power structure, claims that the 'traditional element' in the rural power structure consists of 'Buddhist monks, Ayurvedic physicians, village school teachers and village headmen' ('Elite politics in the new state: the case of post-independence Sri Lanka', in *Pacific Affairs*, vol 46, no. 3, Fall 1973, 373.

3 U. Phadnis, *Religion and Politics in Sri Lanka*.

4 Many recruits to the sangha do not join through religious motivation. It is customary in rural Sri Lanka for poor families with a large number of

children to enter a son into the sangha at the age of 10 or 11, thereby gaining economic relief as well as religious merit. Many of these boys continue in the sangha because it is a sinecure that gives them, at a minimum, food and lodging. Others stay on until they gain a university education (religious institutions pay for residence, books etc.) with the intention of giving up the robes once they gain their qualifications.

5 The Rangama/Devideniya community is not unique in this regard. Robinson states that in 1963 the Morapitiya monk was not a village leader and that the *vihāraya* had been inactive for the past two decades (*Political Structure in a Changing Sinhalese Village*, 83–4).

6 In recent decades the monks of two neighbouring villages have also been forced by the villagers to leave their *vihāra* because they were caught 'in flagrente delicto'.

7 In May 1925 the Assistant Government Agent of Kegalle district wrote, 'one of the subdivisions [of a very large *vasama*] will be made up entirely of Duraya villages and should, I think, be a Duraya *vasama*. There is no precedent for this in this district.' (Diary of the Assistant Government Agent, Kegalle District, 1925.)

8 The Salagama are a predominantly Low Country caste and are found only in small numbers in the Kandyan provinces. The Salagama of Galewala occupy a higher position in the birth status hierarchy than the Vahumpura majority of that village.

9 Diary of the Assistant Government Agent, Kegalle District, Nov 1910.

10 E. Wolf, 'Aspects of group relations in a complex society: Mexico', *American Anthropologist*, 1956, vol 58, 1065–78.

11 A broker is 'an individual who classically plays the role of intermediary through utilising his controls at each level to the advantage of the other' (R.N. Adams, 'Brokers and career mobility systems in the structure of complex societies', *South-Western Journal of Anthropology*, 1970, no. 4, 320.

12 'Both by its history and by the inclination of the personnel who man the co-operatives, the business of buying and selling has taken precedence over development activities like the provision of credit to farmers and the stocking of slow-moving and 'offensive' items like fertiliser and agro-chemicals.' (B. Weerakoon, 'The Role of administrators in a changing agrarian situation: the Sri Lanka experience', *Journal of Administration Overseas*, vol 16, no. 3, Jul 1977, 160).

During my period of fieldwork, all agricultural inputs such as seed paddy, fertilizer, pesticide, credit etc. were, in the Naranhena area, handled primarily by the Agrarian Services Centre.

13 The UNP abolished Cultivation Committees in 1977. Their duties and functions have been taken over by a politically-appointed Cultivation Officer whose area of jurisdiction is the *vasama*.

14 The CO is expected to compile new paddy and high-land registers each year. The Rangama CO, however, makes no effort to secure accurate information for himself. Instead he relies on the people to report any changes in land ownership and land tenure to him. High-land ownership is often underestimated in the CO's register. In the case of paddy land, certain landowners register themselves as cultivators by paying the acreage tax and

producing fertilizer receipts, whilst in fact getting their land cultivated by tenants. The CO does not feel it incumbent upon him to ensure that people who cultivate paddy land for others be registered as tenants.

15 Sarvodaya is a non-government organization predicated on Buddhist principles. It aims to develop rural areas through shramadana (sharing of energy for the benefit of the community).

16 A.J. Wilson, *Politics in Sri Lanka 1947–1973*, 155.

17 The preceding paragraphs have followed closely the argument presented by C.A. Woodward in 'Sri Lanka's electoral experience: from personal to party politics', *Pacific Affairs*, winter 1974/5, vol 47 (4), 455–71.

18 Even the Marxist parties were elitist and were controlled by a small group of urban intellectuals.

19 Provincial Councils were established in 1988 and Pradeshiya Sabhas (divisional-level elected bodies) in 1991 (see Epilogue).

20 J. Blackton, *Local Government and Rural Development in Sri Lanka*, 38. Blackton cites a case where a VC was dissolved following a protracted confrontation between the VC chairman and the MP over the latter's alleged failure to pay his electricity bill to the VC authority.

21 V. Samaraweera, 'The administration and the judicial system', in K.M. de Silva (ed.) *Sri Lanka*, 359.

22 B. Weerakoon, 'Role of administrators in a changing agrarian situation', *Journal of Administration Overseas*, vol 16, no. 3, July 1977, 150.

23 'There is a very real possibility that the efforts which an administrative team are making may be misunderstood as an attempt to extend one's area of influence with a view to seeking future political office . . . and the administrator has perforce to make a special attempt to clear himself from this charge.' B. Weerakoon, 'Role of administrators in a changing agrarian situation', *Journal of Administration Overseas*, vol 16, no. 3, July 1977, 155.

24 In February 1979 the general manager of NADSA told me that land planted with cash crops on Natha Kande estate was being surveyed and would be distributed to the labourers within six months. NADSA was a pet project of the Naranhena MP, but in the case of Natha Kande estate it came into conflict with claims on estate timber for another favoured project: a pencil factory. NADSA could not proceed as planned with the land distribution because the MP kept changing his mind about how much of the estate would have to be set aside for the factory. Sixteen months later, at the end of my fieldwork period, the land had still not been distributed.

25 Susila, a 28-year-old woman from Rangama, was appointed as a clerk on a government co-operative under the last SLFP government. After the UNP victory in 1977 the local UNP organization petitioned the MP that she did not deserve to have this job because she was an SLFP supporter. Susila was first transferred to another estate some distance away, and according to her, a few months later the MP instructed the superintendant of that estate to dismiss her. Her job was given to a UNP supporter.

26 The Malwatte chapter is one of the most influential chapters of the foremost Buddhist sect in Sri Lanka – the Siam *nikāya*.

27 J. Jiggins, *Caste and Family in the Politics of the Sinhalese*, 150.

28 The masculine form is used throughout for convenience. It does not mean that women are excluded from this role.

29 Henchmen in some electorates often retain a commission for themselves. For instance B. Jayasena's sister, who lives in a neighbouring constituency, has established herself as one of the most effective intermediaries for securing white-collar jobs in the whole constituency. It is rumoured that the commissions she charges have made her a rich woman.

30 Silverman, 'Patronage and community-nation relationships in central Italy', *Ethnology* 1965, vol 4 (2), 172–89.

31 A. Blok, *The Mafia of a Sicilian Village 1860–1960*.

32 A. Blok, *The Mafia of a Sicilian Village 1860–1960*, 216.

33 F.G. Bailey, *Politics and Social Change: Orissa in 1959*; S. Tarrow, *Peasant Communism in Southern Italy*; A. Blok, *The Mafia of a Sicilian Village 1860–1960*.

34 N.K. Nicholson, *Panchayati Raj: Rural Development and the Political Economy of Village India*; S.C. Jain, *Community Development and Panchayati Raj in India*; G.R. Reddy, 'Some aspects of decision-making in Panchayati Raj, *Economic and Political Weekly* 1970, vol 5 (41), 1699–704.

35 F.G. Bailey, *Politics and Social Change: Orissa in 1959*; A. Beteille, *Caste, Class and Power*.

36 Robinson (*Political Structure in a Changing Sinhalese Village*) is exceptional in attempting to distinguish the concepts of power and leadership; but she does not manage to do so successfully. On p. 106 she claims that 'the leaders have little power though, as they control no important resources within the village'; but goes on to assert of p. 109 that 'the Morapitiyan leaders preserve their own positions as the sole links to important outsiders; it is this which to a large extent constitutes the source of their power in Morapitiya.'

37 B. Weerakoon, 'Emergent leadership at the village level', *Economic Review* Jan 1976, 12.

38 B. Jayasena was a member of the regional Peace Council. When the elective principle in cultivation committees was abandoned in 1973 the SLFP MP appointed Jayasena chairman and allowed him to choose the other members of the Rangama Cultivation Committee.

39 J. Blackton, *Local Government and Rural Development in Sri Lanka*, 43, 45 and 59.

40 During my period of fieldwork the following local-level institutions were nominally present in rural areas – Village Development Society, Farmers' Society, Young Farmers' Society, Co-operative Society, Funeral Aid Society, Sarvodaya. Under the SLFP regime of 1970–7 the number of local-level institutions was even greater and included cultivation committees, people' committees, agricultural productivity committees, and after the 1971 insurgency, crime prevention societies.

41 Although voting patterns are influenced by caste consideration, there is no simple correspondence between caste and party affiliation. For example, one nearby electorate created by the delimitation commission in 1976 precisely because of its heavy Batgam concentration, returned a UNP candidate with a comfortable majority in the 1977 election; and many low-caste persons in that community have remained loyal to the UNP. Thus although it is

true that the SLFP has made a greater impact on the lower castes, party affiliation does not conform to pre-existing caste cleavages, but has emerged as a new form of local disunity.

42 H.M. Raulet and J. S. Uppal, 'The social dynamics of economic development in rural Punjab', *Asian Survey*, vol 10, no. 4, Apr 1970, 336–47; M. Sharma, 'Big men of Arunpur: political leadership in an eastern U.P. village', in B.N. Pandey (ed.), *Leadership in South Asia*, 131–57. F.G. Bailey, *Politics and Social Change: Orissa in 1959*.

43 N.K. Nicholson; S.C. Jain; H. Orenstein, 'The changing political system of a Maharashtran village' in K. Ishwaran (ed.) *Change and Continuity in India's Villages*, 219–40.

44 M. Sharma, 'Big men of Arunpur: political leadership in an eastern U.P. village' in B.N. Pandey (ed.), *Leadership in South Asia*, 143.

45 N.K. Nicholson, *Panchayati Raj: Rural Development and the Political Economy of Village India*, 44.

46 The heads of factions in Indian villages, usually described 'faction leaders', do not have a following which they can command. 'The responsibilities of the faction member do not extend beyond his obligations to the faction leader, his commitment is usually pragmatic and often temporary, and even the actual membership of the faction may be a matter of some mystery. Only within the central 'core' of the faction is there anything resembling the solidarity and diffused loyalty found in kin groups or among party cadres. In short, the faction represents the minimal organizational response to the problem of electoral politics at the village level.' (N.K. Nicholson, *Panchayati Raj: Rural Development and the Political Economy of Village India*, 36.)

47 N.K. Nicholson, *Panchayait Raj: Rural Development and the Political Economy of Village India*, 44.

12: *The Contemporary Ideology of Stratification*

1 M. Marriott and R.B. Inden, 'Towards an ethnosociology of South Asian caste systems', in K. David (ed.), *The New Wind: Changing Identities in South Asia*, 229.

2 The 'superior' *vāsagama* names that Batgam point to are those adopted in recent decades such as Bodhipaksage (loyal to the *Bo* tree); Rajapaksage (loyal to the king); and Nuwarapaksage (loyal to Kandy).

3 At a ceremony held in 1972 to mark the opening of the Rangama Cooperative store and the new bus service to Rangama, food was prepared in my Vahumpura landlady's house. Whilst the Assistant Government Agent and certain other high-caste officials felt obliged to participate in the meal, a Goigama schoolteacher from Rangama made it clear that he did not approve of such commensality. To overcome his resistance, a number of low-caste youths, plied him with liquor until he was sufficiently inebriated to accept the idea of eating with them.

4 A. Beteille, *Studies in Agrarian Social Structure*, 167; J. Mencher, 'Agricultural labour unions: some socioeconomic and political considerations', in K. David (ed.), *The New Wind: Changing Identities in South Asia*, 331–2; F. Frankel, *India's Green Revolution*.

5 K. Gough, 'Harijans in Thanjavur', in K. Gough and H.P. Sharma (eds),

Imperialism and Revolution in South Asia, 234; J. Harriss, 'Ideas, opinions and decision-making problems of farmers in Randam village: a case study of farmer behaviour', 23; E. Harper, 'Social Consequences of an "Unsuccessful" Low Caste Movement' in J. Silverberg (ed.), *Social Mobility in the Caste System in India*, 36–65.

6 For evidence of class consciousness in India see note 4 above.

13: *Conclusion*

1 K. Gough, 'Harijans in Thanjavur' in K. Gough and H.P. Sharma (eds), *Imperialism and Revolution in South Asia*, 222–45; E. Harper, 'Social consequences of an "unsuccessful" low caste movement' in J. Silverberg (ed.), *Social Mobility in the Caste system in India*, 36–65; D. Sivertson, *When Caste Barriers Fall: A Study of Social and Economic Change in a South Indian Village.*

2 For reasons similar to those given here, it would be equally unrealistic to look upon the anti-UNP terrorism of the Janatha Vimukthi Peramuna in the late 1980s as a peasant insurrection.

3 M.E. Gold, *Law and Social Change: A Study of Land Reform in Sri Lanka.*

4 J. Scott, *The Moral Economy of the Peasant*; E. Wolf, *Peasant Wars of the Twentieth Century.*

5 A different kind of discussion regarding the failure of peasants to organize against economic disadvantage is found in M. Moore's article 'Categorising space: urban-rural or core-periphery in Sri Lanka' (1984). Moore is concerned with the failure of certain types of farmers to challenge disadvantageous aspects of national agricultural policy, rather than the question with which I am here concerned – namely insurrectionary action of the rural poor against the landed elite.

6 J. Migdal, *Peasants, Politics and Revolution.*

Epilogue

1 See T. Gunasekera, 'District MPs, provincial councillors and bureaucrats: change and continuity in rural Sri Lanka', paper presented at Third Sri Lanka Conference in Amsterdam, April 1991.

2 Whilst having an MP of any party would be useful, people in Naranhena were in no doubt that having a UNP MP is what would be ideal, since after nearly fifteen years of unbroken UNP rule virtually all regional bureaucrats are loyal to, or at least co-operative with, the UNP.

3 A Pajero is the expensive four-wheel drive vehicle given to every provincial council member.

Appendix I: Kandyan Names

1 G. Obeyesekere, *Land Tenure in Village Ceylon*, 15.

2 R. Peiris, *Sinhalese Social Organisation*, 173.

3 S.J. Tambiah, 'The structure of kinship and its relationship to land possession in Pata Dumbara, central Ceylon, 24; M. Robinson, *Political Structure in a Changing Sinhalese Village*, 42.

4 M. Robinson, *Political Structure in a Changing Sinhalese Village*, 41–2.

5 S.J. Tambiah, 'The structure of kinship and its relationship to land possession', 24.
6 M. Robinson, *Political Structure in a Changing Sinhalese Village*, 26.

Appendix IV: Income/Cost Analysis for 1 Acre of Paddy 1979/80
1 This item of cost remains relatively fixed whether the extent cultivated is half an acre or two acres, and thus represents the kind of scale economies that large farmers enjoy.

Bibliography

Adams, R.N., 1970, 'Brokers and career mobility systems in the structure of complex societies', *Southwestern Journal of Anthropology*, 4, 315–27.

Ahmad, H., 1973, 'Peasant classes in Pakistan', in K. Gough and H.P. Sharma (eds), *Imperialism and Revolution in South Asia*, New York, Monthly Review Press, 203–21.

Ames, M., 1964, 'Magical animism and Buddhism: a structural analysis of the Sinhalese religious system', in E.B. Harper (ed.), *Religion in South Asia*, Seattle, University of Washington Press, 21–52.

Bailey, F.G., 1957, *Caste and the Economic Frontier*, Manchester, Manchester University Press.

——, 1959, 'For a sociology of India', *Contributions to Indian Sociology*, III, 88–101.

——, 1963, *Politics and Social Change: Orissa in 1959*, Berkeley, University of California Press.

Barth, F., 1971, 'The system of social stratification in Swat, North Pakistan', in E.R. Leach (ed.), *Aspects of Caste in South India, Ceylon and North-West Pakistan*, Cambridge, Cambridge University Press.

Benedict, B., 1970, 'Pluralism and stratification', in L. Plotnicov and A. Tuden (eds), *Essays in Comparative Social Stratification*, Pittsburgh, Pittsburgh University Press, 29–42.

Berreman, G., 1960, 'Caste in India and the United States', *American Journal of Sociology*, 66, 120–7.

——, 1971, 'Self, situation, and escape from stigmatised ethnic identity', 70th meeting of the American Anthropological Association, New York.

Beteille, A., 1965, *Caste, Class and Power*, Berkeley and Los Angeles, University of California Press.

——, 1969, 'Ideas and interests: some conceptual problems in the study of social stratification in rural India', *International Social Science Journal*, 21(2), 219–34.

——, 1974, *Studies in Agrarian Social Structure*, Delhi, Oxford University Press.

Blackton, J.S., 1974, *Local Government and Rural Development in Sri Lanka*, Ithaca, NY, Rural Development Committee, Cornell University.

Blok, A., 1975, *The Mafia of a Sicilian Village, 1860–1960*, New York, Harper & Row.

Breman, J., 1974, *Patronage and Exploitation: Changing Agrarian Relations in South Gujarat, India*, Berkeley and Los Angeles, University of California Press.

Brow, J., 1981, 'Class formation and ideological practice: a case from Sri Lanka', *Journal of Asian Studies*, 1981, 40, 703–18.

Dahrendorf, R., 1969, 'On the origin of inequality among men', in A. Beteille (ed.), *Social Inequality*, Middlesex, Penguin Books.

David, K. (ed.), 1977, 'Introduction', *The New Wind: Changing Identities in South Asia*, The Hague, Mouton, 1–58.

Davy, J., 1821, *An Account of the Interior of Ceylon and its Inhabitants*, London, Longman, Hurst, Rees, Orme & Brown.

De Bary, W.T. (ed.), 1972, *The Buddhist Tradition in India, China and Japan*, New York, Vintage Books Edition.

De Silva, C.R., 1953, *Ceylon Under British Occupation 1795–1833*, I and II, Colombo, The Colombo Apothecaries Ltd.

De Silva, G.P.S.H., 1979, *A Statistical Survey of Elections for the Legislatures of Sri Lanka, 1911–1977*, Colombo, Marga Institute.

De Silva, K.M. (ed.), 1973, 'History and politics of the transfer of power', *History of Ceylon*, III, Colombo, The Colombo Apothecaries Ltd., 489–533.

Dewaraja, L.S., 1972, *The Kandyan Kingdom 1707–1760*, Colombo, Lake House Investments Ltd.

D'Oyley, Sir J., 1929, *A Sketch of the Constitution of the Kandyan Kingdom*, Ed. L.J.B. Turner, Colombo, Ceylon Government Printer.

Dumont, L., 1972, *Homo Hierarchicus*, London, Paladin.

Epstein, T.S., 1962, *Economic Development and Social Change in South India*, Manchester, Manchester University Press.

——, 1973, *South India: Yesterday, Today and Tomorrow*, London, MacMillan.

Evers, H.D., 1964, 'Buddhism and British colonial policy in Ceylon, 1815–1875', *Asian Studies*, 2 (3), 323–33.

——, 1969, 'Monastic landlordism in Ceylon: a traditional system in a modern setting', *Journal of Asian Studies*, 28(4), 685–92.

——, 1972, *Monks, Priests and Peasants*, Leiden, Netherlands, E.J. Brill.

Feder, E., 1971, *The Rape of the Peasantry: Latin America's Landholding System*, Garden City, New York, Anchor Books.

Femia, J.V., 1981, *Gramsci's Political Thought*, Oxford, Clarendon Press.

Ferguson, A.M., 1896, *Ceylon Handbook and Directory 1895–6*, Colombo, The Ceylon Observer Press.

——, 1910, *Ceylon Handbook and Directory 1909–1910*, Planting Review, Colombo, Ceylon Observer Press.

Ferguson, J., 1887, *Ceylon in the Jubilee Year*, London, John Haddon & Co.

Fernando, T., 1973, 'Elite politics in the new state: the case of post-independence Sri Lanka', *Pacific Affairs*, 46 (3), 361–83.

Foster, G., 1965, 'Peasant society and the image of the limited good', *American Anthropologist*, 67, 293–315.

Frank, A.G., 1969, *Latin America: Underdevelopment or Revolution*, New York, Monthly Review Press.

Frankel, F., 1971, *India's Green Revolution*, Princeton, Princeton University Press.

Gair, J.W. and Karunatilaka, W.S., 1976, *Literary Sinhala Inflected Forms: A Synopsis*, Ithaca, New York, Cornell University South Asia Programme and Department of Modern Languages and Linguistics.

Geertz, C., 1973, *The Interpretation of Cultures*, New York, Basic Books.

Gilbert, W.H., 1952, 'The Sinhalese caste system of central and southern Ceylon', *Ceylon Historical Journal*, 2, 295–366.

Gold, M.E., 1977, *Law and Social change: A Study of Land Reform in Sri Lanka*, New York, Nellen.

Gombrich, R., 1971, *Precept and Practice*, Oxford, Oxford University Press.

Gough, K., 1968–9, 'Peasant resistance and revolt in south India', *Pacific Affairs*, XLI (4), 526–44.

——, 1973, 'Harijans in Thanjavur', in K. Gough and H.P. Sharma (eds), *Imperialism and Revolution in South Asia*, New York, Monthly Review Press, 222–45.

Greenwood, D.J., 1976, *Unrewarding Wealth*, Cambridge (UK), New York, Cambridge University Press.

Gunasekera, T., 1991, 'District MPs, provincial councillors and bureaucrats: change and continuity in rural Sri Lanka', Paper presented at Third Sri Lanka Conference, Amsterdam, April.

Gunasinghe, N., 1979, 'Agrarian relations in the Kandyan countryside in relation to the concept of extreme social disintegration', *Social Science Review*, 1, 1–40.

Harper, E., 1968, 'Social consequences of an "Unsuccessful" low caste movement', in J. Silverberg (ed.), *Social Mobility in the Caste System in India*, The Hague, Mouton, 36–65.

Harriss, J., 1974, 'Ideas, opinions and decision-making problems of farmers in Randam village: A caste study in farmer behaviour', *Project on Agrarian Change in Rice-Growing Areas of Tamil Nadu and Sri Lanka*, Center of South Asian Studies, Cambridge University.

——, 1982, *Capitalism and Peasant Farming*, Oxford University Press.

Ishwaran, K. (ed.), 1970, *Change and Continuity in India's Villages*, New York and London, Columbia University Press.

Jain, S.C., 1967, *Community Development and Panchayati Raj in India*, Bombay, Allied.

Jiggins, J., 1979, *Caste and Family in the Politics of the Sinhalese, 1947–1976*, Cambridge, Cambridge University Press.

Jupp, J., 1977, 'Political leadership in Sri Lanka – the parliamentary parties', in B.N. Pandey (ed.), *Leadership in South Asia*, New Delhi, Vikas Publishing House, 483–99.

Kirsch A.T., 1967, 'The Thai Buddhist quest for merit', paper read at the American Anthropological Association Meetings, Washington.

Knox. R., 1911, *An Historical Relation of Ceylon*, Glasgow, James MacLehose & Sons.

Kuper, L., 1969, 'Introduction – plural societies: perspectives and problems', in L. Kuper and M.G. Smith (eds), *Pluralism in Africa*, Berkeley, University of California Press, 7–26.

Leach, E.R., 1961, *Pul Eliya, A Village in Ceylon*, Cambridge, Cambridge University Press.
—— (ed.), 1971, 'Introduction: what should we mean by caste?', *Aspects of Caste in South India, Ceylon and North-West Pakistan*, Cambridge, Cambridge Univeristy Press, 1–10.
Levinson, G., 1982, 'Caste rank and verbal interaction in western Tamilnadu', in D.B. McGilvray (ed.), *Caste Ideology and Interaction*, Cambridge, Cambridge University Press, 98–203.
Lewis, O., 1951, *Life in a Mexican Village: Tepoztlan Restudied*, Urbana, University of Illinois Press, 1951.

McGilvray, D.B. (ed.), 1982, 'Mukkuvar Vannimai: Tamil Caste and matriclan ideology in Baticaloa, Sir Lanka', *Caste Ideology and Interaction*, Cambridge, Cambridge University Press, 34–97.
Majumdar, D.N., 1959, *Caste and Communication in an Indian Village*, Delhi, Asia Publishing House.
Marriott, M., (ed.), 1955, 'Little Communities in an Indigenous Civilisation', *Village India*, Chicago, University of Chicago Press, 171–222.
——, 1959, 'Interactional and Attributional Theories of Caste Ranking', *Man in India*, 39, 92–107.
—— and Inden, R.B., 1977, 'Towards an ethnosociology of south Asian caste systems', in K. David (ed.), *The New Wind: Changing Identities in South Asia*, The Hague, Mouton, 227–38.
Martinez-Alier, J., 1971, *Labourers and Landowners in Southern Spain*, London, George Allen & Unwin Ltd.
Mayer, A., 1958, 'The dominant caste in a region of central India', *Southwestern Journal of Anthropology*, 14, 407–27.
——, 1960, *Caste and Kinship in Central India*, London, Routledge.
Mencher, J., 1977, 'Agricultural labour unions: some socioeconomic and political considerations', in K. David (ed.), *The New Wind: Changing Identities in South Asia*, The Hague, Mouton, 309–35.
Meyer, E., 1983, 'The plantation system and village structure in British Ceylon: involution or evolution?', in P. Robb (ed.), *Rural South Asia – Linkages, Change and Development*, Curzon, London.
Migdal, J., 1974, *Peasants, Politics and Revolution*, Princeton, Princeton University Press.
Mills, L.A., 1964, *Ceylon Under British Rule 1795–1932*, Colombo, K.V.G. de Silva & Sons.
Mintz, S.W., 1974, *Caribbean Transformations*, Chicago, Aldine Publishing Company.
Moore, M., 1984, 'Categorising space: urban–rural or core–periphery in Sri Lanka', in J. Harriss and M. Moore (eds), *Development and the Rural–Urban Divide*, Frank Cass & Company Ltd, London.

Nicholson, N.K., 1973, *Panchayati Raj, Rural Development and the Political*

Economy of Village India, Ithaca, NY, Rural Development Committee, Cornell University.

Obeyesekere, G., 1967, *Land Tenure in Village Ceylon*, Cambridge, Cambridge University Press.

——, 1966, 'The Buddhist pantheon in Ceylon and its extensions', in M. Nash (ed.), *Anthropological Studies in Theravada Buddhism*, New Haven, Yale University Press, 1–26.

Orenstein, H., 1970, 'The changing political system of a Maharashtran village', in K. Ishwaran (ed.), *Change and Continuity in India's Villages*, New York and London, Columbia University Press, 219–40.

Perera, A.A., 1917, *Sinhalese Folk-Lore Notes*, Bombay, 1917.

Phadnis, U., 1976, *Religion and Politics in Sri Lanka*, London, C. Hurst.

Pieris, R., 1956, *Sinhalese Social Organisation: The Kandyan Period*, Colombo, Ceylon University Press Board.

Powell, G., 1973, *The Kandyan Wars, The British Army in Ceylon 1803–1818*, London, Lee Cooper.

Rahula, W., 1956, *History of Buddhism in Ceylon*, Colombo, M.D. Gunasena & Co. Ltd.

Raulet, H.M. and Uppal, J.S., 1970, 'The social dynamics of economic development in rural Punjab', *Asian Survey*, 10 (4), 336–47.

Reddy, G.R., 1970, 'Some aspects of decision making in Panchayati Raj', *Economic and Political Weekly*, V (41), 1699–704.

Redfield, R., 1956, *Peasant Society and Culture*, Chicago, Chicago University Press.

Rex, J., 1974, 'Capitalism, elites and the ruling class', in P. Stanworth and A. Giddens (eds), *Elites and Power in British Society*, Cambridge, Cambridge University Press, 208–19.

Roberts, M., 1973, Aspects of Ceylon's agrarian economy in the nineteenth century', in K.M., de Silva (ed.), *History of Ceylon*, III, Colombo, The Colombo Apothecaries Ltd.

——, 1973, 'Land problems and policies c.1832–c.1900', in K.M. de Silva (ed.), *History of Ceylon*, III, Colombo, The Colombo Apothecaries Ltd., 119–45.

—— and Wickremaratne, L.A., 1973, 'Export agriculture in the nineteenth century', in K.M. de Silva (ed.), *History of Ceylon*, III, Colombo, The Colombo Apothecaries Ltd.

Robinson, M.S., 1975, *Political Structure in a Changing Sinhalese Village*, Cambridge, Cambridge University Press.

Rogers, E.M., 1962, *Diffusion of Innovations*, New York, Free Press of Glencoe.

Runciman, W.G., 1970, 'Class, status and power?', *Sociology in its Place*, Cambridge, Cambridge University Press, 102–40.

Ryan, B., 1950, 'Socio cultural regions of Ceylon', *Rural Sociology*, 15(1), 3–19.

——, 1953, *Caste in Modern Ceylon: the Sinhalese System in Transition*, New Brunswick, NJ, Rutgers University Press.

Samaraweera, V., 1973, 'Economic and social developments under the British, 1796–1832', in K.M. de Silva (ed.), *History of Ceylon*, III, Colombo, The Colombo Apothecaries Ltd., 48–65.

——, 1977, 'The administration and the judicial system', in K.M. de Silva (ed.), *Sri Lanka*, Honolulu, University Press of Hawaii, 353–75.

Schneider, D., 1968, *American Kinship: A Cultural Account*, Englewood Cliffs, NJ, Prentice-Hall.

Schneider, J. and P., 1976, *Culture and Political Economy in Western Sicily*, New York, Academic Press, 1976.

Scott, J.C., 1976, *The Moral Economy of the Peasant*, New Haven, Yale University Press.

——, 1985, *Weapons of the Weak*, Yale University Press, New Haven and London.

Sharma, M., 1977, 'Big men of Arunpur: political leadership in an eastern U.P. village', in B.N. Pandey (ed.), *Leadership in South Asia*, New Delhi, Vikas Publishing House, 131–57.

Silverman, S., 1965, 'Patronage and community–Nation relationships in central Italy', *Ethnology*, 4 (2), 172–89.

Sivertson, D., 1963, *When Caste Barriers Fall: A Study of Social and Economic Change in a South Indian Village*, New York, Humanities Press.

Smith, M.G., 1978, 'Social and cultural pluralism', in V. Rubin (ed.), *Social and Cultural Pluralism in the Caribbean*, Millwood, NY, Kraus Reprint Co., 763–77.

Somaratne, G.V.P., 1975, *Political History of the Kingdom of Kotte*, Sri Lanka, Deepanee Printers.

Spencer, J., 1990, *A Sinhalese Village in a Time of Trouble: Politics and Change in Rural Sri Lanka*, Oxford University Press, Delhi.

Srinivas, M.N., 1959, 'The dominant caste in Rampura', *American Anthropologist*, 61, 1–16.

——, 1966, *Social Change in Modern India*, Berkeley and Los Angeles, University of California Press.

Stevenson, H.N.C., 1954, 'Status evaluation in the Hindu caste system', *Journal of the Royal Anthropological Institute*, 84, 45–65.

Stirrat, R.L., 1982, 'Caste conundrums: views of caste in a Sinhalese Catholic fishing village', in D.B. McGilvray (ed.), *Caste Ideology and Interaction*, Cambridge, Cambridge University Press, 8–33.

Tambiah, S.J., 1958, 'The structure of kinship and its relationship to land possession and residence in Pata Dumbara, Central Ceylon', *Journal of the Royal Anthropological Institute*, LXXXVIII(I), 1958, 21–44.

——, 1965, 'Kinship fact and fiction in relation to Kandyan Sinhalese', *Journal of the Royal Anthropological Institute*, 95, 131–73.

Tarrow, S., 1967, *Peasant Communism in Southern Italy*, New Haven and London, Yale University Press.

Turner, V., 1970, *The Forest of Symbols*, Ithaca, Cornell University PRess.

Wadley, S., 1975, *Shakti: Power in the Conceptual Structure of Karimpur Religion*,

University of Chicago Studies in Anthropology, Series in Social, Cultural and Linguistic Anthropology 2.

Wanigesekera, E., 1977, 'Popular participation and local level planning in Sri Lanka', *Marga*, 4(4), 37–77.

Weber, M., 1957, *The Religion of India*, New York, Free Press.

——, 1970, 'Class, Status, Party', in H.H. Gerth and C. Wright Mills (eds), *From Max Weber*, New York, Oxford University Press.

Weerakoon, B., 1976, 'Emergent leadership at the village level', *Economic Review*, 11–14.

——, 1977, 'Role of administrators in a changing agrarian situation: the Sri Lanka experience', *Journal of Administration Overseas*, 16(3), 148–61.

White, H., 1913, *The Ceylon Manual for the Use of Officials 1912–1913*, ed. 1912–13 by E.B.F. Sueter, London, Edward Stanford.

Wickremaratne, L.A., 1977, 'Peasant agriculture', in K.M. de Silva (ed.), *Sri Lanka*, Honolulu, University Press of Hawaii, 236–55.

Wijeweera, B.S., 1988, *A Colonial Administrative System in Transition*, Marga Publications, Colombo.

Wilson, A.J., 1974, *Politics in Sri Lanka, 1947–1973*, London, Macmillan.

Witherspoon, G., 1975, *Navaho Kinship and Marriage*, Chicago, University of Chicago Press.

Wolf, E., 1956, 'Aspects of group relations in a complex society: Mexico', *American Anthropologist*, 58, 1065–78.

——, 1969, *Peasant Wars of the Twentieth Century*, New York, Harper & Row.

Wood, A.L., 1964, 'Political radicalism in changing Sinhalese villages', *Human Organisation*, 23 (2), 99–107.

Woodward, C.A., 1974–75, 'Sri Lanka's electoral experience: from personal to party politics', *Pacific Affairs*, 47 (4), 455–71.

Yalman, N., 1963, 'On the purity of women in the castes of Malabar and Ceylon', *Journal of the Royal Anthropological Institute*, 93, 25–58.

——, 1967, *Under the Bo Tree*, Berkeley and Los Angeles, University of California Press.

Yanagisako, S., 1975, 'Two processes of change in Japanese–American Kinship', *Journal of Anthropological Research*, 3, 196–224.

GOVERNMENT DOCUMENTS

Census Reports:
   1881, 1891, 1901, 1911
Census of Population:
   1971, II (I), Colombo, Department of Census and Statistics.
Kegalle, District Administration:
   Claim under ordinance no. 1 of 1897 and no. 1 of 1889 with respect to Upalagoda Tenna, Hena at Rangama in Tunpalatapattu of Paranakuru Korale in the Kegalle District.

   Diary of the Assistant Government Agent, Kegalle District, 1885.
   Diary of the Assistant Government Agent, Kegalle District, 1886 and each Diary thereafter through to 1925.

Grain Tax Assessment Registers, Kegalle District, 1869–1875; 1877–1884; 1882; 1888.

Highland Register, Rangama Vasama, Thumpalata Pattuwa West, Paranakuru Korale, 1897.

Service Tenure Commission:
Administrative Report 1870 – Report of the Service Tenures Commissioner by Sir John F. Dickinson.

Sessional Paper XXVII, 1935 – Report of the Headman's Commission.
Sessional Paper XVIII, 1951 – The Report of the Kandyan Peasantry Commission.

Temple Lands Commission:
Lands claimed by the Rangama Vihare, submitted to the Temple Lands Commission on February 7, 1860.

Register of Temple Lands rejected and those to be registered in the district of Four Korales, Temple Lands Commission Office, 1864.

Register of Temple Lands in Tumpalata Pattu of Paranakuru Korale in 1876.

Index